CREATIVITY

www.ChironPublications.com

Previously published by Spring Journal Books

Printed primarily in the United States of America.

ISBN 978-1-63051-875-2 paperback
ISBN 978-1-63051-876-9 hardcover
ISBN 978-1-63051-877-6 electronic
ISBN 978-1-63051-878-3 limited edition paperback

Library of Congress Cataloging-in-Publication Data Pending

Cover Image:
Otto Dix, *"Artist and Muse"* 1924 (detail)
© 2020, ProLitteris, Zurich.
Used with permission.

Technical Assistance Provided by:
Northern Graphic Design & Publishing
info@ncarto.com

CREATIVITY

PATTERNS OF CREATIVE IMAGINATION AS SEEN THROUGH ART

PAUL BRUTSCHE

CHIRON PUBLICATIONS • ASHEVILLE, NORTH CAROLINA

PERMISSIONS

CHAPTER III

Figure 1: Marc Chagall, *The Rabbi*, or *The Pinch of Snuff*, 1924-1927, © 2020, ProLitteris, Zurich.

Figure 2: Marc Chagall, *Jew in Red*, 1914, © 2020, ProLitteris, Zurich.

Figure 3: Marc Chagall, *Rabbi with Torah*, 1930, © 2020, ProLitteris, Zurich.

Figure 4: Marc Chagall, *Jew in Green*, 1914, © 2020, ProLitteris, Zurich.

Figure 5: Marc Chagall, *Jew in Black and White*, 1914, © 2020, ProLitteris, Zurich.

CHAPTER IV

Figure 6: Otto Dix, *Self-Portrait with Muse*, 1924, © 2020, ProLitteris, Zurich.

Figure 7: René Magritte, *Attempting the Impossible*, 1928, © 2020, ProLitteris, Zurich.

Figure 8: Edouard Manet, *Luncheon on the Grass*, 1863, Musée d'Orsay, Paris.

Figure 9: Albrecht Dürer, *Adam and Eve*, 1504, Metropolitan Museum of Modern Art, New York.

Figure 10: Julian Wasser, *Duchamp Playing Chess with a Nude* (Eve Babitz), 1963, Pasadena Art Museum, California.

CHAPTER V

Figure 11: Albrecht Dürer, *The Desperate Man*, 1515, Metropolitan Museum of Modern Art, New York.

Figure 12: Pablo Picasso, *Family of Saltimbanques*, 1905, © Succession Picasso / 2020, ProLitteris, Zurich.

Figure 13: Vincent van Gogh, *The Potato Eaters*, 1885, van Gogh Museum, Amsterdam.

Figure 14: Paul Klee, *Carnival in the Mountains* 1924, Zentrum Paul Klee, Bern.

TABLE OF CONTENTS

ACKNOWLEDGEMENTS

With their invitation for my talks at the 2016 Zürich Lecture Series in Analytical Psychology, Nancy Cater and Murray Stein gave me the impetus and opportunity to gather and develop in the form of a book material that I had been working on for many years.

The realization of this book was supported by generous grants from the Susan Bach Foundation (Switzerland) and the Oswald Family Foundation (USA). For the backing of both groups, I wish to express my deep gratitude.

The translator Stacy Wirth not only made of the complicated original German a readable English text. She contributed as well to the final gestalt with proposed contents, editorial suggestions, and in-depth searches for the source literature in English. I extend great thanks for her work, which brought to bear her language skills and professional competence as a Jungian analyst.

Special acknowledgment goes to my wife Diane Cousineau Brutsche, who enabled my immersion in the work with her readiness to sacrifice so much of our shared time together. Her witnessing and accompaniment of the arduous process entailed as well her conscious constraints on her natural, vivacious curiosity and fine judgment. For her enduring discretion and patience with me, I am profoundly grateful.

Dariane Pictet, allowing my writing retreats in her wonderful house in Rougemont, offered an ideal setting for my work on the book, especially during the more difficult phases of its emergence.

To this day, I feel greatly indebted to the deceased Jungian analyst Rudolf Michel. Many years ago, when he was the picture expert and director of the Picture Archive at the C.G. Jung Institute Zürich, he led me into the world of picture interpretation and equipped me with approaches to symbolic understanding that undergird this study.

LIST OF ILLUSTRATIONS

CHAPTER VI

CHAPTER VII

I

Introduction

> Yet we know that every good idea and all creative
> work are the offspring of the imagination, and have
> their source in what one is pleased to call infantile
> fantasy. Not the artist alone, but every creative
> individual whatsoever owes all that is greatest in his
> life to fantasy.
>
> —C.G. Jung[1]

What is creativity? We could answer the question from the perspective of colloquial understanding, academic research, or the creative individual's experience. In common parlance creativity can typically imply artistic ability. This is the general idea when one speaks of creative activity or a creative profession, that is, when we think of the painter, the musician, the dancer, and all other artistic callings. In this sense creativity is understood as the special ability to bring forth creatively designed products.

From the standpoint of academic research creativity inheres in special mental faculties or capabilities that distinguish creative people from non-creative people. Among the attributes are originality in problem solving; ingenious resourcefulness; interdisciplinary thinking; the ability to connect apparently unrelated ideas; mental flexibility; multi-faceted interests and gifts; an extraordinary ability to formulate language and images; an independent spirit; and self-confidence. Research in the area of creativity has dealt with these and similar traits that characterize creative individuals.

Creativity is further understood to involve special approaches that lead to unique new insights. The famous researcher Mihàly Csikszentmihalyi (born 1934) defines the creative process, for example, as a five-step sequence consisting of a preparatory phase, an incubation phase, a ripening phase, an arising of insight or an "aha" experience, and evaluation.[2]

And finally, creativity is seen to be the ability to find innovative solutions for problems posed by the environment. Researchers in the field try to capture the phenomenon of creativity under such aspects. Doing so, they follow James Melvin Rhodes (1916-1976), who introduced the concept of the "4 Ps:" Person, Process, Press (environmental influences), and Product.[3]

What the various research approaches hold in common is their view of creativity as an individual gift and achievement. They refer to special personality profiles that distinguish the creative from the non-creative individual. They observe the individual's bringing-forth of things, his or her modus operandi, the way of reaching creative results and solutions. Creativity is examined on the basis of observing and questioning the creative individual, and by the comparative elaboration of specific traits belonging to his or her creative doing and being.

This approach to the phenomenon places creativity and its special faculties totally within an individual's area of action and competence. It is, so to speak, a finite view, which makes of creativity an instrument in the hands of individuals, who use it to accomplish special achievements, obtain new insights, and produce new values. Such a functional perspective is of course admissible, but it is limited and superficial. It takes account of the creative individual's abilities and skills, but it neglects the phenomenon of creativity as such, its essential manifestations, and its autonomous action.

The more encompassing approach that I take here begins not with the creative individual's doings and abilities, but with the power and direction of creative imagination itself. I basically assume that creativity is essentially the ability to transmit and represent in visible form the contents suggested by the autonomous imagination. The real creative factor here is not the gifted ego but primal imagination, which autonomously undergirds and fuels creativity, and mediates itself efficaciously through the individual's imaginings.

Creativity can be characterized as follows:

(1) It draws from the wellspring of the unconscious, to bring to consciousness ideas that are of especially timely value for the individual or for the collective Zeitgeist. These mediated archetypal ideas have a healing effect, in that contents drawn from the store of humanity's eternally living wealth of experience open up compensatory perspectives and supply consciousness with astounding new meanings.

(2) Creative imagination mediates itself not only along a time axis stretching between the historical past and the present time, but also in a spatial dimension that lies between the inner world of consciousness and the outer world of real things. It creates images that represent spiritual meanings in concrete, sensuous, and perceptible forms—or that manifest inner meaning in the represented objects. The images offered by creative imagination conjoin the mind and the senses, inwardness and outwardness, thoughts and things, consciousness and objective being.

(3) Creative imagination can be experienced as a puzzling erratic process in which darkness turns suddenly to light and new insight— or despair gives way abruptly to a fecundity of new discoveries, ideas, and nurturing thoughts. This *Stirb-und-Werde*—this dying-and-becoming—is expressed in the Greek myth featuring Demeter, the goddess of fertility, and her daughter Persephone. The story of the maiden's abduction resolves with the establishment of annually recurring cycles: When Persephone vanishes each year to the underworld kingdom of the god Hades, the grieving Demeter causes the death of all plants. And when Persephone returns, the joyful Demeter allows the plants to flourish and bear fruit. The myth suggests the basic archetypal fact of these two moments of experience—the sudden end of all imagination, and its abrupt re-appearance. We see it, too, in the Eleusinian Mysteries, which figured prominently in antiquity, in the Mediterranean area. In a central rite, the *mystais* kept silence in a pitch-dark chamber. All of a sudden, the darkness was penetrated by a brightly illuminated sacred ear of corn, held up for their view. Here we have a ritual enactment of the transformative alternations of death and resurrection, a process, which, since time eternal, has essentially characterized the creative experience itself.

(4) Creativity thus involves a force of imagination that takes its own course, both in the creative process with its sequences of produced images, and in the emergence of a set of collected works. Creative activity accordingly manifests an autonomously directed process of

symbolization. In creative individuals, a pair of opposing perspectives keeps the symbolization process going: a "feminine" way of viewing things, that is, a quality of perception that is immediate, sensory, and imagistic—and a "masculine" way of reflecting that is mediated by abstract intellect. The one perspective immerses itself in the concrete or imaginatively apprehended material, and the other reflects on it abstractly. In interplay, the two bring to bear a transcending third—this is the "child," the sensuous and meaningful image called forth by the symbolization process.

(5) Finally, creative imagination gives rise to a particular way of being-in-the-world, a particular relationship of the individual to the world, and a particular way in which the world appears and offers itself to the individual. A person finding himself in a creative mode undergoes an important change in his self-perception and perception of the world. There is an opening of being, and the world is apprehended in the perspective of a perceiving ego as a place where there are things to discover, to change, to realize. Viewed on the stage of this ego with its imaginings and representations, the world turns into a comprehensible and discoverable place. The creative individual co-creates the world or at least re-creates it in the realm of imagination. It is little coincidence that the element of perspective in art was attributed with such great meaning during the Renaissance, this extraordinarily creative period. At this time perspective became the meaningful expression of an enhanced creative consciousness that started to see the world through perspective of the individual observer and as a stage for the individual's action and design.

In this book I undertake to explore the nature and manifestations of creativity by observing its appearance in works of art. My basic assumption is that creativity not only engenders art works, but also that in certain works the creative force of imagination comes to expression. In their works, artists handle this phenomenon, explicitly or implicitly. The thing that thrusts itself into the expressive foreground is a mysterious, intriguing, and autonomous creative reality that participates in the emergence of artistic works. I refer not to allegorical formulations, but to pictures that spontaneously reveal in symbolic form the underlying reality.

Artists are the evident experts, being able to represent creative experience in the symbolic reality of images. So it should behoove us to allow their works to have a say in our understanding of creativity.

Thus their pictures form the basis of this study of the nature of creativity—its basic forms and its many differentiated variations, including its expression in the generally describable varieties of creative imagination. The observations I develop here are valid not only for the field of art, but also for other fields, such as the humanities and sciences, which can just as much evidence creative procedures and the outcome of creative knowledge.

A word to the question of the legitimacy of the psychological interpretation of art works. Pictures reveal psychological wisdom independently of the artist's conscious will and knowledge. Pictures are symbols. Their meanings lie not only in the artist's intentions and not only in the symbolically comprehensible motifs, but also in the inherent reality of the image itself and its formal gestalt. In other words, the formal elements in the picture speak just as much symbolically as do the picture's main subject matter. Moreover, these formal elements are equally supplied and called forth by the autonomous force of imagination. However, as much as we are generally confident in this independent force to provide symbolic subject matter, we are equally at odds to recognize it as the creator of formal gestalts. This is because we proceed from the erroneous idea that the artist's will and faculty alone determine and achieve aesthetic design. This point of view, while granting psychological interpretation of the picture's subject matter, does not tolerate psychological interpretation of the formal elements. Such interpretation, it is mistakenly thought, would insinuate meanings and intentions that exceed the artist's own will.

According to the same misguided notion, artists alone are considered to be competent interpreters of their works—except, for instance, when art historians are tolerated in their opinions on questions of stylistic coherence and variations, historical context, technique, and biographical circumstances. Psychologists, too, are accepted for their interpretation of themes, motifs, biographical influences, and even the possible influence of psychopathology. However, psychologists tend to be seen as interlopers and hyper-interpreters when they attribute a picture's stylistic elements or artistic design with psychological meaning.

There is no denying that artists compose their pictures according to their own will, faculties, and direction. But their decisions are attuned as well to the inherent demands of the image itself. That is, the emerging image itself wants particular delineations, particular colors, particular rankings of parts, particular spatial relationships, and other particulars related to the properties of the artistic medium. The image steers the creative process, relying on the artist's felt sense of coherence. And the sensed coherence derives from something more than a felt confirmation of personal aesthetic predilections. Which is to say, the artist is satisfied when the visible product corresponds and resonates with the picture's own deeper immanent intention.

The autonomous symbol-making imagination is the reality that underlies the image and compels its particular design. A picture's psychological meanings emanate not only through its subject matter but also through the formal design elements. These meanings are part and parcel of an autonomous creative reality *sui generis*, one that encompasses but lies ultimately beyond the artist's conscious will. The fact that a picture represents such a reality makes of it a timeless and biography-transcending document, open to on-going interpretation and understanding. For this reason we can read such pictures as timelessly valid expressions of creative imagination.

The artistic products generated by the creative force of imagination contain a good deal of knowledge about the nature of creativity and its manifestations and also about the reality of the soul. Conveyed in the form of symbolically rich images, this knowledge is all at once timeless, vivid, stimulating, astonishing, and unfathomable.

II

MANIFESTATIONS OF CREATIVITY
A PHENOMENOLOGICAL SKETCH

The aim of this book is to explore basic forms of creative imagination by observing and interpreting its products and developments in art and culture. What are the distinguishing signs of creativity? To begin, we can sketch out and elaborate on four typical manifestations.

2.1. Discovering Possibilities in Existing Things

Creativity is, first, the ability to discover possibilities in existing things. It envisages the potential to change things, to use them differently, to understand them symbolically, or to render them in artistic form.

The creative drive to discover and re-shape things manifests itself markedly in the play of young children. Several small stones, a couple of scarves, the odd object left lying around—these suffice to build castles, discover dramas, and to develop narratives. At this stage, and under the best of circumstances, there are no rules but those of the child's own invention.

But also the worker, the technician, the inventor—each of them open to creative fantasy when they discover new uses for things that already exist.

Creativity is always at play when concrete things are perceived to mean something that goes beyond their practical purposes—that is, when poets use things as metaphors, psychologists interpret them as symbols, theologians discern them as meaningful signs, and philosophers try to understand their depths.

Ultimately creativity is present both in the artist's shaping of an object and in motifs that appear in the created object itself, be it a painting, a sculpture, or a work in some other medium.

Common to all such manifestations of creative imagination is its reach beyond being in the mere here-and-now. That is, it reaches toward other kinds of being, which are envisaged in play, in invention, and in a pointing-toward and a giving-form-to the other. In this context one could speak of a transcendent trajectory: creative imagination exceeds the given as such and opens up the possible, the coming, the other, and the surprising.

2.2. Confronting Inner and Outer Images

Creativity spawns the kind of knowledge that is obtained through imagination and in particular through a confrontation with inner and outer images. Fantasy both flows from and also nourishes itself from vivid inner, visual perceptions. They can be either pre-determined, or they can crop up spontaneously from within—or even better, they might result of explorations between the two, between pre-given outer images and an emerging inner vision.

The attainment of new insight through the encounter of inner and outer images is well illustrated by the artist, who is never occupied only with a motif as such, but also always with the resonances of its foregoing representations. An artist's particular handling of a topic emerges out of the tension and dialogue between historically preceding images and the new image arising from inner sources of inspiration.

This transforming quality of creative imagination can be discerned in artists who have taken up and re-interpreted the works of preceding masters. We think of Claude Monet and Vincent van Gogh, both of whom picked up motifs from Jean-François Millet—or Paul Cézanne, who reinterpreted the pictures of the nude Olympia painted by both Diego Velazquez and Edouard Manet. Pablo Picasso, too, borrowed from the pictures of many old masters, re-creating and infusing them in his own way with meaning.

The dialogic influence that comes to light especially with painters is present as well in non-artists, whose imagination is also often ignited by pre-existing ideas. A good example can be found in C.G. Jung's exploration of psychological types, which dealt intensively with a range of foregoing typological models to produce his own new version that combines introversion and extraversion with the four conscious orientations.

Creativity rooted in a world of pre-existing images points to its fundament in the stock of archetypal "ideas." When creative fantasy is at work, primordial human experience is easily envisioned, and the images emanating from it form direct links to the basic repertory of the soul's imaginative possibilities.

Creativity is marked as well by the property of deriving from a known image insight that exceeds the image itself, that emerges from behind the familiar image, that questions the usual image, or that even penetrates into realms far beyond it. A figure like Sigmund Freud as the founder of psychoanalysis well exemplifies this exploratory impetus.

2.3. Binding to Concreteness

It ought to be said further that creativity is most typically activated when it can bind to concrete experience and/or to a sensuous medium. "*L'imaginaire est une fonction du réel et non pas de la cervelle.*" "The imaginary is a function of the real and not the brain." This motto of the French cultural revolution in the late 1960s was one among many that set into motion a mass movement of creativity. It tells us concisely that creative fantasy is not just a matter of brain convolutions, but is tethered to an outer reality. Social reality was meant above all at the time, and the prevailing principle was that creativity should not unfold in service to a non-political art for art's sake. But nevertheless there was the fundamental thought that creative fantasy is not the idle start-up of a solely self-occupied intellect. To be creative in the truest sense, fantasy requires some *materia* within which it can compose itself and develop. Lacking a mediating observer and the sensuous prescience of a shaping hand, imagination is purely mental and does not lead to truly new creative insight.

Sigmund Freud relied on the precise observation of his patients and his detailed perceptions of their free associations, and obtained creative insights from these rich materials. With his discovery of the unconscious, Freud contributed substantially to a Copernican turn from the nineteenth to the twentieth century.

Over the course of sixteen years C.G. Jung found himself compelled to grapple with his own inner life, doing so among other ways by painting the images in his *Red Book* with artisanal skill and aesthetically satisfying detail. This activity formed the fertile soil for Jung's entire later work. Lacking the sensuous imagery that portrayed his intuitions from the unconscious, Jung would not have discovered his creative understanding of the reality of the soul. He may have contributed a few clever psychological thoughts inspired by the academic Zeitgeist, but his qualitative leap to a new concept of the soul's autonomous reality would have been missing.

To be stimulated, creative imagination needs to experiment, to handle things in processes of trial and error. The experiment should not be too narrowly viewed as a scientific method that strives to refute or verify a given hypothesis. It is as well a rehearsal for the orchestration of creative thought, the cradle of emerging theory, the sensuous substrate of new insight.

Creativity is characterized by the tendency not to persist in a vacuum of inconsequential conceptualizing. Rather, it pushes itself into visible action and sensory works. Creative imagination does not linger in the sphere of trivial, aesthetic, intellectual art for art's sake. It demands concrete form and generates enduring effect with palpable consequences and lasting changes.

2.4. Individual Experience, Self-Observation, Insight

Creativity is, moreover, expressed in insight that emerges through an individual's experience and self-observation. As such, creativity is inscribed in the horizon of an individual's experience and it inheres uniquely to that individual's personal sensitivity, life circumstances, typological constitution, and cultural anchoring. Such subjectivity is both a fact of and a basic prerequisite for the effectiveness of creative fantasy. Bereft of relationship to personal reality, fantasy would not be creative or there would be no creative fantasy. At best one might speak of an imagination without substance, or of an uncreative, randomly reiterating imagination. It would lack the commitment and directionality of a creative will.

Scientific understanding seems to be defied or baffled by this reality that imagination becomes creative by the binding of creative imagination to the personality. For it is known that science aims to validate only objective findings, and this, by eliminating as far as possible the arbitrary subjective factor. Is the scientific method thus uncreative—or the other way around, is creative fantasy an unsuitable vehicle for scientific discovery?

The answer could lie in the fact that, in the realm of scientific research, creative fantasy is at work, coming through in the researcher's individuality and in his or her accompanying personal circumstances, emotional interests, premonitions, imagined solutions, irrational considerations and decisions. But differently from the poet, the artist, and the psychologist, scientists submit their discoveries to objective test methods that validate the findings based on proof of their repeatability and predictability. In other words, the scientific laws of proof remove the personal factor. And yet, the subjective conditions do nurture and enliven the discovery process. Indeed, would scientists succeed to bracket out entirely their personal reactions, imaginative anticipations, and early trials and experiments, there would be little or no fresh insight. Their discoveries might be repeated and expanded upon, but it is doubtful that the procedure would generate truly creative new understanding.

The poet epitomizes the ability to mediate creative fantasy, to express in language that which is personally experienced or inwardly imagined, and to express it with meaning that holds universally for human experience.

The psychologist, too, obtains creative thoughts about the soul's reality by following the path of his or her own experience, limits and difficulties, ways and solutions. The Jungian notion of the psychologist as "wounded healer" points to the psychotherapist's personally experienced vulnerability, the *condition sine qua non* that constitutes the creative therapeutic fantasy. Without personal suffering and pain, the therapist in practice suffers a lack of creative resource. In *Memories, Dreams, Reflections*, Jung appraises the relationship of the suffering soul to creativity:

> After the illness a fruitful period of work began for me. A good many of my principal works were written only then. The insight I had, or the vision of the end of all things, gave me the courage to undertake new formulations. I no longer attempted to put across my own opinion, but surrendered myself to the current of my thoughts.[4]

The tendency of creative fantasy to incarnate in the individual is clear especially in the figure of the prophet. Alongside the "chosen" ones who receive divine vision in the Old Testament, there is also the seer, John of Patmos, who in the last book of the New Testament beholds the revelation of the apocalypse. Creative revelation of this scope manifests itself always to outstanding individuals who can shape and transmit it for the benefit of the common good.

Yet the significance of each individual in the realm of creative vision emerges through a remarkable detail in the history of art. Centuries of artworks devoted to the apocalypse portray not only the vision itself, but also always the seer John, who is only scantily mentioned in the biblical texts. Moreover, in the artworks John appears in the foreground of the biblically documented revelation. The artists thus underline the necessity of an intimate relationship between the creative vision and the visionary, who serves as the living vessel that brings the vision to bear. (See the series of sixteen woodcuts by Albrecht Dürer, 1496-1498, and the eighty-four-part "Apocalypse Tapestry" of Angers, 1377-1382.)

Likewise the prophetic chapter in C.G. Jung's *Red Book*, "The Way of What is to Come," is bound essentially to the person, depicting Jung's entirely personal path of experience. But it is thanks to the binding in the man that a visionary scene opens up, revealing itself to be all at once new, singular, and yet infused with general meaning. As Jung himself put it far later, in 1957,

> The years, of which I have spoken to you, when I pursued the inner images, were the most important time of my life. Everything else is to be derived from this. It began at that time, and the later details hardly matter anymore. My entire life consisted in elaborating what had burst forth from the unconscious and flooded me like an enigmatic stream and threatened to break me.[5]

Creative fantasy needs a person within whom it can lodge itself as an embodied process structured by the qualities of creative experience. The melancholic, skeptical process is an essential dimension, the manifestation of which depends upon a living, suffering, and experiencing "I."

2.5. Anti-Creativity, Deconstruction, Destructivity

Thus far the nature of creativity has been described in terms of four essential aspects. To these must be added now a fifth, namely the dimension of the anti-creative, the destructive, the deconstructive. Not being simply something other, destruction is an essential ingredient that belongs intimately and imparts to creative fantasy its own imminently opposing force.

The inherent, large power of negation is experienced in and by creative people, as witnessed in their characteristic capacity to renounce pre-supposed ideas. They break the "ten commandments" of good taste, proven codes of conduct, and conventional norms and values. The destructive side of creativity ferrets out, questions, and overturns that which is approved and customary. A diagnostic sense is at work, honing in on signs of inauthenticity, lifelessness, parroting, and all forms of determination by the collective.

All great creators are distinguished by this kind of creative destructiveness, which embodies initially the need to free one's self from habitual thinking. The revolutionary gesture that creates a tabula rasa, negating the existing and familiar, clears the way for what is to come.

The negating impulse itself evidences a fundamental aversion to all inauthenticity. Such sensitivity imparts the creative person with a creative "nose" for dubious human behavior. Among the impressive examples of thinkers who display it are Pascal, Voltaire, Nietzsche and Kierkegaard, all of whom are distinguished by ingenious abilities to sniff out the dubieties of human existence. They show moreover that the capacity comes hand-in-hand with the creative gift of annulling, critical analysis.

Of course, examples of critical creative imagination can be found as well in the field of psychology, beginning in particular with the founders of modern depth psychology. A case in point is, again, Sigmund Freud. His highly developed sense for all forms of neurotic inauthenticity engendered his maxim, "Wo es war, soll Ich werden."[6] In translation, "Where it was, I shall become."[7]

In his *Red Book*—a document of creative fantasy *par excellence*— Jung revolts against the all too human habit of apish imitation:

> Imitation was a way of life when men still needed the heroic prototype. The monkey's manner is a way of life for monkeys and for man as long as he is like a monkey. Human apishness has lasted a terribly long time, but the time will come when a piece of that apishness will fall away from men.[8]

The de-masking, polemic trajectory of the creative impulse is well illustrated in Jung's insight that, "Man doesn't only grow from within himself, for he is also creative from within himself."[9]

Negation is a power and a capacity that belongs to the original force of creation, as evidenced especially in philosophical teachings and religious ideas.

For a philosopher like René Descartes, it is the means of challenging all false ideas and of reaching the final certainty, "*cogito ergo sum.*" Thus according to Descartes, the capacity to think is the ultimate signpost of the individual's creative selfhood.

In the philosophy of Immanuel Kant, a superb creative gift of critical analysis is expressed in his three works, *Critique of Pure Reason*, *Critique of Practical Reason*, and *Critique of Judgment*.

For Hegel, too, the element of creative negation assumes central meaning, for instance in his *Phenomenology of Spirit*. Here he conceives a "naïve consciousness" that traverses a long path of skeptical experiences, undergoing progressive sublations of its partial knowledge before attaining "absolute knowledge" of the absolutely negative freedom of being. ("Negative" here is meant not in a moral sense, but as transcending the finitude of all restricted perspectives of the conscious mind.)

Indeed it can be said fundamentally that there are no philosophers for whom critical scrutiny does not play a central role, which again evidences the analytic reflexive nullifying impulse that is intrinsic to creativity.

Religious ideas as well show how very much negation is inherent to creation. For instance, the Buddha's own beginning begins when he receives the revelation of human suffering. His enduring vibrancy is drawn from his later vision of the fundamental ills of human existence. At the same time, Nirvana represents the highest aim of transcending and negating all earthly ties. Negation, as an experienced fact of life, is the starting point for constructive creative vision. It is the vehicle of a critical coming-to-consciousness of suffering as the source of life and it defines the human goal to become free of suffering.

Negating creativity is central also to Christianity, where human redemption rests on Christ's crucifixion. Here, the sublating creative act—the sacrifice of the Son—is a counterpart in the founding gesture of the Father, itself revealed as a sign in the Father's creation of the world.

In his lectures and seminars at the Swiss Federal Institute of Technology Zürich (ETH) Jung investigated Ignatius von Loyola's "Spiritual Exercises."[10] Loyola's exercise book provides another good example of the potential of creative imagination in a space of negation. The practitioner has to spend the complete first of four weeks confronting the fact of his sinfulness. In all conceivable ways and in all possible realms, past and present, he must envision his personal sins. His task is to recognize how far he has fallen from the original creation, from the so-called "fundament," and how hopelessly he stands in the balance of life. One could disparage such a relentless process of self-scrutiny as nothing but religious moralism, perhaps also as Christian-inspired masochism or pathological compulsion. Conceding that such factors might play a role, it is ultimately about something else, namely the stimulation of creative energy by activating and recognizing the negative pole of creativity. It is not a demoralizing undermining of the self, but a paradoxical enlivening that flows from experience of the destructive power of creation and from the knowledge of redemption by the "negative" symbol of the cross. The cathartic effect of the encounter with this darkness evidences a confrontation with the shadow, as Jungian parlance puts it. The cleansing effect lies not only in becoming conscious of the shadow and the resulting possibility to deal with it more adequately. Viewed in the present context of thought, a purging occurs just as much with our acceptance of negation as such being an inherent activator of creative energy.

The arts often embrace destruction as an intrinsic aspect of creation—an alternative, a mirror, the dark side. Artists of the twentieth century as well as those of our own century have been especially fascinated with it. But it is just as present in earlier paintings, music, and plays that deal with the topics of war, aggression, sickness, injury, destruction, and other distresses and adversities. Let us call to mind, for instance, the great number of medieval portrayals of the passion of Christ and the sufferings of so many martyrs. Hieronymus Bosch's paintings nearly relish in images of lust, other vice, and punishment. Rembrandt famously depicted the slaughtered ox and also Dr. Nicolaes Tulp's anatomy lesson with the corpse. Francisco Goya painted the man-eating monster, the witches' Sabbath, and the eerie allegory of war and madness. Auguste Rodin's bronze casting enshrined the burghers of Calais, not as heroes, but as anguished human beings. We think as well of *Guernica*, Picasso's memorial to the Spanish civil war; Edvard Munch's *The Cry*; and Francis Bacon's contemporary triptychs with disfigured bodies. Also in our time, Niki de Saint Phalle created abstract "shooting pictures" by the violent gesture of firing a gun at paint containers, allowing the exploding colors to bleed at random along blockboard surfaces. The list could go on indefinitely.

Recognizing the constancy and visibility of destruction in artistic expression, we can conclude that an often apparent fascination with such darkness is crucial for the creative process. Destructive creativity is just as rich, mysterious, and large as its constructive counterpart, and as such, pushes repeatedly for its own realization.

Five features that typically characterize the presence and experience of creative fantasy have been discussed here, namely: fresh insight enabled by the visualization of new possibilities of meaning discovered in known things; the confrontation with outer and inner images; the mediating quality of the sensuous medium; the binding of the creative impulse to the individual person; and the paradoxical creative power of negation. Artists experience such dimensions in their own being and creative processes, and their artworks often contain implicit reflections on the nature of art and the fundaments of the artistic process. Therefore we should not be surprised to encounter these particular aspects of creativity expressed in the works of artists to be explored in the coming chapters.

III

DIMENSIONS OF CREATIVE CONSCIOUSNESS IN EXAMPLES OF PAINTING

3.1. Marc Chagall: The Rabbi, or the Pinch of Snuff

To begin to visualize the dimensions of creative consciousness, I would like to examine five of Marc Chagall's paintings that hold in common the motif of the Jew. One of them, a painting of 1912, portrays a rabbi with a penetrating gaze. In his left hand, resting on the table, he holds a small snuffbox, in his right hand, a pinch of snuff. Chagall took up the same motif again between 1923 and 1926. Figure (1) shows a later version of the same portrait, which bears the title, *The Rabbi, or the Pinch of Snuff*. In the summer of 1914, at Chagall's first solo exhibition at the Herwarth Walden Gallery in Berlin, the catalogue listed this painting under the French title, *On dit*, meaning "one says," or "it means," or "it is said."

On the surface, the painting portrays a rabbi sitting in a *shtiebel*, a little room reserved for prayer. Seated behind a table, and having been immersed in the lessons of the Talmud, he allows himself a break with a pinch of snuff. However, the painting doubtlessly intends more than the reproduction of anecdotal details from Chagall's Jewish surroundings. The seemingly incidental motif provides fodder for a more basic proposal.

(Fig. 1): Marc Chagall, *The Rabbi*, or *The Pinch of Snuff*

We see a man with deep-set, profoundly gazing eyes. He has a striking head shape, and waves of hair protrude dramatically from both sides of his face. His profound gaze and unruly curls create the impression of an original, inventive character, a man of perspicacity and unconventional views. A creative spirit is plainly visible, one that apprehends new images from within (eyes); one that generates unusual ideas (curls); one that has an intuitive bent and ability to "sniff out" the new (nose); and one that is in the grip of an unnamable great power (daemon-like face).

This rabbi wears a long pointed beard, which is mainly green, corresponding with the color of the wall-hanging in the background, affixed with the Star of David. However, his beard is marked also by the contrast of an overlapping black goatee. A symbolic understanding of these elements could tell us, perhaps, that the rabbi's spirit embodies the cultural inheritance of his Judaic tradition—an inheritance, which, however, is overlaid by and finds expression in the life of the creative individual.

The rabbi's left hand, clasping the snuffbox, is poised over the open Talmud, while his right hand guides a pinch of snuff toward his mouth and nose. The gesture recalls Goethe's words, "What we are born with, we must make our own / or it remains a mere appurtenance / and is not ours: a load of unused things ..."[11] The Talmud lying beneath the snuffbox could symbolize the traditional wisdom and foregoing experience from which the creative individual, in the here-and-now, draws a "pinch" of new personal life and insight.

This particular creative spirit stands in an existential dichotomy, facing on one side the outer world of long-held religious symbols (the Star of David). Emerging from the other side is the world of symbols that emanates from within, from the center of the personality, the Self, symbolized in the pearl-strung disc, which is only partly visible in the upper left hand corner of the painting. To extrapolate more generally: On one hand, creative fantasy works with the outer determinant of pre-given culture and within the horizon of the given time—and on the other hand, it is nourished from within by the image-giving Self, which transcends all time and space.

The creative spirit manifesting itself in the figure of this rabbi sits behind the table in such a way that it seems there would be very little space available for him. The image obviously concerns some kind of confinement, a constriction from which the spirit would free itself, as if it were in existential distress at the break lines of life. And with this, it is as if creative spirit per se would well up primarily from the experienced fragility of being.

3.2. Marc Chagall: Jew in Red

(Fig. 2): Marc Chagall, *Jew in Red*

A second painting by Chagall brings to expression another aspect of the creative experience, the dimension we described earlier as the dialogic confrontation of old and new representations. I have in mind now the portrait of 1914 entitled, *Jew in Red* (Fig. 2). This picture belongs to the portraits of old Jews that stem from Chagall's second return visit to his home in Vitebsk, and that established the painter's world renown.

With the *Jew in Red* Chagall again intended to portray more than an old beggar from the poor quarter, the *schtetl*, knocking on someone's door by happenstance. While Chagall stated the concern to "document" his witnessing of the threatened Jewish culture, we detect here more than this, especially in the symbolic magnitude of the beggar and the wall at his back.

A close look at the wall's bright outer arch shows that Chagall inscribed it with painters' names, the names of the artists whom he considered to be his important predecessors. Among them: "Giotto," "Courbet," "El Greco," "Chardin," "J. Fouquet," "Cimabue," "Tintoretto," "Vincent." Chagall's homage to these painters attests to the will to reflect his artistic lineage and beyond this, to reflect his experience of creativity as such.

The *Jew in Red* reminds us of the Eternal Jew Ahasver, a figure of legend, the contemplative and shy mystic who wanders for all time, carrying with him nothing but his sparse belongings. His enigmatic presence puzzles onlookers who encounter him without warning. An independent, freely roaming spirit, one that never comes to rest, never arrives, never sits squarely with fixed theories. A spirit that exists outside of established norms. A loner who observes from the outside and looks into the inner workings of society. One who occupies the fringes, having no roof of his own, moving about like a vagabond—as often belongs to the life of the artist: a critical observer of society and life, always somehow foreign to and never at home in his familiar surroundings.

The untethered spirit in Chagall's painting carries his own experiences like a priceless treasure, bundled in a brown sack. The bundle is the sum of his undergone experiences, a container with the function of preserving. But in its form, it likens as well a stomach or a placenta, that is, organs of processing and transformation, which can symbolize the potential to bring forth new images and insights from the substance of experience. As in an alchemical vessel, retort, or vial, in which the essences of one's own new ideas may be distilled from the stuff of experience.

One of the beggar's hands, likening that of a magician's, is assigned to this "bundle of experience." Luminously white, and rendered in primitive a folk style, so to speak, this hand displays four fingers that may allude to a special creative faculty. As the number four conventionally symbolizes a differentiating quality of consciousness, it could mean that, in this aspect, creative fantasy encompasses an ability to shape and frame consciously that which is experienced, for instance in the formulation of theoretical concepts, the plotting out of typological structures, the composition of programs, manifestos, and the like.

Opposite the beggar's white hand and brown bundle we see his other hand, a red one, guiding a walking stick. This hand, a supplely formed and sensitive one, displays all five digits, and seems to be flushed with blood, with the sensibility of feeling. With the thumb and forefinger probing the way forward, this hand appears to perform the function of meticulous yet sensitive examination and judgment. Symbolically akin to the scepter, the walking stick could stand for tradition and authority. Thus this motif suggests the ability to relate with empathic scrutiny to the traditional values that one leans on. As in the sense of the Biblical thought, "Prove all things; hold fast that which is good." (Thessalonians 5:21)

Indeed, the bond with the past, from which new meaning can be discerned, is a special gift that characterizes this particular dimension of creative fantasy. Such attachment has been observed already in Chagall's tribute to his spiritual kin and artistic origins, in the form of the artists' names inscribed on the triangular surface of the white wall. The bond is expressed again in the lower left-hand corner of the painting, where the bright triangle is positioned above the Russian house that refers to Chagall's birthplace and biographical origin.

In summary, we can say that the *Jew in Red* describes creative fantasy in the specific aspect that distinguishes itself by the ability to draw from past experience conscious insight and self-awareness. And this, again in the sense of Freud's dictum, "Where it was, I shall become."[12]

3.3. Marc Chagall: Rabbi with Torah

Rabbi with Torah (Fig. 3), painted by Chagall in 1930, should help to illustrate the third aspect of creativity, namely its manifestation in a mediating, sensuous medium. Depicted in a winter landscape, the rabbi is attired as a devoutly religious man. A tallit, the traditional prayer shawl, drapes his head and shoulders. On his forehead and

(Fig. 3): Marc Chagall, *Rabbi with Torah*

upper left arm he wears the tefillin, the two leather boxes containing
verses from the Torah. The tefillin strap is bound around his left
forearm and hand. In the embrace of his arms he carries a red Torah
scroll. The expression on his face emanates trust and warmth. His
wide-open eyes, gazing attentively and expectantly upward, bespeak
the confidence and ardor of a believer.

The rabbi's binding in a reality greater than his own is symbolized by the circular wrapping of his prayer shawl, his spiraling tefillin strap, and also by the circle of his arms bearing the Torah scroll. He is, in other words, encircled within an all-containing world. While he gazes toward something higher and greater, he finds grounding in the Torah—itself appearing in the circular form of a scroll. Such outer signs of a binding in something larger express the inner attitude of a deeply devout person. One could assume that Chagall intended to convey this quality in the portrayed rabbi. But we might discern in the painting something beyond the artist's intention, namely an expression of the creative process that Chagall himself experienced. In other words, we can view the painting not only as a portrait of a rabbi, but also as a description of the artistic sensibilities of the individual, "Chagall." And from this we might extrapolate a more general, imagistic testimony about a quality of creativity as such.

In this painting creativity is encountered and depicted as a power greater than one's self, a power which incarnates and makes itself palpable in the individual, physically and sensuously. The individual experiences himself as the site of the revelation and realization of a higher creative power. Apparently striving toward wholeness and completion, the creative spirit concretizes itself in circular form and in the shape of the body.

The rabbi's arms and hands are visibly involved in the manifestation of this greater power. His left forearm and hand, uncovered and wrapped with the tefillin strap, stand symbolically for direct apprehension and sensuous experience, but also for hands-on, pragmatic action. Creative fantasy relies on one's concrete doing, on the skill of one's hand, and on knowledge gained through practice. In contrast to abstract thought, creative fantasy requires visible example, manifestation in concrete material, and playful experiment with observable things. In this sense the arm is an organ that anticipates and prepares the way for creative fantasy's emergence. The reliance of creativity on the sensitivity of the hand and on patient doing is well illustrated in the *Red Book*, where the meticulous paintings and texts in Gothic script bear testimony to the religiously diligent practice by which Jung not only rendered the images of his inner life, but also paved the way for all of his later creative insights. The arm and hand serve to "lever open" what Jung calls the transcendent function, the function by which sense and meaning arise through the creating of sensuous images.

The concrete making of things does in the truest sense lever creative fantasy, for the autonomous reality of the creative force becomes activated with the transfer of the inwardly imagined image to an outwardly perceptible form. In the process, consciousness is led beyond that which is known, and helped to transcend its existing views.

The rabbi bears in his arms a Torah scroll, the Jewish Bible containing the five Books of Moses. Considering the meaning and symbolism of the Torah beyond the Judaic context, we can say the following: The Torah is a piece of writing that documents the encounter of a group of people with a higher being, a being which itself determines the history of these people. The Torah remembers and commemorates the effects of a creative entity that reveals itself in astonishing autonomous happenings and discoveries, which themselves convey the experience of being called, guided, and endowed in mysterious ways. (For instance, as in the case of the Jews, the experience of being God's chosen people.)

This kind of Torah experience is characteristic of creative individuals, who find themselves fundamentally thrust into the living reality of a creative force that manifests itself in personal revelation and establishes consciousness of a personal task. It is the immediate grasping of new and surprising connections between known things that develops the sense of a mysterious, guiding force that brings new insights to consciousness step by step, according to its own purposeful strivings.

Jung, too, provides an impressive example of an encounter with an autonomous creative entity. It can be witnessed initially in the "Black Books,"[13] the yet to be published notebooks in which Jung recorded his insights before refining them aesthetically in his *Red Book*. These imaginative materials in turn express the fundaments of his psychological discoveries. The *Red Book* thus contains all at once the foundations, the basic model, and the propaedeutic groundwork of what would become known as Jung's Analytical Psychology.

Likewise the fundaments of Hegel's future and complete philosophical works show in his *Phenomenology of the Spirit*. Such high-density experience appears over and over again in creative individuals, be it at the beginning or in the course of their work. That which foists itself upon them in the sense of nearly overwhelming revelation obtains visible design only afterward with painstaking work. In other words, there is a happy phase of divinely given discovery. The later translations into shareable forms refer back to this fundus or store of numinous insight that comes into being with the creative force as the director, par excellence.

The basic stock of material offers itself to the individual in the framework of a primal preparatory experience, which encompasses as well an encounter with universal archetypes and initiation into the basic, experiential pattern of creativity. The creative individual manages this treasure, using it, actualizing, and visualizing it. He or she draws on both the fundamental personal experience of the creative force, and the archetypes, the determinants of the history of human creativity. This is so to speak the "Torah experience"— the experience of the creative individual, who both works and produces inspired by the treasured material. This portrait of the rabbi can tell us the same thing when we separate its motifs from the context of surface meaning and try to understand them in their more fundamental symbolic depth.

Let us now have a look at this rabbi's surroundings. Cold winter prevails and the country village is veiled in a shadowy, twilight mood. In contrast, the rabbi is wrapped in his radiant prayer shawl, holding on to the warm red Torah. A symbolic view suggests that warming insight can arise through an introverted retreat to the reality of the soul with its eternally living symbols. It requires a distancing from what Jung in the *Red Book* calls "the superficial spirit of this time," which considers things only outwardly and in their materialistic properties, or which travels on the tracks of spiritless factuality, or which is determined by a cynical worldview, a dog's world.[14] In other words, distance is required from the proximal world that comprehends only a materialistic, surface view of things, a world led by the dim light of rationality, like a man relying on streetlamps to find his way, but finding himself more in the dark than in the light. Chagall opposes this chilling worldview with the truly enlightening and healing experience of meaning that arises from the Torah-like inner spirit of the depths.

To sum up, Chagall's *Rabbi with the Torah* concerns essentially the experience of creativity as a *sui generis* numinous and effective reality. It is moreover about the bodily incarnation of the creative spirit in the doings of individuals who feel themselves to be chosen, compelled, and guided by it.

3.4. Marc Chagall: Jew in Green

(Fig. 4): Marc Chagall *Jew in Green*

In 1914 Chagall painted *Jew in Green* (Fig. 4), which he attributed by name to the storyteller Sluzker Maggid. This impressive, worthy beggar with the bodily bearing of the melancholic character sits weary and exhausted amidst pages of religious text, which he recites in the hope of gaining some income for it. We shall let him stand for our exploration of the previously mentioned fourth dimension of creative fantasy, namely the discovery that arises from the experience and self-observation of the individual, and that pertains specifically to that individual.

This is a portrait of a man who appears to bear the weight of much experience and to be marked by the wisdom gained from it. It seems that he has internalized and carries within himself this complete inheritance. Somehow, he echoes Rembrandt's *Old Man in Red* (1652). Then, too, he recalls the pensiveness of Rodin's *The Thinker* (1880/1882), and the metaphysical skepticism of the angel in Albrecht Dürer's *Melencolia I* (1514), as well as the sadness of *Boy in a Red Vest* by Paul Cézanne (1888/90).

What all of these works have in common is their depiction of a certain relationship of the arms to the torso that is understood in iconography to signify a melancholic consciousness. The melancholic seems always reflexively bent or collapsed into himself. This bodily bearing is the visible expression of an inner dynamic whereby the striving for some kind of end or fruition always leads back to the starting point. In the *Jew in Green*, we can imagine the cycle beginning with the old man's left hand, that is the white hand, the unsullied one, seemingly child-like, a *tabula rasa*. It proceeds up along his arm, which bears signs of many incisive experiences. It progresses to the wise old man's head, where all his experiences are "sublated." From his head the movement extends downward along his right arm to his yellow hand. His clasped hands, resting on his knees beneath his downcast gaze, mark the return to the beginning, the place where the melancholic languishes.

Chagall's old melancholic is portrayed with a green head, the large size of which intimates his all-encompassing wisdom. Green, the color of nature and the color of becoming, might symbolize his closeness to nature and his vivid, concretely manifesting spirit. Perhaps also a holy spirit of the kind we associate with the green liturgical vestments worn by Catholic priests during Pentecost, or with the green *Khdir*, the enigmatic spiritual guide of Islam. In other words, the melancholic embodies not the mind of abstract logic, but the mind in awe of the creative spirit that reveals itself in sensuous and artistic form. It is a mind with the faculty to perceive spirit in things found in nature, in the documents of culture, and in one's own history.

The man's right eye is open, his left eye closed. Covering one and then the other, we note the symbolization of two contrary but simultaneously functioning modes of consciousness: an entirely outward one (the open eye), oriented toward the world of outer objects—and a completely introspective one (the closed eye), oriented toward the Self and its world of inner objects. Thus the spirit etched into this man's face appears not only to access both modes of recognizing and perceiving, but also to link them to one another organically. Outwardly perceived forms evoke inner understanding, and inner self-experience finds analogy in the external field of perception. This is the poetic gift by which inner experiences are converted into the sensuous reality of observable events, and vice versa, outer perceptions become imbued with sense and meaning for inner life.

A closer look at the furrowed landscape of this melancholic's impressive face allows us to infer further symbolic meaning. First of all, as the head is the fundamental site of the spirit's expression, the pronounced forehead could signify a rather cerebral spirit, a quality of consciousness directed by linear thinking. Next, the green face contrasts with the tufts of yellow hair that frame the head. The unusual green and yellow coloring here recalls the portrait of the rabbi with his snuff box (Figure 1). In both paintings, yellow stands for light and illuminating revelation from above, from the beyond. In fact, such connection to spiritual transcendence is characteristic in both paintings.

Notably, the yellow hues appear in relationship to the five sense organs: The witty yellow curls on the right side of the man's face align with his eye and the sense of vision. On his left side, his yellow hair frames a remarkably configured ear, highlighting the sense of hearing. His yellow mustache highlights his nose and the sense of smell. His flowing beard surrounds his chin and mouth, marking the sense of taste. And finally, his yellow hand, clasped by the other, evokes the sense of touch.

Thus the painting might symbolically impart the meaning that the five sense organs serve as portals to the experience and mediation of higher, sublime, and transcendent realms. Vision as the physical faculty of the eye can encompass spiritual vision, such as when our observance of Chagall's pictures generates unexpected insights. To hear can be to attune to a spiritual reality as happens, for example, when we listen to a moving piece of music. The sense of smell can bear the presence of a creative force, evident when one' "sniffs out" surprising insights or uses that "nose" for what is to be done in the here-and-now or what should be noticed in the sense of synchronistic events. The transcendent can be mediated when the sense of taste becomes an inner savoring of things, a meditative attitude recommended by Ignatius of Loyola for attaining spiritual fulfillment. Finally, the transcendent can manifest itself in the sense of touch, as in the ingenious handling of brush and paint, so impressively exemplified by Chagall himself. Higher spiritual reality here always becomes manifest in empirical, sensuous experience and in this respect it is bound to the individual's bodily reality.

Approaching the end of our look at this picture, let us devote some words to the background. The old man sits before a dark black backdrop, which aptly bespeaks the black bile humor, that is, the melancholic disposition of the overall scene. Indeed, close inspection of the backdrop reveals that it is overlaid by a yet darker shadow cast by the man's upper body and appearing as a black halo. Heightening the contrast with the bright yellow tufts of hair, this aspect of the composition points to a simultaneous incarnation of the light and the dark. Here the individual experiences the spirit in its total reality—and therefore, too, the condition of spiritlessness. To embody this dark side is to fall into nihilistic emptiness, meaninglessness, and absolute incapacitation. Thus belonging to this aspect of creativity is the experience of negative evidence, the inability to bring forth any creative insight whatsoever. As undergone repeatedly by creative people—be they artists, thinkers, mystics—this negativity can be felt as the *noche oscura* (the dark night of the soul, John of the Cross), a fall from God, an absolute dearth of imagination, a total lack of inspiration, the soul lost in a desert.

It could be said as well that such states of being evidence one's earthly existence and finitude, one's utter lack of access to a living and transcendent spirit, one's experience of a kind of hell. The connection with a fulfilling and invigorating creative spirit is now radically disrupted and replaced by melancholic certainty in nothingness, in existential emptiness and creative impotence. Albrecht Dürer (1471-1528) is among those who lived the creative person's constitutionally borderline existence. Before starting work on his engraving *Melencolia I* (1514), he opined, "What is beautiful I do not know." And yet in that depleted state, he created ingenious works of art.[15]

Intrinsic to this shadow of creativity is as well a fruitless logic of the kind that might be symbolized in the white and red squares appearing at the right-hand border of Chagall's painting. These two basic geometric shapes allow us to imagine an abstract, analytical logic that formally determines and differentiates but that does not encompass a synthetic or descriptive approach. This is on one hand an either/or, anemic type of thinking (the white square) and on the other hand it is sheer emotion (the red square)—all to the effect that such thinking lacks recognition of imagistically conveyed meanings and their feeling-toned impacts.

Thus the suffering of spiritlessness and abandonment by all good is inherent to the individual in whom the creative spirit incarnates itself. Archetypal images show how such creative experience conjoins the absolutely distant spirit and the absolutely near. Among them are God's abandonment of Christ on the cross; the Jews' exile from Egypt; and the Christian Stations of the Cross with fourteen points marking the subjection of the immortal God to the mortal conditions of human existence.

In the *Jew in Green* the old man sits upon scattered sheets of religious text. A surface view might lead us to believe the image recalls simply the texts that were recited by the story teller Sluzker Maggid. However here too a more careful look reveals a deeper meaning. In the lower right-hand side of the image's frame, the text begins with the Yiddish title, "Sluzker Maggid." Following the title is a Hebrew blessing that recalls the Jews as God's chosen people and their binding to the one God and the teachings of the Torah. On the left-hand side of the frame the text runs upside-down and consists of two passages from the 4th Book of Moses, the Book of Numbers. Chapter 30:1-4 cites the command for all Jews to uphold their sworn oath to God. Chapter 32:1-40 refers to the division of Transjordan amongst the ten tribes of Israel. The text in Chagall's painting ends with the closing words of the daily prayer, the Kaddish: "He who makes peace in His heights, may He make peace, upon us and upon all Israel."[16], [17]

These texts emphasize the meaning of the portrayed individual and the task of the Jewish people, and in so doing, they confirm and recollect a particular creative calling. In this sense the words intend to thwart self-doubt—but perhaps they mean as well to afford protection against a dangerous hubris that attributes to the gift of knowledge to one's own abilities. What we have here is an objective written charter of successful interaction between the individual and a greater creative being. We might be reminded of various kinds of documentation that function similarly—for instance a bibliography, a catalogue of works, an exhibition list, a professional résumé. These serve to avoid both absolute self-doubt and self-aggrandizement while they also bring to memory the value of one's creative work as well as the duty of seriousness towards one's calling.

3.5. Marc Chagall: Jew in Black and White

(Fig. 5): Marc Chagall, *Jew in Black and White*

For the *Jew in Black and White* (Fig. 5), in later versions entitled *The Praying Jew*, the model was an old beggar whom Chagall had persuaded to sit for a few kopecks, draped in his father's prayer shawl. The string held in his right hand, a *tzitzit*, is worn for the performance of the morning prayer. The centerpiece of the service is the *Schema*, the profession of faith taken from Deuteronomy 6:4: "Hear, O Israel: the Lord our G–d, the Lord is One." In the morning prayer service there immediately follows a reading from the 4th Book of Moses, Numbers 15:37-40, which cites the commandment for the "people of Israel" to "make [fringes] in the corners of their garments." In the painting such a fringe hangs from the Jew's hand, a sign that he keeps the commandment.

This portrait was painted in 1914 when Chagall had returned to Vitebsk in Russia, where he had planned to stay for only three months. But finding himself unable to leave due to the outbreak of World War I, he remained in Russia for eight more years. The painting shows the lively presence of a person sitting upright, his alert gaze and warm face looking from beneath his white prayer shawl into the darkness of a torn world.[18] The image as such might stand for the aspect of creativity that we previously linked with the dimension of fantasy that is anti-creative, destructive, and deconstructive. The man here finds himself in a dark, cold, rejecting, winter-like world, confined by dire fear and existential need. (In German the words for "confined" [*eng*] and fear [*Angst*] are closely related: fear means confinement.) Wedged between cubistic split surfaces, he is condemned to non-action. Impotent, he is completely at the mercy of his own fate.

He seems to live in absence of a visible and palpable God. He is no longer borne up by such a presence. We might think of the Old Testament figure Job, who because of God's wager with the devil was deprived little by little of all signs of a happy existence and merciful God—and who against all common sense and against all his experiences of an unjust God keeps firmly his belief in the same God as the eternal and only one. Just as the Jews, despite their constant persecution and homelessness, did not allow themselves to be dissuaded from their fundamental convictions.[19]

Beyond this, the *Jew in Black and White* could point to a general and fundamentally human condition. Namely that in which creativity itself springs from a painful absence of creativity and that "despite all," things move forward when one abides by one's own calling or task. The fundament and fueling of creativity are built on experiences of meaninglessness, experiences of restriction, experiences of absent inspiration, and experiences of doubt in the value of one's own and others' creative endeavors. Such dark times (re-)invite belief in one's own possibilities. They challenge us in direct proportion to the very evidence they engender for an absent or no longer flowing source of creativity.

We find again an example in C.G. Jung, who was afflicted by an illness that nearly cost him his life—and yet he emerged from it strengthened and transformed. From that time onward he devoted himself entirely and without compromise to his creative task. The existential threat awakened his creative resolve:

> After the illness a fruitful period of work began for me. A good many of my principal works were written only then. The insight I had had, or the vision of the end of all things, gave me the courage to undertake new formulations. I no longer attempted to put across my own opinion, but surrendered myself to the current of my thoughts... . It was only after the illness that I understood how important it is to affirm one's own destiny. In this way we forge an ego that does not break down when incomprehensible things happen; an ego that endures, that endures the truth, and that is capable of coping with the world and with fate.[20]

Before this, the break from Freud had already caused the deep shock that resulted in the emergence of the *Red Book*, which contained the fundaments of Jung's own creative ideas. Without the crisis Jung would not have become the originator of Analytical Psychology. Likewise without his loss of the traditional god image, Jung would have been unable to undertake through the *Red Book* the creation of his own god image. When God is no longer a given, then he is given as a task. When the entity of god is no longer self-evident, then god becomes a creative endeavor.

Existentially earnest creative activity uncovered by the vehicle of one's own limits is a general and basic experience to which many examples from art and culture bear witness. René Descartes' (1596 -1650) methodic doubt illustrates. From his standpoint, when all appearances are merely empty illusions, when all existential security must be surrendered, when humanity no longer feels the containment of a world made by God and infused with his presence, then the only remaining individual certainty and reason for being is, *cogito ergo sum*. Such unshakeable belief in one's self despite all adverse conditions is personified in Miguel de Cervantes's (1547–1616) sad figure Don Quixote of la Mancha. This *hidalgo* or nobleman is compelled to fulfill his own mission—even when his seduction by an anima-like illusion and the absurdity of his doings become all too apparent. The centuries of enduring interest in this rather strange story with its hapless protagonist suggest that it touches on an archetypal idea: the person who pursues his task to the bitter end, despite the destruction, the injustice, and the malice he wreaks along the way. We think also of the existential courage of Friedrich Nietzsche (1844–1900), who—despite his dreadful certainty that "God is dead"—did not fall into depression because he held steadfastly to his guiding idea that the goal of life is to become a creative person who strives to work beyond him- or herself.

To sum up thus far: Destruction and loss lead to consciousness of one's own creative resources, to the discovery of one's own creative calling, and to recognition of the essential features of one's own creative approach.

Returning to the *Jew in Black and White* and some of its details, we discover that the white prayer shawl displays two different aspects. On the side draping the man's right shoulder, the appearance of a smooth seam line on the outer border is reinforced by the two parallel fold lines. In contrast, the outer seam on the other side is jagged, depicting the fringe that belongs to the tallit. The horizontal stripes on both sides typically adorn the tallit, five on the right, three on the left.

In the differences between the two sides of the tallit we might discern such opposites as continuity and discontinuity, constructive building-up and dissolving differentiation, positing and sublating. The five horizontal lines on the right mark the symbolism of organic development that attributes us with five senses and five extremities (if we count the head). The three horizontal lines on the other side point to the symbolism of a three-step dialectic. The tallit's body-conforming roundness on one side and the pointed triangles on the other enhance the visual representation of two opposing qualities: a building-up, and an annulment—a construction and a deconstruction. Johann Wolfgang von Goethe (1749–1832) in his famous lines in *Faust* captures the same basic dynamic of the creative principle: "… Formation, Transformation, / Eternal mind's eternal recreation."[21]

The *Jew in Black and White* appears to take up the same theme, namely in the man's two hands. The formative pole of creation is described by his right hand: Opalescent in hue, likening the original translucence of an egg white, its yielding gesture forms the shape of a new moon. A basic chord of creation is struck by the index finger unfolding as a curve with five parts. This same hand holds the lower part of the *tzitzit*, the string knotted or twisted into five sections that open at the end with the fringe. Thus this right hand stands as well for service to the constructive logic of the number five, which we already observed in the tallit's immediately adjacent five stripes.

The pole of transfiguration is described by the man's left hand, which is depicted in an active red hue that emphasizes three fingers. Symbolizing the progressive dynamism of the number three, this hand expresses the revolutionary gesture of a new resolve—a dynamism that carries forward in the spiral form of the tefillin strap. Thus the left hand and arm together point to the force of transformation, which both circles and penetrates, participating in this way to complement the yielding gesture of the right hand, involving it in a playful back and forth exchange.

One last detail in this painting does not take up much space but is nevertheless visually impressive. In the lower corner beneath the man's right arm, there is a circular arc, which depicts the *tzitzit* with sixteen knots or twists leading to the fringe. The image as such alludes to a circular movement that likens the systematic direction of the clock or the cosmic motion of the planets. Perhaps here we can discern a basic sign of the creative process. The Jew in black and white, holding the corner fringe in his own hand, is portrayed as an individual who takes up the creative thread and is yet bound in the process as a mysterious reality that unfolds according to its own laws. Connected with such an autonomous reality that reigns like a bewildering fate, he moves along a creative path, encountering many blank spots and dark moments that in the end afford meaning. The whole pathway, in other words, is circular. To borrow from Goethe, it is "the eternal meaning of eternal mind's recreation..."

IV

CREATIVITY AS INTERACTION BETWEEN MASCULINE AND FEMININE FACTORS

The creative force concretizes itself always in a creative work. Being not only a kind of consciousness and not only a conceived possibility, creativity realizes itself in a visibly living, emerging thing. And this thing is the product of the encounter of two qualities of soul that come into interaction with one another. Insofar as these qualities are masculine and feminine, creativity has something to do with procreation, fertilization, pregnancy, and birth. Creativity is the *faszinosum* of a becoming-active and a becoming-fruitful, a joining of the fundamental opposites of a masculine doing and a feminine offering, a goal-oriented consciousness and a containing unconscious, a determining form and an enabling content. Creativity is essentially equal to what C.G. Jung called the transcendent function. It is the specifically imaginative power of the soul in contrast to the ego's linear striving for achievement.

It makes sense to distinguish these two kinds of thinking. On the one side, there is a single-minded, linear thinking, which remains within the scope of the rational, which unfolds coherently and systematically according to the respectively valid rules, and which thereby aims for effective and provable insights. On the other side there is a creative, imagistic thinking, which springs from the experience of opposites, which follows its own typological and procedural principles, and which thereby leads to illuminating and stimulating insights that give rise to further reflection.[22]

In this chapter four paintings will illustrate and support my discussion of this creative constellation, this fruitful cooperation between the masculine and feminine. The making of artworks entails essentially the experience of and practice with the creative force per se, so we should not be surprised to see such experience represented in art as a basic content and central *faszinosum*.

4.1. Otto Dix: Self-Portrait with Muse

(Fig. 6): Otto Dix, *Self-Portrait with Muse*

Self-Portrait with Muse (Fig. 6), painted by the important German expressionist Otto Dix (1891–1969) portrays a pair of subjects with two very different auras. Dix's muse alludes to a feminine Other who places herself in the scene suggestively—nearly hysterically—with an intense, beguiling, sphinxlike gaze, a sensuous red mouth with full lips, a generous mane of hair, a large protruding breast, and a theatrical pose. Facing her, the painter appears with a very controlled, absolutely concentrated ego. Two antithetical factors encounter one another here, helping the creative work to emerge: a side that animates and a side that determines; a side that stimulates, suggests, and opens the imagination—and a side that shapes, defines, and structures.

Dix's painting impressively expresses something that always happens with artistic activity: certain ideas offer themselves—ones that appeal, excite, seductively invite. These ideas seem to develop as if they would have lives of their own and would know in which direction the creative process would have to move.

In *Self-Portrait with Muse* a concentrated and resolutely observing consciousness, the artist, stands opposite this image offered from within. His neatly combed hair contrasts with the curly mane of the inner feminine counterpart. Insofar as hair stands symbolically for thoughts, we have in the figure of the artist a personification of ordered thinking facing a diversity of chaotic inspirations. His head appears distinctly in profile, rather than in the diagonal three-dimensional perspective that portrays the muse. The lateral view underlines the thinker's straightforward and categorically directed perspective.

The artist wears a dark blue pleated smock, conveying the impression that he would administer and prevail over his office and celebrate his job, so to speak. His habit contrasts very much with the nakedness of the muse. It shows a quality of reliable form, which corresponds to the social norms that the artist is embedded in, and which carry the traditional knowledge that he uses in his confrontation with the muse. The artist represents the established viewpoints, the tried and tested values, the rules of social communication—and this, as opposed to the muse's new views and propositions.

The encounter of the two worlds so plainly and intriguingly portrayed in this painting belongs fundamentally to creative work. The "feminine" conveys the fascinating and imaginative offer of images and ideas that aim at an inner gestalt and encompass suggestive new insights and creative possibilities—while the "masculine" holds the world of internalized social norms, rules of communication, historical tradition, and the binding criteria of reality.

There are always two agents: an actively shaping, structuring, and goal-oriented consciousness that stands in a cultural context—and a suggestive unconscious that gives, offers, and suggests fantasies. Creative activity arises from this fundamental constellation: the inner encounter, dialogue, tension, and cooperation between two different and antithetical agencies—one that inventively gives-shape-to and one that stimulates with the offer of fantasy. In Dix's painting the creative activity that occurs between the two poles—the artist's masculine "consciousness," and his muse's feminine "unconscious"— is portrayed symbolically in motifs that occupy the space between the two. Such motifs join and yet also transcend the two sides.

We observe first of all the motif of the hands. The hand symbolizes *par excellence* the act of creating. In the history of art we find God as the creator time and again depicted in relationship to the creating hand. The hands painted on the walls of ancient caves reveal the inhabitants' consciousness of their own creative possibilities. These hands arguably expressed the astonished and fascinated certitude that being was not only to be suffered, but could be creatively shaped, thanks to the power of image.

Let us observe first the painter's left hand, which is centered visually between the antithetical subjects, and which guides a fine brush that joins the two. His two very curved fingers emphasize the gesture of a particular conjunction of man and woman, artist and muse. It is the gesture of a direct bond and amalgamation between sense and sensuousness—a pair of antagonists that together bring forth startlingly vivid and pregnant figures, and that generate the feeling of immediately emerging creativity. The painter grasps in his right hand a long staff. In the powerful gesture suggested here, a prince-like painter holds a scepter to embody his spiritual authority. In earlier times, the scepter signaled the power of kings. With his own scepter Moses drew water from the rock. Thus the staff or scepter could stand symbolically for the capacity to create new values, ideas, methods, or perspectives that open to the future and that promise to become generally binding cultural assets, or to usher in a new era, or to establish a decisively new rule of collective behavior.

The feminine counterpart, also actively and equally involved in this creative experience, looks very different from the usual artist's model. Her left hand extends high into the ether, like an antenna or a concave mirror intercepting hidden messages and meanings from the skies, from the horizon of the *Zeitgeist*. The muse appears to express the artist's intuitive feel for the "high time," for some imminence on the verge of revealing itself. This would be, then, something that distinguishes art and creativity through all time: the expression of the unknown in prophetically anticipatory and creative form.

The utopic, prophetic dimension of creativity realizes itself precisely in the artist's devotion to a concrete, sensuous image or to his/her artistic task—not in elevated, intellectual speculation. The phenomenon can be read symbolically in Dix's painting, where the woman's right hand rests on her own body and her extended left hand suggests the counterbalance of an intuitive faculty. The curve formed by her two arms suggests a functional linking, a kind of balancing movement: The touching of one's own body and the delving into the matter of artistic appearance and sensuous beauty serve together as a lever that pries open the revelation of something to come.

C.G. Jung's *Red Book*, which opens with the chapter, "The Way of What Is to Come," contains imaginings and images of a creative encounter with inner fantasies. The fact that this book anticipated new spiritual developments that were not only Jung's personal insights but were relevant in the realm of collective consciousness is thanks to the painstaking and concrete manner by which Jung entered into the flow of fantasies and committed himself to their best possible expression. Had he not delved deeply into his fantasies and had he not cared enough to attribute them with imagistic form, he would have been unable to portray "what was to come." Intuition of that which is to come results not from intellectual speculation, but from the creative expression of the sensuous and meaning-making fantasy itself.

Creative activity is a mysterious process, moving in two directions. In the horizontal trajectory it takes the form of cooperation between an actively directed and determining moment of consciousness that interacts with an autonomous, stimulating fantasy. In the vertical trajectory it is the realization of an idea that arises between the poles of imagined possibility and concrete fulfillment.

Otto Dix's painting might tell us how he personally experienced creative activity—but it can also help us to understand the fundamental experience as such. It is an endeavor on a vertical plane, where a timely creative idea concretizes itself enigmatically in the here and now— and an endeavor on a horizontal plane, where a current consciousness interacts with an eternally young inner source to create new images.

4.2. René Magritte: *Attempting the Impossible*

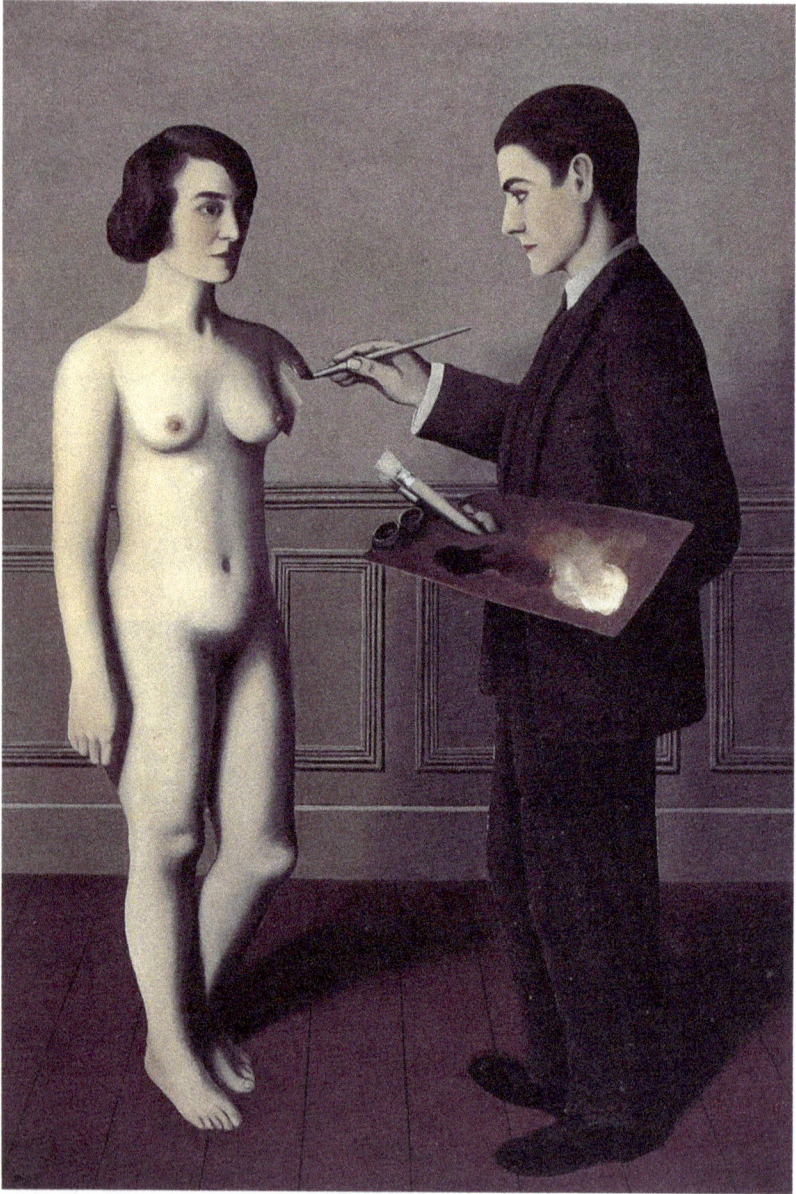

(Fig. 7): René Magritte, *Attempting the Impossible*

Attempting the Impossible (Fig. 7) by the Belgian painter René Magritte (1898-1967) may help us to glimpse another dimension of creativity as it manifests in creative people. Here again I assume that the portrait of the artist and his model not only interprets a theme typically handled in the history of art—but that it also reflects on the mysterious nature of the artist's creative act. As is so often the case with such self-portraits, we find in Magritte's painting, too, his enquiry into the basis of his own work—an enquiry that is, in a way, his own self-analysis and self-affirmation. What is it that finally and repeatedly determines the painter's innermost and most personal activity? This is the existential question lying behind the image. What is the secret of artistic creativity? And beyond this, what is the mystery of the creative phenomenon as such?

Just as it seemed to be for Otto Dix, Magritte's basic creative experience as a painter seems determined by his awareness of a suggestive feminine counterpart to his directed masculine consciousness. This elemental opposition provides the basic frame for the formation of the creative force as a third factor between the two. In Magritte's painting, we see on one hand a consciousness represented in a lateral view of the person looking intently at the Other.

The painter's attentive gaze on his subject reveals the intrinsic properties of consciousness per se, such as directionality, intentionality, and focus. These correspond with what Jung in *Symbols of Transformation* calls "directed thinking," which he distinguishes from "non-directed thinking" or "fantasy-thinking."[23] In the context of creative work, directed thinking may correspond with the deliberate choice of a theme for a painting, or with the decision to deal with one's own or some previous translation of the theme, and/or with playful attempts to access a theme through various techniques and efforts that aim to strike balances amongst the choices of form, color, proportion, medium, and tools. It is through such aspects that the dimensions of directed consciousness come to play in creative activity—and it applies not only for painting, but also for every kind of creative expression, be it in the medium of the word, music, or theater, dance, or otherwise.

On the other hand, in Magritte's painting a feminine counterpart stands opposite to the masculine consciousness. In the creative process it is the inner Other that transmits stimulating insights, that inspires, that offers gripping hunches, that lays the ground for and triggers new insight. She is experienced typically as an independent personality, an autonomous entity, who has advanced knowledge of new ideas that will emerge. Her given perspectives don't feel tentative or random, but convincing and binding.

It is interesting to observe Magritte's portrayal of the painter's hands. They convey above all the impression that *conscientious work* is being done. With this basic work atmosphere Magritte offers a further glimpse into the creation of the work and its concrete realization. Seemingly in line with this practical approach, he envisions it as a hands-on manufacturing process that entails the orderly use of the tools of the trade—i.e. the palette, the paints, and the brushes. Our sense of the laborer's morale is enhanced as well by the painter's simple brown suit.

What could the artist's left hand, balancing the palette, say about the experience of the creative process? It suggests the artist as the individual whose creativity inheres in the capacity to render sublime realities from limited resources. In other words, the painter can produce awe-inspiring images from within the confines of his palette, which could stand symbolically for an ego consciousness aware of its own boundaries and preconditions. Here the creative impetus consists of the return of creative consciousness to its own basis and critical reflection on the fundaments of the creative work. For this reason Magritte gives special attention to the palette as the starting point of the painterly act. The palette with its boundary surface, and the spectrum of paints, oil media, and brushes, all together depict the practical preconditions for painting in the vein of task-oriented work.

Let us now try to understand the possible meaning of the right hand. It holds a brush with serene mastery. Hand and brush appear to be one, suggesting that the painter's hand is entirely a function of the brush's autonomous movement. The hand serves the brush; the hand is more guided by the brush than the brush by the hand. It is as if the artist were given in service to a creative process that takes its own course. He is no impulsive exponent of subjective feeling, but rather the matter-of-fact renderer of an objective occurrence. He makes his know-how available to the creative force, which realizes itself through him and in his own way.

In Magritte's painting the attitude of sober service to this purpose is so prominent as to suggest that the artist's rendering hand is led by a mysterious presence rather than by his personal will. This hand is entirely subservient to the emerging image, which itself seems to be anchored not in his incidental want and desire but in a creative reality of its own. The creative force is grounded not in the immediacy of the artist's expressive gesture, but in the artist's ability to subordinate himself to the objective dynamic of the creative process. He wields his brush as he follows its movement. Thus here creativity is experienced and described essentially as an autonomous principle of design, in the service of which the creative individual is moved to action.[24]

With a closer look at the woman in Magritte's picture, we see that she appears partly as an art object but also partly as an actual human being. Partly she is being conjured into life by the painter's brush, and partly she is the living model who poses for the painter. In this paradoxical image Magritte produces a feminine being that is at the same time pre-existing. He creates a vivid reality that already exists, in the realm of his inner vision at the very least. With this representation of a pre-existing inner image, we are not surprised to find that the woman's facial features nearly mirror those of the painter's. We note the similarities in the design and expressiveness of their eyes, noses, mouths, and heads.

As for the ways and means by which creativity is experienced and expressed in this painting, we can conclude as follows: A fundamental interaction transpires also between directed thinking and the emerging fantasy, but the opposite fantasy is seen merely in analogy to masculine consciousness. To come to full expression, this fantasy requires the masculine act of rendition. The feminine counterpart reveals herself little by little, corresponding with the artist's probing actions and the progression of the creative process—and ultimately, she emerges to have the quality of an alter ego. Such a step-wise creative process corresponds with an artist's actual practice with models, with sketches, with drafts, with tentative thoughts and brainstorming. To varying degrees, these are the familiar means by which creative activity invites fantasy and interprets the imminent meanings of its contents. Encountered in this way, the inner image doesn't overwhelm the artist or creative individual with evidence of its visionary immediacy. Far more, it manifests itself gradually, through the artist's patient and tentative attempts at formulation.

All psychologists who work with groups know that the participants' brainstorming is needed to uncover new creative thoughts. Only in this way can habitual ideas and approaches be abandoned in favor of fresh ones. Likewise the artist's relinquishment of trusted forms and proven formulas relies on experiment and non-committal sketching. An unfinished sketch is the midwife to the birth of a new work and serves to activate its opposite, the generative fantasy. Indeed, it is actually only the rendering hand that calls creative fantasy to be involved in the production of a work. Only by probing and following the fantasy that appears to the inner eye does the artist's hand finally summon that fantasy as an autonomous counterpart. Magritte's painting describes creativity as being initiated all at once by both the rendering hand and the lively, autonomous fantasy itself. His curious title, *Attempting the Impossible*, may well point to the paradox in the creative endeavor to produce the living reality of fantasy and to know that it is very fantasy itself that guides the whole work.

4.3. Edouard Manet: Luncheon on the Grass

(Fig. 8): Edouard Manet, *Luncheon on the Grass*

To further explore the theme of the artist and his model in relationship to the creative experience, I have chosen the example of *Luncheon on the Grass* (Fig. 8), which was painted by Edouard Manet in 1863. Precise observation and symbolic interpretation will bring to light another feature of the creative experience. While it is again a specific characteristic that has to do with the picture of a single painter and his work and era, it can serve to illustrate a special dimension of creativity that is also valid for other painters and for creative individuals in general.

Compared with the previous two examples in this chapter on the motif of artist and his model, Manet's painting depicts a greater number of human figures and other contents: The artist himself reclines in the grass on the right-hand side. Opposite him sits a naked woman—the model—and next to her, a clothed man. In the background another feminine figure is bending over in knee-deep water. The artist gazes upon a feminine/masculine presence, a dual presence that is doubled by his own connection with a feminine counterpart in the background.

Creativity here is experienced as a process in which multiple autonomous factors are at work. Thus Manet's discourse concerns not only the artist and his model, but also the several people who join for a *déjeuner sur l'herbe*, a lunch in the midst of green nature. The artist lying in the grass is distinguished by his painter's beret and his scepter-like walking stick. Sitting directly across from him are two people, a nude woman and a man in a suit.

The woman has brought along a luncheon basket, introducing the gifts of Mother Nature into the circle. In the parlance of C.G. Jung, she represents the anima, a personified gestalt of the bearer of gifts from the collective unconscious, which manifests itself in a particular "here and now." She brings maternally nourishing food to the creative rendezvous—nourishing metaphors, archetypal images, and primal fantasies—all springing from her basket as if from a fertile womb. Beyond this, she has a transforming and renewing function: she opens creative consciousness to the archaic images of the soul as timely discoveries and fascinating, lively realities.

In Jung's terminology, the masculine counterpart represented in parallel to the anima figure is the animus. Anima and animus together form a couple, a so-called *syzygy*. The soul itself is a syzygy, which consists of, "paired opposites, where One is never separated from the Other, its antithesis."[25] The animus embodies the side of the soul that engenders sense and meaning. The spiritual value of this aspect is emphasized in Manet's beautiful depiction of the sitting man's face, with his intelligent eyes, fine nose, and open countenance.

The masculine/feminine bi-polar reality of the soul is elucidated in the parallel placement of the nude next to this man and in the nearly sibling-like resemblance of their faces.

Symbolically speaking, Manet's picture brings across a specific experience of creativity marked by the artist or by creative people in general who find within themselves a soulful wealth of fascinating design prototypes and an *a priori* sense of beauty, all transmitted through the image-giving anima. At the same time, these people can access within themselves the archetypal concepts and ideas that are communicated by the meaning-making animus. According to this particular variety of experience, creative people experience themselves not as a *tabula rasa*, but as individuals who are first and foremost filled with and led by the imagistic treasures of their own souls.

This giving aspect of the creative experience is complemented by a function of the psyche, an agency that can actively "handle" the given things. In Manet's painting it is personified by the woman in the background, whose hand reaches toward the water—and by the artist, his right hand outstretched and his left hand holding the walking stick.

The woman bathing in the background wades in the waters of the unconscious. A boat is docked at a nearby shore. In contrast to the anima figure on the left, who is associated with the fruits of nature and the archetypal images grounded in the soul, this woman is connected with the water and the boat. She is thus linked to future possibilities to be gleaned from the unconscious and to the vehicle, this means, for exploring new shores. With this, a prospective, finalistic trajectory affects the creative happenings: The originally intuited goal or gestalt, the end in itself, influences the steps of the creative process and the thing that is becoming and that is to come. It is this future-oriented dimension that compensates the previously mentioned archetypal imagination that nourishes creative fantasy from sources of the past.

The painter himself performs a meaningful gesture with his right hand, as if to make visible or stress an idea or concern of his own. It is, so to speak, a rhetorical gesture that wants to convince and clarify. We might understand that the painter's creative impulse here consists of the desire to express some point, or to work out a pregnant idea, or to strengthen its archetypal relevance. The gesture could mean also that the artist understands his creative act to be the generation of a symbol. This he conjures from within the inner space of his soul— from the images and thoughts transmitted by his anima and animus—

and converts them from intuitive perceptions (see the bathing woman) into a visible gestalt. The artist is the author in the sense that he realizes and consolidates the inputs flowing from within the circle of the participating creative factors.

In his left hand the painter holds a stick. But it apparently serves less as walking support than to steady or anchor his earthly being, to ground him in concrete reality. Or like a sounding rod, it serves to tap into aspects of reality that can contribute to the emergence of a creative work. We might recall certain reality factors that are involved in every creative achievement and for which there must exist a certain sensorium: the feel for temporal circumstances, for synchronicities, and also for the materials and tools that enable the concrete realization and work.

A look at the picture as whole suggests that, in the picnic round of two couples, it expresses and distinguishes four different factors that interact in a creative experience. These bespeak the four functions of consciousness that Jung designated in his model of the psychological types. There is the feeling function, which could be represented by the nude anima woman. Her scrutinizing gaze on us, the picture's observers, and the self-reflexive gesture of her right arm express an attitude of evaluation, self-relatedness, and judgment according to subjective criteria—qualities that all intrinsically belong to the feeling function. The animus man next to her corresponds with the thinking function, suggested in Manet's far-reaching reduction of this figure to a head, a symbol of the spirit or intellect. The dimension of thinking is emphasized by the fine, intellectual characteristics of the man's face.[26] In the background, the woman bathing near the rudder boat corresponds with the function of intuition. Dipping into the waters of the apprehending unconscious, she possesses the capacity to anticipate things that are to come.

My attribution of the four Jungian functions to Manet's four figures requires some precise explanation. Obviously it is not the case that Manet tried to illustrate the functions of consciousness in his painting. Indeed when this painting was created Jung had not yet been born and his concept of the four functions of consciousness was not yet known. It is rather the other way around: The four modalities of consciousness constitute an archetypal fundament that takes shape symbolically in Manet's painting and that Jung would later develop on the basis of his own observations. The ways and means by which Jung arrived at his description might, however, suggest that the four types have not to do with an archetypal structure but rather with a more or less complete enumeration of possible perspectives of consciousness. Jung developed his own model by discussing and comparing other typologies, and for a certain time he hesitated to define the functions conclusively. Thus we might deduce that what evolved was a coincidental differentiation of potential viewpoints rather than an archetypal structure of orientations of consciousness. However, even if Jung did not discern the schema of the four functions all at once, *in globo* he nevertheless came to grasp this functional structure and its *a priori* archetypal validity. Jung's pathway involved many attempts and comparisons, but the goal manifested the one fundamental structure.

Edouard Manet's painting reveals how this specific experience of creativity is realized through an interaction of the four different perspectives of consciousness. The creative endeavor begins with feeling, with the discovering Eros, expressed here in the figure of the nude and her lunch basket.[27]

It is feeling that furnishes the interesting, nourishing contents; that allows the discovery of satisfactory ideas; and that sets the creative search in motion. Feeling grasps the value of a creative idea and stimulates the *curiosity* that fuels creative action or realization. Moreover, feeling establishes an *intensive relationship* to an object and charges it with meaning. The object of interest is perceived as beautiful, worthy, and appealing. Feeling also mediates, as it were, an *instinctual sense* of the elemental beauty, truth, and good that surface in creative thoughts or images.

Finally, feeling is able to identify an object as a gestalt and to *focus* creative consciousness upon it. The recognition of psychological types is above all a capacity of the feeling function. The other functions simply lend help, in forms such as those of precision of thought, intuitive amplification, and a sensation-oriented confirmation with observable materials. I refer as well to the discourse of a "beautiful" schizophrenia: Feeling sets the criterion of beauty. The somewhat questionable expression "beautiful schizophrenia" intends to say that feeling recognizes the particular kind of schizophrenia in which all of the characteristic features are present and visible in picture perfect ways. Other examples of the significance of feeling in the artistic process and its ability to free creative energy include such phenomena as the artist's affection for his or her model or for particular paints and tools—or the writer's fondness for a particular author, certain books, or themes. Love of something, feelings of Eros, are needed to enable symbolic insight and thus creative action. All such aspects make clear that feeling is attributed with an initiating quality. Feeling marks the beginning of a creative endeavor and through its perceiving Eros it determines and provides the subjective starting conditions of the creative act.

By the means of Logos, the thinking function defines and refines a theme, and understands what it is really about. At the same time it connects the theme with one's own earlier thoughts and with the thinking of other authors and their standpoints. Finally thinking realizes the possible intellectual or technical approaches and methods by which a theme might be best approached. In these aspects, thinking can be noted as a function of defining. It subjugates things that are seen to a structuring Logos and determines the objective intellectual context of the creative task.

Intuition grasps in advance a difficulty that need be resolved and meets it as a creative challenge. Thus intuitive people who encounter such challenging difficulties are attributed with an *a priori* sense of certainty, to the effect that, despite all not-knowing, they will find a solution. Intuition produces the urge to overcome the barriers of familiar ideas and to discover new ways to perceive and create. Further, it opens the dimension of symbolic meaning in relationship to the imagined contents. Finally, intuition implements the development of perceived possibilities by means of play with models, images, and imagined contents. In other words, intuition trusts the transcendent function of imagination. In brief, then, it encompasses essentially an exploratory quality. Intuition points toward new shores and new insights that are opened up by its creative dealings with difficulties.

Sensation translates into concrete form things that have been seen and recognized. Sensation gets to the heart of the matter. It connects the theme with concrete data and observable facts. Thus the theme, the recognized thing, is enriched and confirmed. Moreover, sensation lends an artistic work a certain order, in that it structures the creative process stepwise in time and with methodological segments. Finally, the sensation function creates the image or work as a sensuous and symbolic gestalt.[28] In this sense, sensation is the function that brings the creative idea to bear as a living symbol expressed in sensuous, material form.

Taken together, the four functions serve as a vessel that allows creativity to become conscious experience. It is thanks to this vessel that creative people gain conscious access to the creative force itself—or the other way around, their consciousness becomes an instrument of the creative force. Here we understand creativity to be a subjective power of insight and design, which exceeds the mere coping mechanisms of normative thought and action, and which through the mediating individual brings to light new contents, values, and patterns. Observed objectively, creativity is a consciousness-transcending and transformational reality, at the heart of which is the transcendent function itself.

Manet's *Luncheon on the Grass* expresses creativity as a functionally conveyed and soulful experience. It is this kind of experience, alongside the three others, that we examine on the basis of art works in this chapter.

4.4. Albrecht Dürer: Adam and Eve

The 1504 copper engraving of Adam and Eve (Fig. 9) by Albrecht Dürer (1471-1528) offers another example of the artist wrestling with the creative experience by employing the juxtaposed images of man and woman. In this case the motif is not the artist and his model, but the ur-couple, the ur-parents. Although this couple shifts us away from the artist's personal situation, and although the artist's reflection on his own work process is less evident, nevertheless the motif of Adam and Eve, in its depth, could intend the theme of creativity. Dürer's engraving is maybe less concerned with subjective creative experience than with a portrayal of the puzzle and wonder of the creative force as an objective, fundamental reality that reaches beyond the artist himself and yet also grounds his own work. It can be said, perhaps, that this metaphysical approach, as it were, still evidences a view through a medieval, pre-modern lens.

Adam and Eve gave Dürer the chance to portray man and woman, showing each in their differing characteristics and also their creative interaction. Adam's specifically masculine being is marked by his aimful gaze, by his open extremities that penetrate and stake claim to the surrounding space, by his strong and finely sculpted muscular body, and by his connection with the public world—a hint of which appears

(Fig. 9): Albrecht Dürer, *Adam and Eve*

in the sign hanging above his shoulder, an attribute of the persona that displays the artist's name, and the origin and date of the work. As in the previously discussed paintings, the specifically masculine is depicted here, too, with the elements of outwardly directed consciousness, the power of self-assertion, the capacity to differentiate, and finally the connectedness to the reality of a social world.

Eve on the other hand is characterized as the epitome of the feminine. Her gaze turns both inward and toward the apple in her right hand. The compact contours of her body suggest the form of a closed vessel. She is self-contained, tranquil, at peace with herself. She embodies an unfathomable depth, like that of the forest animals associated with her. Thus we can say that here the feminine is attributed with the quality of a container that contains itself, that gives birth from within itself, and that reveals and mediates the mysterious depths of nature.

Creativity encompasses both poles, the masculine and the feminine, working together. This is the fundamental subjective experience, as has been shown in our discussions of other artists' works. However, a specific dimension of creativity coming to light in Dürer's engraving distinguishes it from the three foregoing pictures. Leaning on the language of the typology of temperaments, I would call it the melancholic/schizoid dimension of the creative experience.

At the center of the picture Adam and Eve extend their arms toward each other, as if expressing cooperation between an outwardly directed masculine consciousness and a quiescent, self-contained feminine consciousness. However the image is enlarged by a third element, the snake. The interaction between the two opposing poles is mediated by the presence of this "serpent of paradise," that is, by the mythical embodiment of evil. We can understand evil symbolically as the appearance and experience of negativity. Thus creativity, experienced basically as an exchange between a mysteriously revealing anima and a structuring mind, here takes place with the participation of a third: the dynamic of negation.

Negation comes to play in a variety of ways as a creative factor. We think first of the negative in a moral sense, that is, the not good, the questionable, the reprehensible, and ultimately evil. In the Judeo-Christian paradise myth, evil is manifest at the beginning of creation. In the symbolic form of the snake, evil leads to a development of consciousness: Adam and Eve are seduced to eat from the forbidden Tree of the Knowledge of Good and Evil, and are so led to recognize each other in their nakedness, in their natural condition, but also in their desire for and dependence upon one another. Evil leads as well to the consequence that Adam would "eat only by the sweat of his labor" (Genesis 3:19) and Eve would suffer pain in childbirth (Genesis 3:16). Both outcomes are clearly related to a creative endeavor, to work, and to giving birth. This mythical imagining of an evil that initiates creative but arduous and painful labor and birth expresses in universal archetypal language the experience of the creative individual per se. For there is no creative endeavor without one's readiness to open to influences that go against the norm, or that are incorrect or morally questionable.

Creative individuals seem especially drawn to negation or negativity as a vehicle of creative energy when it takes the forms of kinkiness and foreignness as well as pathology and uncanniness. Literature and art abound with examples. For creative individuals, negativity as it appears in illness and shadowy phenomena functions as a special stimulus that releases personal fascination and sets creative energy in motion.

Other ways and means by which negation belongs to creativity include the creative process itself. Artistic activity involves not only the building up of forms and colors, words and thoughts; it is also a continuous taking-away, reduction, abstraction. Pablo Picasso, in the well-known documentary film by Henri-Georges Clouzot, *The Mystery of Picasso* (1956), offers an impressive example of the artist's work progressing by means of such negation.[29] Here, Picasso's pictures begin with a few strokes on translucent screens and evolve by rapid successions of interim sketches, which are relentlessly drawn over, re-colored, replaced with new motifs, and otherwise re-worked. In this film Picasso's entire painterly activity consists of creative negation. It is the case not only for the pictures that were done especially for the film, but also fundamentally for his complete body of work.

Creation by negation in the form of reduction is not typical of Picasso alone; it is a potential for creative activity in general. Indeed, negation as the taking-away of material is required for wood-cutting and stone-sculpting—and also for engraving, as exemplified by Dürer, whose technique reached a singular pinnacle of mastery. Such negating and abstracting is a primal creative function, manifesting itself in technical procedures as well as elsewhere in the process.

Alongside the dimensions of creative negation mentioned thus far—the moral, the heuristic, and the artistic—we can distinguish a fourth, the philosophical. Here we find the philosopher's creative renunciation of all that is sensory, concrete, provisional and superficial, and his focusing on the essential, invisible, durable, and profound. This is the philosophical effort to reach authenticity and the ground of truth by doing away with deceptive surfaces. Examples of philosophers using this form of creative negation include René Descartes, whose *Discourse on the Method* (1637) undertakes the path of methodological doubt and leads him to the singular, undeniable conclusion, "I think, therefore I am." In *The Phenomenology of Spirit* (1807), Georg Wilhelm Friedrich Hegel also follows the path of doubt, which he holds to be not only a method but also an existential experience. In Hegel's dialectic, negation takes on the important meaning of an on-going sublation of all certainties, which is simultaneously an act of negation and conservation. Later, in his own phenomenological method, Edmund Husserl used the notion of épenche—the bracketing out of the sensory world—to reach recognition of true essential being and real phenomena. All such philosophical approaches—and there would be many others, for instance in Kant, Schopenhauer, and Nietzsche—are carried by the creative act of negating a concrete and naïve worldview.

Returning to Dürer's engraving, we observe in addition to the snake a number of other animals. They can be held as symbolic expressions of certain drives that are experienced in creativity activity. On Adam's side of the picture, near the top, we see an exotic parrot-like bird, and between Adam's feet, a mouse. On Eve's side, a rabbit huddles near her feet and farther behind her lies an ox. In the center background, nearly hidden behind the tree, there is a deer, and in the utmost foreground, a cat.

The exotic parrot-like bird could symbolize not only the urge to communicate per se, but more specifically, to parrot or repeat existing ideas. The mouse as a gnawer, with a tail straight as an arrow, suggests the directed and penetrating energy of the drive to obtain knowledge. Thus, each according to its own specific characteristics, the bird and the mouse could symbolize two basic instinctual tendencies of directed masculine consciousness. There is the urge to explain made experiences, to verbally communicate and conceptually define them. There is as well the urge to purposefully fathom out ideas and examine them methodologically.[30] Thus, following Dürer's symbols, it can be said that the bird and mouse point to two conjoined qualities of consciousness or particular drives that come to play in creative experience: that of the researcher and that of the scientist. The two together stand for the drives to explore and discover things, to act on curiosity, on one hand, and to explain, to determine, to convey newly gained insight, and to obtain public recognition for such achievements on the other hand.

On Eve's side of the picture we see the resting horned ox and the rabbit. In most cultures the ox is associated symbolically with the maternal nurturing powers of the earth and also with the world of the moon, the latter because of its crescent-phase "horns" and its feminine attributes in general. In Dürer's picture the ox can be understood to symbolize an instinctual sensibility for the depth and wisdom of nature, offered by the anima to the creative individual.

Creative individuals draw special meaning from their experience of nature's stimulating and inspiring powers. It is hardly surprising that their work requires closeness to nature, evidenced by the fact that all creative individuals expose themselves to nature's effects and seek contact with invigorating soul landscapes. The examples are so abundant that it should suffice here to point to only several of the best known: Albrecht Dürer, whose closeness to nature is expressed in his aquarelle landscapes; Jean-Jacques Rousseau with his *Reveries of a Solitary Walker* (1776–1778); Johann Wolfgang von Goethe with his intensive nature studies and extensive walks in the woods of Thüringen; Friedrich Nietzsche with his inspiring stay in the mountains of Sils Maria; and C.G. Jung, who found great meaning in his hand-built tower on the shore of the upper Lake of Zürich, where he chopped wood and lived as simply and as close to nature as he possibly could.

The nearness to nature needed for creative inspiration does not necessarily mean that she need be the object of active exploration and analysis. Nature does not reserve her powers exclusively for individuals who make of her the topic of aimful tasks. Indeed, it is the immediate contact with nature and her effects that release and unfold within the individual her inherent, primal creative potential. The direct experience generates within the individual nature's own maternal qualities—her formative, world-creating dimension, her fertility and fruitfulness.

The second animal associated with the image of Eve in Dürer's engraving is the rabbit. Symbolically connected with the moon gods, the rabbit represents rebirth and resurrection. For this reason the rabbit appears on Easter day when Christ overcomes death, a liturgical context which itself points to nature's springtime re-awakening. Due to its prolific breeding habit, the rabbit symbolizes also fertility and sensual pleasure. And in Native American mythology, the rabbit often stands for the trickster, a cunning and sometimes malicious rogue.

Accordingly the rabbit motif can be understood to convey, in symbolic language, inspiration's jumpy nature, its variability and volatility. Belonging to the basically puzzling and painful experience of all creative individuals is the reality that inspiration does not flow like a steady current, but comes with seemingly arbitrary phases of emptiness and fullness, an absence of fantasy and overflowing imagination. Inspiration does not emerge along a continuum and it does not exist as a certainty. Rather a lunar phenomenon, inspiration is sometimes bitterly missing; it sometimes catches us by surprise; it evades every attempt to be grasped; and it astonishes us again and again.

Sometimes, though, inspiration can manifest itself indeed like the malicious trickster rabbit that appears in Native American myth. It then takes the destructive form of an individual's repetitive, impulsive leaps to vague notions, intuited perceptions, potential actions and projects—to the effect that the concrete realization of ideas can never keep apace. This in turn leads to perpetual beginnings that never find ends, and the hectic consciousness personified in the *puer aeternus*, the eternal child led and overwhelmed by creative impulses.

Insofar as the rabbit is attributed with the symbolism of fertility and sensual pleasure—an attribution underscored by the popular Playboy Bunny—the rabbit alludes to the meaning of responsiveness to sensuality, beauty, and pleasurable experiences in general. An instinctual attraction to this Dionysian life distinguished among others Goethe, Mozart, Picasso, and Tinguely—and it presented them and their likes, in part, with problematic relationships. And yet the Dionysian life is so to speak the biological basis of the creative individual's aesthetic sensibility. The desire to create and experiment playfully with new forms and contents is nourished precisely by primal sensuality and joy in the senses.

Among the animals in Dürer's engraving, it remains to explore the meanings of the deer, and the cat lying at the foot of the Tree of Knowledge. Facing in opposite directions, the two animals allude to opposing but interrelated qualities of consciousness.

In the symbolic understanding of the deer, the antlers have the particular and traditional meaning of spiritual insight. As antlers bifurcate and later develop many branches, they represent the joining of opposites and beyond this, the transcendence of dualistic consciousness. Because antlers fall off and grow again each year, they stand also for renewal and eternal return. As a leader of souls, the deer belongs to the world of spirits and vision. Correspondingly in Celtic myths and fairy tales the deer inhabits the background, the woodland thickets, and as if out of the blue it shows up to guide seekers and lost wanderers to the right paths. In Christianity the deer expresses the soul's natural yearning for God, for instance in Psalm 42:1: "As the hart panteth after the water brooks, so panteth my soul after thee, O God." At the same time, the deer can be associated with epiphanies of Christ in nature. For example in a story about Saint Eustace (otherwise known as Saint Hubert), a stag springs from a thicket in the woods, bearing between his antlers a shining crucifix. This motif was so meaningful for Dürer that he devoted the largest engraving of his entire work to it (*St. Eustace*, 1501).

On the whole, then, it can be said that in the deer we have a symbol of the reality and dynamic of spiritual sensibility. More specifically, the deer represents background and transcendent meaning, that is, experienceable meaning or living Logos. Thus the "deer" quality of consciousness exists outside of dualities and leads beyond everything already existing. It manifests itself as something new and yet ever returning. It reveals itself to seekers, and can take shape unexpectedly as a religious experience of infinity.

With this understanding we can say that Dürer's deer represents the creative experience of being led mysteriously from within by an autonomous spirit. This spirit seems to behave meaningfully according to its own laws, aiming for greater clarity or to reach a far point that is difficult to describe—a Final Point Omega, as it were. It compels the necessary steps according to a living and efficacious Logos. However, other than when determined by intentional scientific research methods, here the contents, steps, and pace of discovery manifest themselves spontaneously, and they do so little by little. In this vein, the process of discovery and form-giving defies speeding-up or foreshortening. It takes its own unhesitating course and leads always to unexpected and compelled moments of re-thinking and detour.

This creative way of discovering, by which one gradually grasps something being revealed from within, could be called phenomenological recognition. It apprehends inner phenomena in their own nature, in their connection with a living whole, and within an experiential process. The creative individual's essential mode of discovery is marked by its adherence to such perceiving-based knowledge rather than by pre-given, research-determined knowledge. As Pablo Picasso famously said, "I do not seek, I find."

The cat lying in the foreground of Dürer's engraving alludes to a different perspective. Whereas the deer may be associated with Adam, the cat's association with Eve is suggested by the tail rolling between her feet. Thus, while the deer would correspond with the viewpoint of the masculine animus, the cat would represent the perspective of the feminine anima. The cat has many meanings in many different cultures, and yet its symbolism boils down to three essential aspects: the feminine as such, sensory perception, and independence. Of significance here is the cat's symbolization of an anima-mediated sensuous orientation to the tangible world, which opposes the sense-making and other-worldly orientation mediated by the animus and symbolized by the deer. As the cat lies in the foreground and at the very bottom of the picture—identical with the ground as it were— we might say that creative experience involves groundedness in the senses and an empirical sensibility for the concrete here-and-now.

Hermann Hesse, in his book *Narcissus and Goldmund*, describes two such essentially different characters: Narcissus, an introverted cerebral cloister abbot—and Goldmund, an artist and wanderer devoted to the sensuous life. With this pair of opposites Hesse reveals two meaningful sides of his own personality that have bearing for the creative individual in general. The two together suggest a collaboration of the symbolic deer and cat, the one being determined by sense, meaning, and order—and the other being led by the senses and pleasurable experience. On the basis of such coupling, it can be said that creative thought is never abstract, but mediated by imagistic ideas. It discovers things not because it knows, but because it sees them. And it discovers and understands thanks to the creative image.

Between the deer and the cat grows the Tree of Knowledge. Meaning that, both within a single image and an artist's work as a whole, the collaborating agents of sense and sensuousness, or meaning and beauty create the reality of a gradually developing process of images. The process, the work, can take the form of an artistic creation by which the material object of beauty contains spiritual meaning, or the form of an intellectual or linguistic creation, which itself mediates meaning through aesthetic appearance. The mark of a specifically creative mind is its connection to images and its proclivity to create symbols that give rise to meaning. Belonging to it as well is the ongoing process of symbol formation, which, like a tree, develops in accordance with its own law—in this case, that of a pictorial Logos.

For further discussion of this engraving's contribution to an understanding of the creative experience, there remains a last motif, namely that of the cooperation between Adam and Eve. Going by the snake-like line joining their arms at the image's center, the two would appear to stand in dialectical relationship, with Adam's extended left hand indicating his leading role. He, so to speak, puts a topic in the room, or in the language of dialectics, he opens a thesis. His point of departure is a pre-given, officially recognized opinion, an expression of the social norm. His position as such seems to be proclaimed by the branch he raises, as if to display the bird and the nameplate. Proceeding from this collective reality Adam posits a new thesis, and is ready for a new experience.

Eve posits a counter position. Dialectically speaking, she asserts an antithesis. In Hegel's language Eve stands for being-for-itself, which counter poses Adam's being-in-itself. Eve's position takes shape through her own impulse to contribute the forbidden apple—symbolically, the fruit of nourishing insights gleaned from vibrant subjective experience. Thus Eve conveys essentially the value of experiential wisdom, the wisdom brought into play by the experiencing subject, the individual. With her left hand cradling another apple from the Tree of Knowledge, Eve enunciates the principle she stands for: experienceable inner knowledge or understanding, which in *The Red Book* Jung calls the "spirit of the depths." The spirit of the depths runs contrary to the collectively determined "spirit of the time," suggested in Adam's display of the bird and the nameplate. The latter is the spirit of traditional knowledge, without the inwardly felt evidence of the kind imparted by Eve and her apple.

Writhing in the tree between the oppositional couple, the snake assumes a mediating position. In the logic of dialectics the snake proposes a synthesis, or in Hegel's precise language it would stand for an aspect of being-in-and-for-itself. The snake in this sense symbolizes the principle of negation sublating existing certainties. For as the snake bites into the apple, so is negated the aspect of subjective experience that Eve brings into play. The snake transcends *both* opposing sides—Eve's subjective experiential certainty and

Adam's collectively determined knowledge—and so manifests a new creative idea. (It bears noting that the dialectical sublation [*Aufhebung*, literally, "to lift up"] encompasses the meaning of both negation and conservation. With this in mind, we note as well that the snake devours the apple and that Eve in the truest sense had lifted up the fruit and so brought its meaning to bear. Dürer's composition thus especially beautifully illustrates sublation in the double Hegelian sense of negation and conservation.)

The dialectic symbolized by the two protagonists and the snake can be viewed as a tripartite schema that structures a creative process. Creative work—with all of its puzzling and manifold procedures—does indeed often take on a dialectical character. Or it does so at the very least with this specifically discussed kind of creative experience. An impressive example appears in the previously mentioned film, *The Mystery of Picasso*, for which Picasso allowed his friend Clouzot a glimpse into his creative process. In the film it becomes strikingly clear how Picasso's pictures came into being, always involving a dialectical dynamic.

Each picture starts with simple, often unsightly, abstract lines drawn with black felt-tipped pens or ink. They build the initial scaffolding of the imagination, a kind of lattice, around which the emerging image will crystallize. With this first creative act Picasso corresponds with Dürer's Adam, who sets an initial thesis.

There follows a second phase in which Picasso, quasi by his own accord, fills in the painterly content. In the course, personal associations and experiences become palpable and infuse the picture with emotion and pregnant forms. Splashes of color are often added, and from these concrete motifs may take shape. It is this phase that corresponds with Eve's "antithesis," whereby personal experiences and memories determine the emerging motifs. This phase is characterized as well by great change—motifs appear, vanish, and re-appear until they are finally voided or kept in transformed shape.

The third and final phase corresponds with Dürer's snake and the aspect of negation that yields a synthesis, a transcending and final image. In the Picasso film this phase is characterized by the artist's intensive application of the color black to accentuate contours and often to utterly re-define the composition. Through Picasso's massive, nearly violent re-working of an emerging image, the picture evolves "in-and-for-itself," as the picture itself wills it.

Creativity that takes shape in a dialectical process is not unique to Pablo Picasso. It shows in all artistic processes that correspond with the kind of creative experience symbolized in Dürer's engraving. Also creative writing, creative dealing and thinking, and all other forms of artistic expression follow the three-step dialectical dynamic— provided that fantasy and imagistic vision are admitted to the process.

4.5. Julian Wasser: Duchamp Playing Chess with a Nude

(Fig. 10): Julian Wasser, *Duchamp Playing Chess with a Nude (Eve Babitz)*

Duchamp Playing Chess with a Nude (Fig. 10) is a photograph carefully staged and shot in 1963 by Julian Wasser. It portrays Marcel Duchamp (1887-1968) engaged in an actual chess match with Eve Babitz, who was at the time a young art student (and has long been an artist and author in her own right).[31] This picture can stand for a fifth aspect of the creative experience as it comes across in the juxtaposition of man and woman.

If our foregoing discussion assumed the expression of artistic reflection about creative experience in works of art, the photograph leaves no doubt. Here it is made explicit by the museum gallery where Duchamp and Babitz compete, and where Duchamp's own works hang in the far background. Moreover, directly behind the two players hangs *The Bride Stripped Bare by Her Bachelors, Even (The Large Glass)* (1915-1923), Duchamp's celebrated masterpiece. Thus the essential object of reflection is Duchamp's art imagined in relationship to a woman.

The photograph, like the foregoing pictures, again depicts the man as representing directed thinking and a social persona, and the woman as an inspiring anima figure who mediates nurturing fantasy. Going by this portrait in particular, art evolves like a chess match progressing by the interplay of two qualities of consciousness: a masculine one, which plans and reflects; and a feminine one, which is enigmatic and stimulating. The masculine side leads with the white chess pieces, the feminine plays the mysterious black ones. The man's face is illuminated, his body clothed in black. The woman's nude body reflects the room's bright light, while her face is hidden behind her dark hair. The picture displays a remarkable encounter of brightness and darkness, white and black. The pair of opposites permeates the space, spreading out to the dark floor and light walls, and to the dark table and chairs that also contrast with the bright background. The dichotomy of lightness and darkness points to the central reality of a dialectic between the feminine and masculine progressing to a synthesis in the course of a shared game.

The contrast of black-and-white describes the most fundamental dualities, such as light and darkness, day and night, good and evil, beginning and end. The polarizing values or non-colors of black and white cast the opposites in the farthest reaches of their difference. And yet the motif contains the idea that the poles belong together, as they appear for example in the Chinese concept of yin and yang, or in the game of chess with its black and white figures.

Wasser's photograph however brings to a boil the extreme difference between the two opponents—directed consciousness and concretely "existing" fantasy. The gulf between the two is underlined not only by the black-and-white color scheme, but also by the apparent isolation and absorption of the two players, each in their own worlds. The portrait indicates no sign whatsoever of communicative connection. The man seems to be fully concentrated on his chess game, planning the next move. Hiding behind a veil of dark hair, the woman evidences no discernable awareness of her opponent. There is as well a nearly obscene contrast between the fully clothed and intensely concentrating man, who seems pointedly unmoved by the nude woman sitting across from him—and the woman, who comes across as having been disrobed and reduced to an object.

However, if we want to understand Wasser's photograph as an authentic expression of Duchamp's creative experience, then we could say that it apparently consisted of the parallel processes of stringent inward thinking and the revelation of objectively evidenced meaning. It is indeed the case that Duchamp used ready-mades, and found again and again symbolic value in these ordinary objects of the outer world. He is best known for *Fountain*, the porcelain urinal that he turned upside down and exhibited in 1917. Among its predecessors is *Bottle Rack*, which Duchamp declared a work of art in 1914.[32]

Going by Duchamp's experience, a creative spirit abides directly in material things. The creative achievement lies not in the artistic making of things, but in lifting things out of their ordinary contexts to uncover and heighten their symbolically meaningful dimensions. Duchamp in this sense experienced creativity as inhering in the artist's capacity to convey the visual appeal and meaning that live in things, given by life's own creative force. Thus creativity is not so much an inner capacity, but far more, a given objective dimension of reality itself. Existing things, just as they are, hold the potential to speak symbolically to discerning individuals. Accordingly in the photograph the woman has a very concrete physical aura: she represents objective fantasy and meaning of the kind mediated and rendered visible by concrete things and physical bodies.

Duchamp was not alone in his persuasion that things and the body inherently contain an imaginative potential and visual appeal for their intrinsic aesthetic quality. His personal perception reveals a general and fundamental possibility belonging to the creative experience per se. Let us illustrate with some other examples.

The artist's creative activity depends on his or her experience and awareness of the beauty or meaning in encountered things. To create beauty the artist first has to discover and come upon it. He or she requires an eye, a sense for the noteworthy material and for the added creative value that lends plain things their appealing gestalts and symbolic meanings. With a visit to Paul Cézanne's atelier in Aix-en-Provence one is astonished to find the abundant assortment of objects that we recognize from his still lifes—pots, tables, fruit bowls, jugs, and also the famed putto. It is not only astounding that these objects remain in place, but also that they are utterly banal as compared with their appearance in Cézanne's paintings. The amazing contrast between the banal object and the magnificent painterly motif is a measure of the artistic genius that led Cézanne to create art from ordinary things. It is as well a measure of his creative eye for, recognition of, and response to the beauty and meaning inherent in being. Creative activity begins always with this sense of the hidden and discoverable, a sense of the beauty that is already at hand. It is especially the case for an artist's work with a model. For as the artist searches for and tries to portray the individual's own truth and beauty, he or she is all the more receptive and uncovering. Creativity is expressed already in the artist's recipience.

The importance of objective given beauty extends as well to nature and landscapes. Both have their own auras and primal characteristics, which lend themselves to the same interest of exploration and creative interpretation. Cezanne's paintings abound with the special atmospheres and colors of the region around Aix-en-Provence. So much so, that a stroll through those woods and meadows today creates the impression of a walk through one of Cézanne's pictures. Georgia O'Keefe's paintings, too, create the impression of a direct encounter with her New Mexican landscapes and with the objects she found there—bones, skulls, flowers, clouds, and the like. These two examples stand for the many other artists whose creative vision is determined by contact with real landscapes and their imminent beauty and meaning. The British artist Andy Goldsworthy goes a step further with this typically creative ability to draw inspiration from nature. In a manner of speaking, he asks nature herself about her expressive potential, for he works in nature with materials offered by her, creating wonderful ephemeral sculptures, which he documents photographically. His works creatively accent and stage the gestalts that nature herself creates and offers. Creative individuals possess to an extraordinary degree this capacity to empathize with nature, and to recognize her aesthetic power and the symbolic potentials of her reality.

Just as the material world is considered to mediate imagination, so are certain materials important for each individual's creative work. Henry Moore collected and studied bones, integrating into his own sculptures their beautiful contours, proportions, volumes, and structures. Jean Tinguely's preferred basic substance consisted of wheels, rusty iron, and machines, from which he took his idea for kinetic sculpture. For his own point of departure Joseph Beuys used fat, felt, and wax. These few examples serve to illustrate that one's relationship to the imaginative possibilities in concrete things is typical for the creative experience.

It holds not only for the visual arts that, before there is any concrete realization, creativity begins with creative perception. The same phenomenon occurs in intellectual activity, where the discovery of illustrative material often precedes the building up of a body of thought. It may well be, for instance, that C.G. Jung intuited the relevance of alchemical thought and imagery to his own lines of psychological thinking. Premonitions arising from illustrative material can anticipate with great certainty things for which scientific hypotheses are later developed. Here, too, it remains that creative perception registers potential sense and meaning in advance of actual recognition or proof. It is as if one's hand reaches for the illustrative material that proves to be key for later cognitive processes. Hand and eye seem to detect in the chosen material the hidden potential of discovery. The explicit thing to be found reveals itself gradually, with the subsequent working out of the implicit sense.

Let us now return to Wasser's photograph. As we have already observed, there is no evident connectedness between the woman and the artist, between objective fantasy and directed thinking. Nevertheless, the chess match underway suggests a third factor that brings the two worlds into creative relationship with each other. It is in part the element of time, signified by the chess clock at the table's far end. In the spirit of this game the players are not left to their own devices, but are determined also by timing. Psychologically speaking, time and synchronicity steer the creative process by mediating between outer reality and inner consciousness. Synchronicity correlates the meanings offered by outer realities and the contents of inner consciousness, and vice versa.

As if to underline the playful collaboration, the chess table in Wasser's photograph is placed such that between the two players there appears a shape from the lower half of *The Large Glass*, a shape that hints of a process of concrete actualization. Creative activity here lies actually in the hands of a meaning-making third, which is the creative dynamic itself, symbolized in the puzzling motif of the *The Large Glass* that appears between the two players. The depicted object gives shape to what we might call a creativity machine. While a direct interpretation unavoidably pushes boundaries, the rich symbol merits an attempt at speculative understanding.

If Duchamp's machine can be taken as a symbol of the creative dynamic per se, it would be likened to a set of moving rollers that stand for the present, the future and the past, forever circling in a symbolically elevated level in the sense of Nietzsche's "eternal return of the same." Thus creativity would be characterized not as a purely primal or natural phenomenon, but as a spiritual activity in the service of sublime meaning-making.

Above this elementary course of time a central disc with a two-pronged brace turns at the machine's center. This aspect of the construction points to the idea of sustaining the tension of opposites. It recalls the Chinese wisdom of "Wuwein," non-doing as the way of tolerating dualities until creative resolution arises; or similarly, the attitude of holding-one-self-in-the-middle proposed by Loyola with his spiritual exercises. The tall rod attached to the disc forms the central rotating axis, which provides the elevation needed to enable sublimation at a higher level. (See Jung's concept of the "transcendent function" that can be understood as the actual dynamic of the creative process.) The elevation symbolizes the unfolding of a spiritual order with new coordinates, represented by the four directions in the pair of crossed horizontal rods. These in turn effect an arc of change progressing in seven steps, reminding us of the seven days of creation recorded in the Book of Genesis as well as Rudolf Steiner's notion of human development transpiring in seven-year cycles. Last but not least, Goethe's understanding of creativity comes to mind, expressed in his well-known poetic lines, "Formation, Transformation, eternal minds in eternal recreation."[33]

To sum up thus far, we can read Duchamp's machine symbolically to describe the creative dynamic as follows: Creative activity consists of a spiritual process of centering and transforming, which transcends the rotating process of time and leads to a qualitatively different vertical dimension in which creation and re-creation take place. Looking again Wasser's photograph, the background machine motif can be associated with the foreground chess match, allowing us to take our understanding a bit further: Creativity's autonomous quality and its properties of meaning-making and synchronicity are background phenomena that realize themselves in the foreground interplay of opposing poles.

So far, we have understood the two chess players in Wasser's photograph to express symbolically the interplay of directed thinking and fantasy. However we could as well take the image to portray the real relationship of two individuals, be it an artist and his model or man and woman. The naturalistic display of the couple underlines the meaning of a relationship between two concretely existing persons. In this light, we could say that the creative dynamic as discussed above manifests itself especially in the actual couple, or the other way around, the couple itself sets the creative dynamic in motion. However, this would be not just any couple, but one characterized by or open to play—perhaps a couple whose relationship even functions like a chess match. It would be a couple with the capacity for playful argument, creative conflict, and for a conscious encounter with Eros. Indeed, Duchamp often signed his own works with the pseudonym, "Rose Sélavy," which cryptically contains the phrase, "*Eros est la vie*," "Eros is life." And with this he asserted his fundamental conviction about the central meaning of Eros in relationship to life and art.

It goes without saying that creativity can be inspired by the relationship of creative individuals and their soul partners. There are in particular many examples of women attributed with the power of the muse thanks to some special aura, be it imbued with human kindness, erotic beauty, or another emanation. The same holds true for men playing the role of inspiring soul mates for creative women. To mention but a few of the renowned ones: Mathilde Wesendonck, Richard Wagner's muse; Charlotte Stein, who inspired Goethe with her cool reservation, her ingenuity, and her acute sensibility; Dora Maar, who was an inspiration during a particular phase of Picasso's work; and Lou Andreas-Salome, whose charm and liveliness captured a whole round of artists, including her own husband Paul Rée, Richard Wagner, Friedrich Nietzsche, and Rainer Maria Rilke. Jean Tinguely was not only Niki de Saint Phalle's husband but also her inspiring artistic partner. We should not neglect to mention Toni Wolff, who stood by C.G. Jung as a creative partner and contributed significantly to the development of his work. Many less known and unknown examples certainly abound.

To conclude this chapter, it can be said that, in his person and work, Marcel Duchamp brings across a sense of the creative spirit that is incarnated in material things and experienced in the process of creative relationships.

V

THE CREATIVE INDIVIDUAL

Creativity is more than an intellectual or aesthetic gift, more than an imaginative or visual capacity, more than a skill or special dexterity. It entails a task that makes demands on and realizes itself existentially through the whole personality. The task is absolutely compelling and binding. It tolerates no excuse, no subterfuge, no detour. It is in the truest sense inescapable. This holds not only for great creative individuals but also for every individual, insofar as creative energies within each of us compel meaning-making and goal-orientedness—a phenomenon that in Jungian parlance can be understood as the principle of individuation.

For the person who lacks or fails the creative task, there looms the sanction of an inauthentic and depressingly arbitrary existence. Common knowledge tells us that everyone is dispatched with a creative task and that its failing bears negative consequences. As it is said for example in the Gospel of St. Thomas, Saying 70, "If you bring forth what is within you, what you bring forth will save you. If you do not bring forth what is within you, what you do not bring forth will destroy you." Similarly, Nietzsche in his book *Human, All Too Human* writes, "'Disease' is always the answer when we wish to have doubts of our rights to our own task, when we begin to make it easier for ourselves in any way. How strange and how terrible!"[34]

The coming-to-consciousness about one's creative task entails reflection on one's own personality as the basis of creative activity.

Creative individuality differs from private existence. It is an aspect of individuality, which out of necessity creates something from within and beyond itself. It is an individuality that is not simply given, but that creates and projects itself. It is an individuality that experiences itself as being invested in a task assigned by a creative power, and that translates and realizes that task. It is a labor-oriented individuality, which experiences itself as complete only when it realizes the given and larger task. It is an individuality that exists only in the evolution of the creative task. It is an individuality that stands in service to and connects with something greater than itself, and that only in this wider horizon can be itself, alive and healthy.

In the pages to come my discussion will focus on selected artists who illustrate this particular aspect of creativity, which has to do with the phenomenon of the creative individual as such. In these pictures we will always discern several persons who represent the different aspects of personality or part-personalities that constitute the larger creative consciousness.

5.1. Daimonic Individuality in Albrecht Dürer's The Desperate Man

I refer now to another of Albrecht Dürer's images, his 1515 etching, *The Desperate Man* (Fig. 11). Art historians are undecided about the meaning of the picture. Because Dürer himself did not entitle it or otherwise provide information, it received this more or less arbitrary name. It obviously points to a central figure in the foreground, but raises questions about the surrounding figures and the idea of the image as a whole. The care with which Dürer rendered it—probably his first engraving on iron—makes clear that it was not a preparatory study, but a fully viable, completed work.[35] Dürer's atypically missing signature and year of completion appear to relativize the etching's importance. And yet these omissions could be taken as Dürer's intentional nod to the timeless presence of the subject matter and/or its closeness to his own personality as it was in the here-and-now. The image is quasi an expression of Dürer the individual in a moment of utter directness and presence. I will try to interpret the symbolic meaning in three steps.

Step One: The etching depicts four men with expressions of pain or even illness, and a reclining woman who appears like a mother sleeping or withdrawn in a death-like state.

The masculine figures seem to emanate basic knowledge of non-creative inauthenticity. The man standing in the background, nude and holding a metal tankard, makes us think of the depressing dependency

(Fig. 11): Albrecht Dürer, *The Desperate Man*

of addiction. Next to him, a demonically glaring face conjures up madness and its hysterical being-beside-one's-self. The man sitting at the far left with his meticulously groomed hair and otherwise flawless appearance suggests a compulsive character and its loss of self-determination. And finally, the main figure in the foreground, nude and contorted in despair, alludes to existential anxiety and its schizoid self-alienation.

Thus we see the personification of four different sufferings of the soul: addiction, mania, compulsion, and anxiety. In the classical language of the temperamental types, with which Dürer was well familiar, the four figures would portray respectively the phlegmatic, the choleric, the sanguine, and the melancholic. Indeed, according to the great Dürer scholar Erwin Panofsky, the temperaments must have been envisioned here.[36] Dürer's work often dealt with the motif of the four temperaments, as witnessed by *The Four Witches* (1497), *The Four Horsemen of the Apocalypse* (1498), and *The Four Apostles* (1526). We could say that, as a composite image, *The Desperate Man* describes the experience of a complete loss of self, expressed in terms of these four basic temperaments that constitute conditions of the creative individual.

The man in the center background radiates depressive melancholy and sadness, and, as previously noted, with his tankard he suggests addiction. Thus he could stand for the phlegmatic temperament, or, according to the German psychologist Fritz Riemann, a depressive personality.[37] The man's unprotected body, his torso bowed in indifference, his head drooping sadly, his hopeless gaze, and his downturned mouth, all express unmistakably the sensitivity of the phlegmatic/depressive and his or her regressive mood.

The face in the background on the left, casting a critical glare, could stand for the choleric temperament or the hysterical personality. Projecting not directly, but shiftily from the corner of the eye, his gaze is one of a person who enviously compares and calculates.

The man at the far left comes across as a person who is very much concerned to comply with proper, outward appearances. In contrast to the other figures, he is entirely clothed. Going by the evident fastidiousness expressed in his carefully chosen hat, jacket, shirt, and hairdo, he appears to be a person of particular importance. He seems to attach special meaning to a social persona, that is, to the way others perceive him. Such identification with collective norms and values is characteristic of the sanguine/compulsive temperament.

The main figure, quasi kneeling in the center foreground, could bespeak the melancholic/schizoid temperament. This man appears to be trapped in a cramped fury of melancholic self-centeredness, defending himself with merciless self-scrutiny against the losses of inner ground and existential stability.

Second Step of Interpretation: These four figures can be seen also in relationship to the reclining mother figure. That is, they all appear to be severed from a maternal ground. The impression is conveyed that they lack the feeling of primal maternal holding.

The "sleeping mother" could represent a personal mother who is missed, or who is remembered as having been doubted or unreachable. Or the image can point to one's irretrievable past and childhood. Or this mother can express symbolically the loss of the feeling of belonging to nature and life. Or she can stand for the primal ground of creativity that has ceased to provide nourishing images and insights. Such particular kinds of maternal loss seem to be reflected in the four masculine figures.

In this sense, the desperate man in the foreground could stand for the creative individual's ever recurring torturous experience of complete unfruitfulness, of an absolute dearth of inspiration, of being cut off entirely from the original maternal ground of creation and imagination. He suggests the anguished inability to bring forth any creativity whatsoever, because inner images do not arise, no inner idea sparks the creative impulse. With the lack of inward guidance, thinking collapses into an abstract empty dialectic. The fruitful synthesis of ideas is missing. Instead, head and eyes are obscured by mere thoughts, to the effect that thinking encompasses only a divisive back-and-forth exchange between the antagonists of assertion and negation, thesis and antithesis, yes and no. In Dürer's picture the condition is expressed in the desperate man's divided body: On his right-hand side, his forearm and lower leg form vertical lines that suggest an affirmative exclamation point—and on his left side, his arm and leg are angled transversely and bent in upon his own center, suggesting a gesture of denial.

A severed connection with a maternal reality intensifies the opposition of abstract thinking and basic bodily being. In Dürer's picture, this discrepancy shows on one hand in the dominance of the desperate man's head, and on the other hand, in the raw or hyper-plastic representation of his other body parts. With the loss of relationship to the inner mediating image, consciousness succumbs to a soulless dissociation of mind and body. The rational mind yields to abstract logic, while the body caves in to the concrete reality of muscle and bone.

The clothed man at the far left, whom some art historians hold to be Dürer's brother, could echo the missing mother in the sense of a lost family background. Such loss can engender the alienation, loneliness, and insecurity that so typically constitute the creative individual's experience of being-other and not-belonging-to his or her social context. In Dürer's portrayal this condition is expressed in the man's relationship to the other figures: by all appearances, he is at odds with them, unconnected like an isolated foreigner.

The castigating face in the background could allude to a real mother who was experienced as never there, or with whom one was unable to forge a secure relationship, or with whom a problematic relationship still exists. Projecting a theme that is often a central one for creative individuals, this face conveys something of the "son lover" and his unresolved relationship to a mother who was ever-present but never emotionally available.

The nude man standing in the background with his tankard emanates the missing mother in the sense that his source of life seems depleted, dried up. Like a depressive person, he appears to be cut off from nature's own vitalizing energies. The feeling of a basic inner life drive is missing. The mother imago has vanished, and along with it, its given physical and psychic energies.

The creative person's painful point of departure consists of these four dimensions of maternal loss: being unfruitful, alone, unloved, and unheld. They constitute the original wounding and fundamental theme, and explain creative individual's characteristic fragility. At the same time these wounds form a basic pre-condition of creativity. The artist and other creative individuals who belong to this gestalt of creativity create out of an existential deficiency. They write or paint against it, and they survive it only by thematizing and giving shape to it. And doing so, they give birth to themselves anew. They are essentially re-born persons, resurrected by and in their creative work. They are the creators of themselves, whose new life is no longer given by a real biological mother, but by a transcendent archetypal Great Mother.

In Dürer's etching the reclining mother points to both meanings: that of the personal mother—and that of the archetypal Great Mother, the source of all origins and transformation. Just above the reclining mother's breasts, at the level of her shoulder girdle, we see a peculiar, anatomically unexplainable contour. It could create the impression of a technical error and a modification, a so-called *pentimento*, having to do with Dürer's handling of what was for him the new and unfamiliar medium of iron engraving. Similar irregularities in some of Dürer's other works suggest that this explanation cannot be ruled out. However, an equally plausible reason can be found for the strange contour: It would seem that, above the line, the maternal figure embodies a personal mother, her head resting upon a pillow or mattress. And beneath the line, we discern a sculpted breastplate, which points to the archetypal mother. The breastplate here would evidence Dürer's use of the motif elsewhere to characterize certain figures as otherworldly beings, to distinguish them from earthly reality. Thus, rather than perceiving artistic error in Dürer's seemingly anomalous contour, we could speak of his depiction of the mother's double aspect, here encompassing the personal/biographical dimension of maternal loss—and also the symbolic/archetypal dimension of potential renewal, given by the Great Mother.

Third Step of Interpretation: In *The Desperate Man* the *dramatis personae* are situated underground, in a dark cavity of the earth, occupying the root area of a great tree. The remarkable placement points symbolically to the fundamental reality of the creative individual's rootedness in an elemental substrate, a deep layer of the psyche that contains the rhizome of creative being.

The underground place, with its emotionally tinged figures, suggests that the dark substrate of creative work consists of a paradoxical experience of painful and destructive negativity. For creative individuals who mainly act within the horizon of this gestalt of creativity, the creative impulse unfolds above all within the paradoxical experience of pain, negation, and destruction. Here creativity is rooted and extends itself in nocturnal or shadowy experience, which purely contradicts or opposes all new gestalts that are constructive, inspiring, becoming; it is anchored in the hell of manifold, anti-creative adversities.

We could as well speak of creativity's shadow, or of the existence of an active and influential anti-creative factor. Just as much as there exists a factor that gives rise to creative energy as if out of nowhere, there exists a factor that renders creativity impossible or systematically obstructs it. This factor, which inheres in the creative individual to a high degree, appears to have its own energy and destructive intentionality.

In the four temperaments as personified in Dürer's etching, we observed various dimensions of this anti-creativity that is so familiar to creative individuals. It is from this perspective that we will gradually come closer to the notion of daimonic individuality.

To begin, I want to recall the depressive phlegmatic, who could stand for the experience of anti-creative adversity in the forms of illness of body and soul, attributes which are laid bare in the man's sad face and drooping body, and his tankard that points to addiction. Yet uncountable examples from the history of art and ideas evidence the fact that pain, illness, and soul suffering can be mobilizers of creative activity and can become also the content of the creative work itself.

It is a truism that creative individuals are often physically ill, emotionally labile, or driven by compulsions and addictions. But the mere predisposition to extraordinary sensitivity, to a fragile constitution, or to an unstable nervous system cannot be held solely responsible for it. We need consider as well the determining creative principle, which would contain inherently illness and destruction as existential antitheses to creation per se. We think of Frida Kahlo's impairment by polio and her later severe injuries suffered in a bus accident. During his whole lifetime, a chronic lung disease impeded the philosopher Karl Jaspers. Nietzsche suffered delusions of grandeur. The hypochondriac Thomas Mann obsessively maintained his daily journal. James Joyce was an urban neurotic. The painter van Gogh, driven by madness, cut off his own ear. Edvard Munch was consumed by anxiety and jealousy. This is not to mention the many artists, musicians, and poets who have succumbed to alcohol and all kinds of drugs. The examples connecting illness and creativity could form an endless list.

As for Dürer himself, alongside the present etching with its theme of desperation, there is as well his famous self-portrait, a drawing that points to his painful melancholic suffering. Indeed the themes of illness and death run throughout his entire body of work.

Edvard Munch and Pablo Picasso thematized illness in some of their earliest works, respectively in *The Sick Child* (1885/86), and *Science and Charity* (Barcelona, 1897). This makes clear that for both artists, wrestling with illness and death was in the truest sense an existential matter that provided an initial impulse for their creative work. Indeed it can be said that bodily and mental maladies not only determine one's personal experience—but also, they can furnish both departure points for creative activity and motifs for the work.

Let us now return to Dürer's image of the hysterical choleric and his ferocious face, which lends itself readily to the idea of the daimonic. "Daimonic" describes the experience of being driven and determined by forces that exceed one's own will—forces that can lead to one's undoing, or to one's doing of great deeds and creation of great works, or to both. In this sense, all genuine artists recognize that their achievements and failures spring not from themselves, but from a force, a daimon, that possesses and releases them, that takes control of them, that enables their deep and far vision, and that suddenly throws them back into the void.

Socrates was indebted to his own daimon, which he described as a constant objector, nay-sayer, and disabler. It is, he said, "a voice which comes to me and always forbids me to do something which I am going to do, but never commands me to do anything... . And rightly, as I think."[38] Wolfgang Johann von Goethe, too, acknowledged his daimon and his lifelong attraction to the theme. In conversation with the poet Johann Peter Eckermann, Goethe said, "'The Daemonic [*sic*]... lies not in my nature, but I am subject to it.'"[39] For Goethe the daimon is, in essence, "that secret, problematical power, which all men feel, which no philosopher explains, and over which the religious help themselves with consoling words."[40] Goethe asserted as well, "the Daemonic [*sic*] throws itself willingly into many figures of importance."[41] Accordingly, Goethe saw daimonic personalities in the commander and self-proclaimed emperor Napoleon, and also in the musician Paganini.

To further exemplify the daimon as a stimulator or motor of creative work, we can invoke other artists and writers who were especially subject to it and/or thematized it. For his creation of so many characters that were possessed by daimonic energy, Fyodor Michailovich Dostoyevsky (1821–1881) need be mentioned here. Coming also to mind are authors like Edgar Allen Poe, Hugo von Hofmannstal, and Stefan Zweig.

Experience of the daimonic resonates in the works of composers like W.A. Mozart (1756–1791), Ludwig van Beethoven (1770–1827), Robert Schumann (1810–1856), and Johannes Brahms (1833–1897). The daimonic aspect of Albrecht Dürer's personality appears through his interest in the Apocalypse, which he portrayed in a magnificent woodcut that imagizes the destructive works of God in all their ghastly ferocity. Dürer's vivid articulation of the disturbing material leads us to assume easily that it expressed his own experience of daimonic power, his feeling of subjugation to an autonomous destructive force that equally compelled his creative work.

In the framework of psychotherapy we find as well examples of people who are especially inclined to creativity and vulnerable to the effects of a factor, a daimon, as it were, that diametrically opposes the creative impulse. It is this factor that again and again seems to set the stage for the massive hindrance of creative activity and works, doing so emphatically, systematically, as if casting a spell. This "something" can torpedo creative efforts with external distractions and irritations, and also with inner confusion. It disrupts what the Hungarian psychologist Mihaly Csikszentmihalyi holds as one of the most important attributes of the creative individual: the capacity to *concentrate*. In the presence of the daimon, attention may be derailed, narrowed by overvalued ideas or by the intriguing powers of exaggeration and absolutism. In the course, initially coherent thoughts and creative ideas develop *ad absurdum*, led by the grand demand to explain everything all at once and on principle. Creative flow arrives at a dead end, the original idea on the wrong track.

The tendency to intemperance and exaggeration, a particular characteristic of creative individuals, hinders the patience needed to accomplish creative realization. Behind the tendency lies the daimonic energy, which with the help of blindsiding aimfully wills the production of non-productivity. It appears to employ actively and deliberately all possible means to obstruct creative advancement. It behaves as if it were creativity's adversary, like an entity determined to mislead and to engender failure. Justifiably characterized as daimonic, this factor correlates as the shadow of creativity, its counterpart and destroyer. With astonishing energy and efficiency it wants to and succeeds to prevent creative emergence. Revealed here is the creativity of anti-creativity.

Let us return to the clothed man, the figure in which Dürer connotes the sanguine temperament and in which—following Fritz Riemann—we have observed a compulsive personality. In this type anti-creativity could take the form of annihilating critical intellect. The attitude would be judgmental, one that slays every fantasy in advance by the criteria of the "true," the "right," the "generally acknowledged"—or the "illusory and invalid." It relegates the flow of imagination to the overvalued need for absolutely formal clarification, until the artist or author doubts himself and his own competence. This is a straightjacket for every creative person.

Creative block appears often in these forms. It appears, for one, in impatient thinking that spawns hasty conclusions following the conviction that things are or should be known in advance. This kind of thinking is trapped in prejudice, relying straightforwardly on what is already known and customary. It is not able or willing to enter into creative imagination to discover unexpected and astonishingly new things, new shores and insights.

Creative block appears also in over-critical thinking, derived solely and at the wrong time from collective measures of truth and scientific viability. Creative imagination is thereby hastily buried in Procrustean beds of dos and don'ts. Denied the right to unfold in an atmosphere of free play, imagination is disciplined and duly trimmed before it even has the chance to express itself spontaneously. And so it necessarily remains within the realm of "tried and true" ideas. A creative opening to the entirely new is made impossible.

A third aspect of creative block is the striving for perfect form, for the ideal rendering of an image or the ideal rationale for a body of thought. Such formal efforts supposedly provide the evidence needed to persuade an imagined public, which itself should then have no cause for doubt. However, it is not creative to shift creative activity into the external domain of potential observers and readers—that is, as it were, for the purpose of journalistic or pedagogical scrutiny. This is the instrumentalizing orientation that does not serve the gradual unfolding of ideas—to the contrary, it leads inevitably to creative block. The realization of creative ideas requires a child-like, playful absence of intention.

Finally, creative block can manifest itself in agonizing self-doubt. Creative flow is hindered by qualms about the validity of one's own fantasies, impulses, and notoriously, one's own capabilities. Constant self-scrutiny and self-correction prevent the essential movement forward. The flow that belongs naturally to creativity is stopped by one's treading of water and formalistic backward movement.[42]

To sum up: Experience from the psychotherapeutic practice shows that people with creative block suffer repeatedly the effects of anti-creativity, which appears in various forms of negativity, including excessive self-criticism. They succumb to impatient thinking and to over-critical thinking; they strive too much and too soon for formal perfection; and they despair about their own capabilities.

Let us return again to Dürer's desperate man, whom we have already observed to emanate the melancholic temperament or Fritz Riemann's schizoid character. A further dimension of experienced negativity could be expressed in this figure, namely the shaming evidence of the creative individual's impotence. Shameful impotence is the negativity sine qua non that arises in the creative process. It is the unavoidable recognition of the inability to fulfill one's own demands, of having no say about it, of losing command of one's intellectual and creative resources. It is, in short, to be subject to daimonic powers that make us uncreative and unable to produce anything enduring that goes beyond ourselves.

Creative individuals succumb again and again to this radical self-doubt. Behind it there is no neurotically driven perfectionism or narcissistic vanity, nor the exaggerated self-ideal that brings overly ambitious people to the inevitable experience of failure and inadequacy. Rather, doubt in one's own ability is an imminent phenomenon inherent to the creative force itself.

The despair that belongs to creativity entails an extreme splitting of consciousness. One side longs for transcendence, for an otherworldly domain, for the absolute and eternal. The other side feels trapped in the immediacies of earthly mediocrity, foreground ordinariness, and superficial contingencies. Again and again, melancholic despair is induced by the existential incongruences of transcendent desire and the reality of the here-and-now, of ideal yearnings and concrete being. To borrow from Sören Kierkegaard, it is a condition of "sickness unto death." It is to suffer all at once the unattainability of transcendence, which alone provides creative satisfaction, and unfulfilled immanence, which alone provides a solid foothold and confidence in the real world. Thus creative individuals live often with a difficult to bear tension of opposites, in the realm of the either/or, or betwixt-and-between, where they are neither fulfilled by a higher calling, nor held in the warmth of secure being.

The seemingly unbridgeable gap between temporality and eternity forms yet another split in which creative individuals abide, and which explains their existential despair. Here, they strive for enduring forms that would withstand all change—and at the same time, they experience their work as being fragmentary, transient, and subject to falling out of date. In the face of its limited life and sustainability, the meaningfulness of one's own activity comes into doubt.

Finally, despair is evoked by the encounter with the oppositions of freedom and necessity. Uncertainty presents itself—be it related to the context of free choice connected with one's own work, or to necessities arising from one's social surroundings, typological conditions, or personal biographical data. Either way, qualms about the degree and quality of one's self-agency or authorship lead to fundamental doubt in one's own capacities.

It remains for us to further explore the reclining woman in *The Desperate Man*. Thus far we have considered her personification of the mother whose meanings come to light in connection with the four surrounding masculine figures, each of whom have been seen to emanate some aspect of anti-creativity. Let us now consider more carefully the image of the mother in terms of her own symbolization of an anti-creative force, a daimonic, anti-creative mother principle. Seen as a mode of action, her figure comes across as crippling and life hindering. She posits the impulse to annul, to deconstruct, or to reduce life that would otherwise be brought forth, built up, and nurtured. In symbolic language, she alludes to the death aspect of the Great Mother. This negative pole, it need be said, belongs to creativity just as death belongs to life—and it belongs not only as life's end, but also as life's original and interlinked antithesis.

In the image of the sleeping mother Albrecht Dürer seems to picture the psychological obstruction and paralysis that so many creative people endure. At the same time he alludes to the recurring experience of a mother daimon that absorbs and destroys creative fantasy—but that acts also like a black hole, a destructive cosmic entity that is "'pregnant' with creative energy."[43] In the mother's apparently passive and powerless gestalt, the creative negation of creation is traced to its archetypal wellspring and retained as an objective power.

The negating principle is creative in its own paradoxical way. It is creative in its negation of creativity, in its ways and means of suspending creation. In this sense, sickness itself provides a unique bounty of creative fantasy, an astonishing wealth of images of bodily and psychic illness. Maladies that initially obstruct creativity can function as well to lift creative individuals out of their healthy mid-grounds. Sickness shakes down their familiar ground; it opens their horizons, and makes them receptive to the uncertain and the unexplainable.

Creative potential is also contained in the experience of daimonic energies that seem to work against creativity itself. Awareness of the active anti-factor strengthens creative people in the certainty that their creativity depends not on their own insights, but on some autonomous power. It opens up creative resources that lie far beyond the individual's knowledge and skills, making him or her receptive to them and grateful for their guidance.

Also critical negativity, although seeming to oppose creative flow, contains creative potential. While a skeptical attitude blocks creative movement, from the failure of creative fantasy it can just as much evoke awareness of a transcendent reality that holds and wants to realize its own creative insights.

To conclude, we should acknowledge the creative potential in the laming experience of melancholic despair, which would seem to tear the creative ground from under our feet. As the ego loses its own grounding and sense of self-control, it becomes all the more the instrument of a creative reality par excellence. The state of despair opens the way to the transcendence of the controlling "I" and its narrow horizon. In this way the creative force realizes itself, going beyond all the efforts of a failing ego.

5.2. Muse-Inspired Individuality in Pablo Picasso's Family of Saltimbanques

Created in a different time, in a different medium, and by a different artist, Picasso's *Family of Saltimbanques* (Fig. 12) on close examination shows some surprising parallels to the motifs and composition of Dürer's *The Desperate Man* (Fig. 11). Setting aside the possibilities of coincidence and Picasso's conscious reference to Dürer, we are left to assume the spontaneous emergence of an archetypal design idea that expresses the two artists' similar experiences and aesthetic intentions.

Seen from a depth perspective, the basic experience and intended theme is that of the artist's encounter with the creative force and his query into the grounds of his existence as a creative individual. And this applies, in my view, despite the surface subject of *Saltimbanques*. Through the consciously chosen subject a more existential theme asserts itself, such that the painterly medium conveys reflections about the basis of the creative work and the artist's creative drive.

(Fig. 12): Pablo Picasso, *Family of Saltimbanques*

This is the leading thought we are following in this book. It assumes that it is not only the consciously envisioned theme of an artistic work or other creative act that merits attention. Just as important are the meanings that manifest themselves through and beyond or even against conscious intention and design. In other words, we want to uncover meanings that emerge from the creative unconscious, expressed in the form of symbols and other formal design elements.

The two pictures, *Saltimbanques* and *Desperate Man*, show astonishing similarities of composition. Both show a group of individuals positioned opposite a feminine figure poised at the lower right-hand side of the frame. The earth itself forms the ground and background of both scenes. While the group in Picasso's painting is enlarged by the presence of a young girl, it remains that, just as in Dürer's etching, the four masculine figures are distinguished by their expression of the temperamental types. Similarly, too, the woman in the lower right-hand corner of Picasso's picture emanates a hieratic quality of dignity that suggests a transpersonal being.

One cannot help but think that the two pictures portray and contemplate one and the same theme—the creative force as such— even if it is cast in different lights and from different perspectives. What is it, or what is it about the creative force, that ultimately determines the creative work? To what source can the work be traced? What constitutes the mysterious power that compels creative work and design? Or asked another way: What is the real reason that one is not only a human being but also a creative individual? What is the basis of the expanded creative personality?

Such are the questions that could underlie Picasso's circus motif. It cannot be assumed that the artist himself posed such questions explicitly. But they could have played subliminally, and come to expression as the voice of the unconscious in the artist's search for the satisfactory design of his chosen subject.

In the four masculine figures of Picasso's picture we again recognize the classic four temperaments, although in distinction to Dürer, Picasso may not have intended it. At any rate I am not aware that Picasso was familiar with or explicitly meant to thematize the temperaments, with the possible exception of *Melancholy Woman* (1902), a painting belonging to his Blue Period. But the four temperaments comprise an archetypal pattern that belongs essentially to the creative force and through which this force manifests and makes itself visible. It should therefore come as no surprise to find the schema personified in the troupe of circus figures. For this, Picasso's conscious knowledge was not needed, nor was his declared painterly intention. Rather, variations on the motif of the playful and creative circus performer correspond with the temperamental structures that are given by the creative force itself.

As compared with Dürer's *Desperate Man*, we encounter in Picasso's painting a slightly different staging of the four masculine figures and their respective temperaments. The sanguine/compulsive character—personified by the boy dressed in blue and red—now has wandered from the left toward the picture's right. The melancholic/ schizoid personality—Dürer's desperate man—now appears at the left-hand side of the frame, garbed in the harlequin's traditional chequered costume. The choleric/hysterical aspect takes shape in the big-bellied "Tio Pepe," Picasso's familiar buffoon, who is dressed in red, wears a fool's cap, and here occupies the same spot as the face with the daimoniac glare in the background of Dürer's etching. The nearly nude young man next to Tio Pepe can be associated with the phlegmatic/depressive personality.

Each one of Picasso's circus entertainers suggests a certain quality of pensiveness. Unlike the figures in Dürer's etching though, they do not create so much the impression of disturbance or illness, or of being plagued by creative daimons. Nevertheless they seem somehow burdened and sad. They carry the stigma of the creative person, exiled to loneliness and a life outside of an ordinary, containing reality. As circus performers they exist in the truest sense as players and progenitors of illusion, abiding and functioning in a kind of desert, as Picasso suggests; that is, they inhabit absolutely new territory, bereft of guiding pathways. The otherness of this existence, the bohemian status, the exposure to a totally open and undefined being—all such things are both the burdens and gifts of an unusual fate.

All of Picasso's figures wear or carry something on their shoulders: the tall harlequin, a warming scarf; the girl, his companion, a butterfly vest; the boy in blue, a red shawl; the paunchy Tio Pepe, a large sack; and the young man, a big barrel. Even the woman in the foreground wears a shawl over her shoulders, and also a straw hat that seems to hover over her head as if it would not belong to her. This all suggests the idea that something is up with these characters—perhaps a calling, a task, or maybe a special charisma. Let us explore each one more closely.

The artiste in the background, carrying the barrel, can be compared with Dürer's phlegmatic/depressive figure holding the tankard. Now, however, instead of the hand-held mug we have the big barrel, which, carried at head level, would appear to contain and offer something larger—something upon which consciousness can *fall back*. It would be something one can "get one's head around," an underlying reality that exceeds an ego perspective, and is yet something the ego can grasp. It has to do with potentials contained in primordial ideas, to which the ego is subordinated, but which the ego actualizes and *makes its own* (see the artiste's hand, holding the load in balance). We can think of the collective unconscious, which holds ready for creative consciousness multitudes of forms and contents that are not personally acquired, but are always available and given from a wellspring and pool of imagination. With this we can say that among the characteristic attributes of the creative personality is its proximity and receptivity to the unconscious.

The figure of Tio Pepe corresponds with the hysterical choleric of Dürer's etching, the detached face with the daimoniac glare. Despite the obvious differences in appearance, Tio Pepe nonetheless emanates something of the characteristic madness. It comes through not in an image of daimonic possession, but rather in a clownesque playfulness and originality, suggested by Tio Pepe's ruffled collar and fool's cap. The tip of his cap hangs amusingly to one side, as if forming a hook that can catch insights that are "in the air," and that also can produce skewed and thwarting thoughts. With his majestic bodily mass, his dominant red costume, and his cap recalling a crown, Tio Pepe is staged as a king of fools. As a king he represents a *decisive principle*, that of the fool as the underminer of all values, the scrutinizer of fixed norms. He stands for the creative person's alternative perspective on things.

Art in general, of course, encompasses some notion of the transcendence of ordinary views and a corresponding proximity to the unfamiliar. It is no coincidence that in the history of art this motif takes form repeatedly in the figure of the acrobat, the clown, the harlequin, the fool, or some other kind of outsider. Such figures range from Hieronymus Bosch's grotesque creatures, to Velazquez's dwarves, to Goya's lunatics, to the clownesque characters of Watteau, Toulouse-Lautrec, Rouault, Derain, de Saint Phalle, and all the way to the caricatures of the Zen artist Sengai. Creative work always has something to do with the abnormal and the strange. The clown motif in particular alludes to the revolutionary and playful desire to turn things up-side-down, an impulse which, according to Faust, belongs fundamentally to the creative drive.

Tio Pepe, the king of fools or foolish patriarch, shoulders his sack such that its line of tension arcs from his back to the front of his body and extends to the roundness of his belly, where it creates the impression of a mill-like circular motion. This line and circular dynamic point to the transformative power of inherited and age-old knowledge and abilities, which are contained in the sack symbolically. That is, the inherited contents are *carried* and brought into circulation by personal processes of acquisition, digestion, and actualization. Generally speaking and in a nutshell, Tio Pepe can be said to personify resourcefulness and the yen for change, further pillars or basic structures of the creative personality.

In Picasso's painting the boy in blue is analogous to the compulsive sanguine character represented on the left-hand side of Dürer's etching. Of Picasso's figures, this boy is the most normal one, or at least the most unobtrusive. The one reservation would be his jacket, which is so long and so dignified as to lend him the appearance of being older than his face and body size would tell. While his jacket is unsuited to his age, and is in this sense not entirely normal, it does suit the sanguine/ compulsive pole. The impeccable style corresponds generally with the compulsive tendency to project a persona that emanates correct and orderly behavior, and that can as well create the pointed impression of maturity or in this case, of being *grown-up*.

Yet the very same sanguine/compulsive character brings into play the creative sensibility for measure, proportion, and order, and it is thus responsible for the composition of an image, for the visualizing of structures, and for the differentiating and joining of opposites. It is this aspect of the personality that enables the recording of gestalts, ideas, and themes, and that accesses the sense of the decorative, the musical, the rhythmic, in short, the moment of beauty. The boy's stylish look—his carefully coiffed hair, his elegant ballet shoes, his decent outfit—underscores the dimension of aesthetic discernment that is bound essentially with this temperamental function.

Grasping in one hand the tip of his shawl, the boy expresses symbolically a connection with a superordinate dimension, just as the artiste with the barrel expresses a relationship to the unconscious and Tio Pepe with his sack expresses a relationship to a cultural inheritance. Insofar as a shawl stands symbolically for an office of power as it did in antiquity, or for a priestly and sacral function as it does in the Roman Catholic Church today, the boy's shawl could symbolize a greater "task" or "calling." It could stand for the awareness that one's painting and creative engagement transpires not only by personal will, but also by virtue of one's captivity and service to a mysterious entity whose investment in the realization of certain tasks and creative progress sustains for the sake of the common good.

A fourth pillar in the structure of creative individuality comes to expression symbolically in the tall harlequin standing at the left-hand side of the picture. He bespeaks the schizoid/melancholic type that we saw in Dürer's etching of the desperate man himself. While Picasso's harlequin shows no trace of desperation, he nevertheless emanates a typical schizoid/melancholic kind of self-division that entails a splitting of opposing needs, interests, and attitudes.

The sense of self-division in this figure can be discerned in a number of different ways. We can observe first his harlequin costume, noting especially the colors that make up the typically chequered design. In the realm of color symbolism the juxtaposed opposites of red and blue stand for the antitheses of emotion and reason, instinct and reflection, extraversion and introversion, energy and contemplation. Brown and other colors set next to black symbolize the antagonists of being and nothingness, affirmation and negation, life and death, reality and the void. Dark and light represent the opposites of surface and depth, lightness and shadow, positive and negative. Viewed under the variety of aspects, these color contrasts on the whole suggest the schizoid/melancholic's typical emotional conflict and divided sense of self.

For artists like Picasso, whose works foreground especially the melancholic element from within the four-fold creative profile, such basic contradictions engender acute self-division and abrupt ceasures in their lives. At the same time, artists tend to thematize such experiences. See for instance Søren Kierkegaard's *Either/Or* (1843), the book in which he distinguishes two diametrically opposed life views—the aesthetic/hedonistic and the ethical. We have already mentioned Hermann Hesse's dealing with oppositions in *Narcissus and Goldmund*. Robert Schumann wrote his critical music reviews in the voices of two different imaginary characters, the introspective "Eusebius," and the exuberant "Florestan" (beginning 1831). The German poet Jean Paul Friedrich Richter thematized his own split in the characters of "Walt" and "Vult" (1863). Creative people experience recurrently the existential sense of being at variance with themselves, as symbolized in Picasso's harlequin by the antitheses of red and blue, dark and light, color and black.

The harlequin alludes to self-division in yet another way, namely in the overt collision of the vertical and horizontal axes formed by his bodily bearing. He stands straight and tall, directed toward the ground, but in sharp contrast his head tilts to the left and his gaze is directed outwardly to the right. His left forearm, crossing his back horizontally, forms a remarkable contrast to his long body axis and the vertical line emphasized by his right arm. Finally, as if woven into the fabric of the overall image, division appears in the crisscrossing horizontal and vertical planes, where harlequin's shawl is slung around his neck, and the loose end of it falls down his back.

Understood symbolically, vertical and horizontal directions express the antitheses of transcendence and immanence, the ideal and the real, the life beyond and this life, and finally, the absolute and the realizable. As we already observed in the discussion of Dürer's *Desperate Man*, the existential tension evoked by such opposites characterizes in large measure the melancholic individual's creative sensitivity that finds no reconciliation between existing and envisioned being, between experienced and possible reality.

We note again however the great difference between Dürer's and Picasso's portrayals of creative individuality in its four constitutive temperamental dimensions. Whereas Dürer's *Desperate Man* represents it under the sign of the daimon and its creative negativity, Picasso's *Saltimbanques* represents it under the sign of a positively animating muse, symbolized in part by the girl with her basket of flowers. Held by the harlequin's hand, the girl's function is analogous to that of the barrel for the artiste, the sack for Tio Pepe, and the red shawl for the boy in blue. Just as these objects symbolize larger and wider resources for the benefit of the creative individual—the *a priori* images of the collective unconscious, the cultural background, the greater dimension of one's own task—so does this girl, too, point to something larger, to the offering of some greater autonomous inspiration.

The girl wears a sort of ballet dress, in pastel pink, which conveys a feeling of airy lightness that contrasts the harlequin's angular qualities and Tio Pepe's mighty body weight. She implies a playful levity that compensates the dialectic tension of the schizoid aspect and the cyclic heaviness of the hysteroid aspect. As elfin ballet dancer, she introduces a light-footedness that moves the creative process away from both of these aspects. She represents the creative flow out of which the creative force generates itself. It goes without saying that creativity requires movement, or a relatively unbounded sequence of steps that allow the emergence of unexpected new ideas that manifest like sparks ignited in a sudden turn.

The girl's black butterfly-like vest characterizes her as a flying being, an elf or a small angel, a guardian angel perhaps, or a cherub. She represents the element of ether and the realm of ethereal being that oversees and conveys spiritual insight, intuition, and fantasy. Her black wings make clear that she functions not primarily to communicate heavenly thoughts, but above all to transmit unfamiliar ideas that arise from the dark of the night and the underworld.

A red flower adorns the girl's black hair. If we understand symbolically hair as the expression of thoughts and the red flower as feeling and Eros, then we find in this girl an image of an inspiring muse with the special ability to establish through feeling the relationship of things, that is, the ability to think poetically and to symbolize. She personifies a symbolic quality of thinking that adds Eros to sensed meaning. We can speak of the "kiss of the muse," the inward relationship between an inspiring force and the artist. Yet in addition to stimulating the creative ego per se, the muse effects the ego's awareness of connections between things and its interest in things as such. This is, then, among the attributes of creative thinking and activity that is repeatedly confirmed in the literature on creativity: the creative person's ability to draw meaningful relationships and unusual perspectives of meaning from things that appear otherwise in separate categories.

The capacity for qualitatively new and integral vision owes itself to the aspect of the muse symbolized in the red flower. Astonishing connections and surprising insights, taken not as self-made products but experienced as gifts from some other source, lead to the notion of a muse. Like the notion of the daimon, the muse might belong to the vocabulary of by-gone times. Yet phenomenologically viewed, the language conveys precisely and authentically the creative individual's satisfying and grateful experience of receiving from an inner Other gifts of insight that come in the forms of fascinating discoveries and the revelation of astonishing connections.

The elfin girl of Picasso's painting holds a flower basket, which points to something larger that might have something to do with the creative process as such. The flowers spring out from her basket as if from an opening seashell, such that the basket not only contains them but also seems to bring them into being. This could hold the larger meaning of a creative process that draws on a pool of possibilities taken from the history of art, from the development of one's own work, and from the primary structures of creative imagination.

Creative painting and thinking do not unfold according to one's own desire and mood or capriciousness. Far more, they follow the larger will of a pre-given program that realizes itself gradually and with its own intention in the form of a creative work. The program is inscribed within and also re-writes the given realities of the current time and the history of art and thinking. And finally, the program is also co-determined by given patterns of imagining and designing, which themselves steer the steps of the creative process.

Just as in Dürer's *Desperate Man*, in Picasso's *Saltimbanques* the group is staged opposite a woman in the lower right-hand corner. We can understand Picasso's woman, too, to represent the creative feminine principle that lies behind the four modalities of experience. Yet in *Saltimbanques* the woman's nature corresponds with the wholly different atmosphere and perspective of this picture, whereby the muse features as the mediator of the greater force of creation and the fundament of the creative work. Thus the woman here displays the engaging, animating qualities of an enlivening and primordially feminine energy.

Moreover, as the woman in *Saltimbanques* is pictured to be young, her figure describes the primal creative force to be an eternally fresh spring and origin of new possibilities and change. This woman's epithet could consist of Hermann Hesse's wonderful words, "In all beginnings dwells a magic force …"[44] Her jacket is depicted in a beautiful eggshell white, which symbolizes all beginnings and becomings *ex nihilo*. Her outfit contains as well the primary opposites, red and blue, both rendered in spring-like virginal, fresh, and tender tones. In other words, her figure in itself holds the inherent creative tension that springs up between the yearning for sensuality, materiality, and *materia* (red), and the yearning for sense, meaning, and spirituality (blue).

The woman's gestural language makes clear that a process of transformation is taking place, steered by the feminine principle. Her right hand, poised horizontally in her lap, shows a gesture of giving and providing in the here-and-now, while her left hand points upward toward some other sphere. This could allude to a process whereby natural realities are sublimated into higher imagistic levels, that is, to become symbols and carriers of sense and meaning. Such transformation transpiring by the influence of an underlying feminine principle suggests again that ideas, images, and symbols are not so much created by the ego but far more, are offered by the underlying reality itself.

The underlying reality here is nothing other than what Jung called the soul, the container and creator of images. However as portrayed in *Saltimbanques*, the image-making soul is not to be understood as the individual, personal one but as the general archetypal soul, the actual ground of creative being, the world soul. Picasso associates this creative force *par excellence* with two further symbols: the woman's water jug and her straw hat adorned with flowers. The jug, alluding to water drawn from the depths of the earth, stands for the mysterious world of the unconscious that contains a wealth of "figures"—or as Albrecht Dürer put it: "[T]he imagination of the good artist is full of figures, and were it possible for him to live forever, he would always have from his inward ideas, whereof Plato speaks, something new to set forth by the work of his hand."[45] On the other side, the straw hat, almost as if hovering slightly above the woman's head, imagizes a higher spiritual principle that lends to the creative process the qualities of wholeness and centeredness. This principle is symbolized in the hat's mandala-like form built up on the disc-shaped brim with the rising central crown and the circular flowered band.

The woman's association with the water jug and straw hat implies that both attributes belong to her and that in her figure both dimensions are offered: the wealth of inner "figures" and the principle of meaningful connections. Even more astonishing, her figure represents the potential of mediation between the two, that is, between the inner contents of the unconscious and the meaningful events in the visible world. For this reason we can see in this woman an astounding picture of what C.G. Jung called synchronicity.

Once again I must emphasize, I do not submit that Picasso attempted consciously to represent such a picture or even the concept per se. His sole purpose was to achieve the genuine, coherent, and artistically satisfactory production of a picture that offered itself from his inner experience. Symbols that appear as result offer interpretive possibilities that exceed the artist's explicit intention and view. They express meanings that are posed by the co-determining unconscious, that are taken up by a symbolically attuned consciousness, and that thus stand open for our interpretation.

The young woman with her water jug and straw hat points to the soul that underlies the creative individuality portrayed in Picasso's *Family of Saltimbanques*. It is the image-and-meaning-making-soul, the soul that governs meaningful coincidence and synchronicity. This is the factor that animated Picasso to say, "I do not seek, I find."

5.3. Ingenious Individuality in Vincent van Gogh's The Potato Eaters

(Fig. 13): Vincent van Gogh, *The Potato Eaters*

The Potato Eaters by Vincent van Gogh (1885) (Fig. 13) offers a third example of the artist's visual query into the roots of creative individuality, a theme that runs in the background of the image itself. The formal structure is again the same: Among the five figures portrayed, four form a group that represents the four temperaments, while a woman with archetypal implications sits apart at the right-hand side of the frame. On close examination, we will see that van Gogh's representation of creative individuality in its four constitutive dimensions follows a specific perspective that differs from the two paintings discussed so far.

The Potato Eaters is van Gogh's first large-scale work, and one of his earliest. He had taken up painting rather late, at the age of twenty-eight, after working as an art dealer and later as a preacher. In view of the occupational background, the painting at hand can be held as the outcome of an initiation process. With this work, van Gogh not only launched his earnest artistic endeavor, but he also found his self-understanding as an artist. In other words, in his portrayal of the simple potato eaters he expressed parts of his own creative personality. Or said more correctly: His variations on the potato eaters presented the four constitutive temperamental perspectives in a manner that would serve his awareness of himself as a creative individual. In a letter to his brother Theo on April 30, 1885, van Gogh described the pains he had taken to render his subjects' "heads and hands," and he indicated the large extent to which this painting amounted to a ground plan for his future creative work.[46] With the creation of *The Potato Eaters*, van Gogh initiated himself as a self-sovereign creative individual. As is always the case with the vivification of an underlying mythos, the process stimulated van Gogh's new consciousness and new energy. For him it entailed the resolve to continue as a painter with his own concerns and calling, and to affirm his own creative being without external encouragement.

The above-mentioned letter makes it clear that with *The Potato Eaters* van Gogh's explicit theme was that of creativity as such. He wrote, for instance,

> You see, I really have wanted to make it so that people get the idea that these folk, who are eating their potatoes by the light of their little lamp, have tilled the earth themselves with these hands they are putting in the dish, and so it speaks of manual labour and—that they have thus honestly *earned* their food.[47]

Van Gogh wanted to portray authentic people who produce their food by working the soil with their own hands. Understood symbolically, he was captured by the idea of creative individuals who were involved directly and with their own hands in the process of generating soul-nurturing products.

He wrote further about *The Potato Eaters*, "I wanted to give the idea of a wholly different way of life from ours—civilized people."[48] He was thus concerned to portray a natural way of living, one that precedes all education and that embodies an unmediated, primal relationship to life. Van Gogh's interest in this vein was shared by many other artists, including for instance: Brueghel, with his idyllic villages; Dürer, with his dancing peasant couples; Gauguin, with his Breton and Haitian women; Jean-François Millet, with his farm scenes; Picasso, with his African motifs and interest in children's art;

and Jean Dubuffet with his enthusiasm for *Art Brut* or Outsider Art—an absolutely non-professional genre. Such interest in "simple folk" who are not yet formed by education, training, and social pressure shows the fascination of the idea of a creative life that self-generates from its own source.

"So I certainly don't want everyone just to admire it or approve of it without knowing why."[49] This confession is van Gogh's proud acknowledgment to his brother that his initial work, *The Potato Eaters*, affirmed his inner and unmistakable calling. And with it, he realized that he would not rely on outside approval, and that quick collective applause would cast doubt on his work's creative uniqueness and depth.

Let us now turn to the picture itself. The scene is set at night, in a small room reminiscent of a cellar or cave. So we can say that the scene transpires in a subterranean or other dark interior, pointing symbolically to the fact that the fourfold pattern of creative individuality is fundament (cellar) or origin (cave) of creativity. There is a recurring motif here, namely the connection of creative individuality with the dimension of the elemental, the fundamental. In Dürer's *Desperate Man*, it takes form in the image of the dark cavity of the earth, and in Picasso's *Saltimbanques*, the arid desert. Independently of any given era, its surrounding circumstances, and the artist's personality, the query into the theme apparently comes hand-in-hand with consciousness of its fundamental meaning.

In van Gogh's picture, the spatial staging of the four characters with their psychological attributes virtually mirrors their appearance in Dürer's *Desperate Man*. In the center background, the man raising his cup emanates the depressive/phlegmatic tendency. The woman on the left personifies the hysterical/choleric inclination. The man at the far left embodies the compulsive/sanguine bent. The girl in the center foreground, her back turned to the onlooker, represents the schizoid/melancholic leaning. Finally, on the far right-hand side, an old woman set slightly apart from the others alludes to the archetypal mother and the deeper collective unconscious. The round of characters gathered at the table can be said to picture a unified whole consisting of specific creative perspectives that belong and work together. Each part has its own value and meaning, and yet they are all joined in communication and by a common activity.

The representative of the phlegmatic tendency, the man at the far end of the table, is portrayed typically with a container. This time it is neither a tankard (Dürer) nor a barrel (Picasso), but a cup, which the man extends toward the woman who is serving coffee. His gesture has the double meaning of a plea and an offering. On one hand it expresses need, his cup being held up in the hope to have it filled. Yet a quality of determinedness in the same gesture suggests also the awareness of having something to contribute. Expressed symbolically in this figure, then, is an aspect of consciousness that knows about its reliance on a greater, giving and inspiring entity—and is at the same time having a container at its disposal, that is, a capacity of understanding. There is thus a giving and a taking, a forming and a receiving, an exchange emblematic of an intrapsychic creative process: Ego consciousness puts forth an original idea—a trial notion, a sketch or a draft, an initial hypothesis—and from the other side, from the creative unconscious, the idea is validated or amplified and filled with contents. It is the method of trial and error, a playful tinkering, or a "bricolage," in Lévi-Strauss's sense of an archaic quality of thinking.[50]

Still following the image of the man with the cup, held out from the level of his breast, we can say further that the original idea comes to play from the heart, from one's center. Perhaps it is born as well from the experience of distress and infirmity, a condition that characterizes this person as a whole and that is signified especially by the man's cane, propping up his left hand. The phlegmatic tendency as personified here brings to the creative process the ability to condense and express emotion and existential adversity in a personal container, such that the collective unconscious may manifest in its universal significance.

The woman on the left in the white bonnet, holding her fork over the plate of potatoes, personifies the choleric tendency. Her wide eyes and imploring gaze are especially striking, and correspond with the hysteric bent of the choleric, as we saw in the analogous figure of Dürer's etching. But in contrast, hers is equally the expression of a seer. It might remind us of Michelangelo's Delphic Sybil in the Sistine Chapel, although the framework here is far more modest. Rather than the monumental chapel, we have a humble cellar or cave-like kitchen. And yet this woman's face emanates a hieratic dignity and the faculties of intuition and prophetic vision. Her beautifully rendered bonnet creates the impression of a sensitive organ that enhances her reception of inspiration from above. At the same time, she is about to take a piece of potato from the plate, while her left arm rests on the tabletop. With these gestures she points symbolically to the here-and-now, to concrete earthly existence.

On the whole, this woman expresses another specific dimension of creative action, namely the capacity to realize inner vision in concrete form, to give it appetizing and nourishing shape that can be taken in by others. As Jung says, creativity lies not in the intriguing imagination per se, but in the capacity to transpose its images into concrete pictures and thoughts. Inward imaginings become truly creative only when they are molded by the ego. The real creative act—not to be taken as self-evident—is this incarnation and implementation of visionary ideas, the process that makes them accessible in the context of the everyday (the plate), in the immediate time, and in basic reality (potatoes). It is this process of creative transformation that constitutes real creative achievement.

Like the analogous figure in Dürer's etching, the man on the far left represents the sanguine inclination and its distanced otherness, projected in a gaze that looks on others from the outside. Riemann's "compulsive" aspect takes the form of a facial expression that emanates compliant self-certainty and moral superiority. Indeed the sense of an authoritative and controlling inspector comes across in the man's almost perfectly square cheek framed under his highly perched cap with the stiff visor. And yet the fact that he sits upright, as if enthroned on his high-backed chair, conveys an attitude of "seatedness" in a worthy tradition backed by collectively recognized values. This latter characteristic corresponds with the norm orientation of the compulsive/sanguine tendency.

Behind this man, hanging high on the wall and not so easy to see, there is a framed picture of a Christian scene, presumably showing the crucifixion with Mary and Joseph at the foot of the cross. There is also a pendulum clock showing the hour to be about 11:40. With these two objects we have on one hand an expression of the Christian myth with the central symbol of Christ's death—and on the other hand, an expression of clock time as such, which is valid for everyone. This sanguine character thus appears to be at home in the collective world of Christianity, a circumstance that would reflect van Gogh's upbringing in a pastor's family as well as his own short career as a preacher. And referring to the clock, the objective measurement of time, it appears further that respect for secular collective standards would be the self-evident norm.

However, the man's right hand reveals an attitude that runs contrary to one of respect for objective rules and collective persuasions. With his index finger he appears to pick and chose which potato pieces should be eaten, in what order, and according to which preferences of taste. Implied here is an entirely subjective choice attuned with personal predilection. The decisive factor with van Gogh's portrayal of the compulsive/sanguine tendency is thus not the generally recognized rule, but personal judgment. It is not the impersonal socially relevant truth that matters, but a personally nourishing and inwardly experienced certainty.

The man's right forearm functions like a free boom, the long spar that extends the foot of a sail, alluding to the art of free choice and trial and error by subjective criteria whereby something new can develop—a novel methodological approach, a fresh worldview, unforeseen guiding thoughts. Creativity consists also of this strength: to spawn new ideas on the basis of personal experience and testing as well as on the basis of a Zeitgeist that requires new forms and contents.

And now to the mysterious girl, who is seated in the center foreground and oriented completely toward the table scene, such that her back is turned to the onlooker. She stands for the aspect of the melancholic. Very much in the shadow and appearing as little more than a silhouette, she wears as well a black cap. With these emphatically dark elements her aura corresponds entirely with the black-biled melancholic. Apart from this, it is hard to decipher who she is, how she feels, what she is doing. Her hidden face and unobtrusive bodily bearing make of her in essence an anonymous presence.

Perhaps it can be said that technical factors are responsible for the girl's invisibility. That is, van Gogh's composition of the group around the table necessarily entailed the placement of one figure in the foreground, with his or her back turned toward the viewer, in the shadow. Even if such consideration did play a role, other solutions could have been found. And so it remains that the girl's missing bodily vitality and face are further indicators of the melancholic temperament.

From the onlooker's perspective, the girl appears almost completely in the dark. She could thus symbolize an aspect of consciousness that is consumed by feelings of not-being and being-nothing, feelings of emptiness and worthlessness, unknowingness and impotence. These kinds of existential negativity that make up generally the ingredients of a melancholic malaise, but they describe here the girl's concrete and initial psychic condition.

We need consider, however, that the wondrous light appears in the midst of night and shadows. There may be an inner connection between the girl and the oil lamp that hangs above her, illuminating the whole room and the other figures seated around the table. The lamp itself can stand for the sudden appearance of a bright idea and warming thought, which enlighten everyone, and cast new light on life and people. This dynamic and meaning bespeak the aspect of creative consciousness that we can describe as experienced "genius" or "ingenious creativity." However, in the literature on creativity opinions are divided as to precisely what characteristics and talents distinguish the genius from other creative individuals. I myself am persuaded, though, that van Gogh's painting reveals something more about it.

The ingenious person holds the potential to be taken entirely into the service of enlightening ideas. It is the person seized suddenly by a great vision and mission and able to function like a lamp in the dark that sheds new light on humanity for the sake of the common good. By analogy to the warming quality of light, he or she brings profound new values to bear; by analogy to light's illuminating quality, brilliantly new viewpoints.

In effect, however, the genius is diminished by his or her identification with the light. In other words, the intense light of the higher goal and task casts the genius into darkness. He or she is driven and consumed by the light, or reduced to being its sheer curved mirror. The genius becomes the instrument of the revealing light itself, living no longer for him- or herself, but solely for the cause. The activity is fulfilling but it eats away at one's substance. Ingenious creativity is then no longer self-sovereign, but captive to the cause, and the creative individual falls into a state of possession.

In van Gogh himself we find a good example of this radical devotion to the work in the absence of self-protection. Only days before his attempted suicide and subsequent death in July 1890, van Gogh wrote to this brother Theo, "Ah well, I risk my life for my own work and my reason has half foundered in it …"[51] Yet in a letter of 1882 he had asserted, "[T]ime and again I return lovingly to the difficulties, to the cares, *to a difficult life*—and think, it's better like this, I learn more this way, I'm no worse a person for it, this isn't the road to ruin."[52] Pressing onward in 1883 he wrote, "… I carry on as *one unknowing* but who knows this one thing—'*I must finish a particular work within a few years*' …"[53]

And yet we need keep in mind that ingenious creativity encompasses also the other creative faculties that come to light in van Gogh's painting and that we have discussed in connection with the three other temperamental aspects. To review, the phlegmatic aspect involves the capacity to shape personal adversity into symbolic forms that make of the contents universally visible and meaningful ones. The choleric tendency contributes the ability to transpose visionary ideas into digestible and nourishing forms. And finally, the sanguine bent provides the ability to create wholly new methods and revolutionizing worldviews and perspectives.

At the right-hand side of the table the woman serving coffee is set slightly apart from the group by a protruding wall and also by her seat between the table and what appears to be an oven. This apartness, along with her solemn and mysterious expression, seems to attribute her with a special status. As in the pictures by Dürer and Picasso, what we seem to have here is an image of the archetypally feminine. And again, what appears to emanate in her figure is the archetypal factor in the collective unconscious that is linked to the specific aspect of the creative individuality.

The woman appears to be sunken entirely into herself. She seems to dispense the coffee at her own discretion, doing so as her spontaneous contribution of a potion to stimulate the spirit. She, that is the deep creative unconscious, is the source of this coffee, this potion, this power of animation that awakens creative consciousness. Like an unfathomable fate, she offers unexpectedly and freely the aptitudes of keen insight and concentrated action.

Symbolically speaking, as the donor of coffee the woman is as well the donor of black bile, or the potential for a heightening melancholy that intensifies the creative potentials of the four temperaments. As she pours this black potion into the white cups, the unmediated meeting of white and black symbolizes her containment of the absolute antitheses of beginning and ending, day and night. Thus her gesture expresses her reign over the mystery of sudden beginnings and endings, and also her governance over processes of pure becoming (white) and absolute fading (black), as well as all transformation that comes of them *ex nihilo*.

Even if van Gogh's talent was initially unrecognized by the collective world around him, his sudden advent as an ingenious painter at age twenty-eight may well be thanks to the soulful power of transformation that presents itself in the archetypal image of the coffee server. It is, so to speak, the feminine factor from the depth of the unconscious, which apparently awakened *ex nihilo* van Gogh's creative power and transformed him into an ingenious artist.

In the course, van Gogh himself became essentially an agent of renewal and transformation. This is, then, the word that can summarize van Gogh's experience and portrayal of creative individuality: transformation by the conversion of personal suffering and other experience into universal gestalts; transformation by the concretization of visionary ideas in a vital reality; transformation by the reevaluation of existing rules and the establishment of new worldviews; and transformation by self-surrender to a given task and its guiding spirit.

There remains one last detail to consider for our symbolic understanding of the woman. While she serves the coffee with her right hand, her left hand seems to have passed over an apparently unused coffee pot, to hover just above her lap, palm down, with her index finger pointing downward. Her paired gestures could imply the tendency of the archetype of transformation to give with one hand, and to withhold with the other hand—to offer from one pot an abundance of suggestive potentials, and to keep the other pot as a reserve of emptiness and dearth of imagination. Said another way, it would be characteristic of the archetype to offer on one hand symbolic understanding, and on the other hand, to thwart it, that is, to allow consciousness to collapse into concrete, immediate being and depressing factuality.

Creative people are often prone to suffer the conflict of creative inspiration and acute feelings of emptiness. Behind it stands the archetype of transformation with its ambivalence or bi-polarity that can both nurture and repress symbolic understanding. When the archetype manifests in the latter sense, and when images, fantasies, and symbols thus dissolve under a literal, "nothing but" attitude, life becomes meaningless and empty in unbearable measure. Anxiety and depression assert themselves on the evidence of a life without any imaginative quality.

The radical incapacity for symbolic doing and perceiving amounts to a hell that can overcome creative individuals in enantriodromic fashion especially at the end of a fruitful phase of creative work. This often observed painful experience is exemplified by the awarded French-speaking Swiss author and painter Jacques Chessex (1934-2009), who died of a heart attack at age seventy-five. Upon his completion of every novel, Chessex fell into a state of loss of soul, to borrow Jung's phrasing, and abandoned himself relentlessly to alcohol and debauched sex.

One's delivery into the dark and gloomy aspect of the archetype of transformation can of course lead to an absolute dead-end and utmost despair, from which suicide offers the only way out. The tragic ends of many creative individuals bear witness. Van Gogh's life ended in this way, dramatically, when he was merely thirty-seven years old.

5.4. Alchemical Individuality in Paul Klee's Carnival in the Mountains

(Fig. 14): Paul Klee, *Carnival in the Mountains*

Paul Klee's watercolor, *Carnival in the Mountains* (Fig. 14), gives us a fourth example of the basic pattern of creative individuality as it appears in artistic work. As ever, the pattern's emergence bespeaks the artist's growing awareness of several factors: the special status of his creative personality; the deeper fundament of his creativity and creative task; and finally, his specific experience of transcendence. The different artists' imagistic variations on the bases of creative being hold in common a certain pictorial design: the elemental setting, and four gestalts that both personify variously the four temperaments and also stand as a unified group opposite an archetypally feminine figure. In the foregoing discussion of selected art works, we identified in detail the specific accents. We have understood that those perspectives that become visible and appear to be specific to the individual artist are in fact not only personal variations, but they belong as well the potentiality of the gestalt of creativity as such.

For Klee, *Carnival* had special personal significance, and he ranked it accordingly among his works. We can assume his ranking had at least as much to do with the content as with the aesthetic quality of the image. *Carnival* recalls *Saltimbanques*, Picasso's family of circus performers, which pictures a playful kind of consciousness that surpasses the gravity of everyday being with imagination and suggestive illusion, and that also thus sets the basis of creative work in general. Klee's idea of the carnival presents a similar quality of playful illusion and creative transfiguration of reality. "Carnival" here means the creative invention of new meanings by the inversion and mixing-up of established norms. A carnival thrives on the reversal of collective roles. It is an institutional opportunity for the discovery and integration of repressed opposites, and thus also inspires creative expression.

As compared with the previously discussed works, Klee's mountain setting presents a new variation on the elemental context in which the act of artistic self-affirmation takes place. In distinction to Dürer's subterranean hollow, Picasso's desert, and van Gogh's simple hut, the mountain landscape points to the displacement of artistic existence from the level of ordinary life to the heights of loneliness and outsiderness. It is a different cipher for the creative individual's exceptional status, given by his or her distance from social custom and nearness to elemental being. Klee described himself in this sense as being, "[s]lightly closer to the heart of creation than usual, but still not close enough."[54]

The pair of mountains flanking the middle ground where the carnival plays recalls "The Two Mountains," a poem Klee wrote in 1903, when he was a young man of twenty-four years:

> Two mountains there are,
> where all is bright and clear,
>
> the mountain of beasts, and
> the mountain of gods.

Between them, lies the
valley of humans in twilight.

When one among them by chance lifts his head,
He is gripped by foreboding and
unquenchable yearning;
he who knows he knows not,
yearns for those who don't know they know not,
and for those who know that they know.[55]

Paul Klee's poem envisions human existence playing out between two orders, the natural and the spiritual. The two poles correspond with the pair of mountains in *Carnival*, where the spirit is symbolized by the one mountain in the upper left, with its steeply ascending and geometrically precise pathway—and nature is symbolized by the mountain range on the right, with its jagged and horizontally spread peaks. In the "twilight valley" human existence plays out between the natural and spiritual orders: in the animal here-and-now, being aware and questioning—and in sublime awe, being more uncertain and doubting. To inhabit this valley, then, is to live the ambiguity of being human, the *condition humaine*. Sometimes, like Klee, we look upward, and are "gripped by ... yearning," knowing (as Diogenes knows) that we do not know. To escape the inevitable painful question, we long for the natural and sheltered existence of the animal that does not know that it does not know, and we long for the confidence of those individuals who, without being plagued by doubt, know that they know.

Klee's poetic lines address not only the general human condition, but also the particular conditions of a creative existence. Creative individuals are acutely aware of their own limited faculties and yet at the same time, they yearn for absolute insight and are compelled by the urge to seek it ever anew. Theirs is Hegel's "unhappy consciousness," or the consciousness of Dürer's *Melencolia*. They are aware of being driven to understand, and of missing the sheltered animal's indifference to not-knowing. Their survival obtains only in creative efforts to obtain ever deeper insight and ever truer expression. Felt less as a source of happiness and fulfillment, the existential need to know is experienced far more as a crisis and fate driven by notions of absolute truth and beauty, waiting to be discovered and designed.

These are the lofty ideas that constitute the creative goal and determine the creative search. By the same token, one's god-like probing of every last hiding place and one's god-like gift of sublime composition are the only and ultimately recognized measures of progress. It is little wonder that creative individuals feel limited and insufficient in their own powers. The melancholy typically induced by creative work inheres in the individual's consciousness of his or her ineradicable inadequacy to reconcile the demands of the envisioned ideal and the concrete task, the demands of the potential and the realizable.

Let us now begin to explore the five main figures that play in Klee's carnival and that symbolize the archetypal pattern of elements that come to play in creative individuality. Because the variety of characteristics appear in abstract form, they may seem a bit difficult to identify. Nevertheless it is possible to discern the expression of the four temperamental perspectives and an underlying archetypally feminine force.

An initial bird's eye view of the scene should be helpful. At the far left-hand side of the picture a figure wearing a hat holds out a container full of globe-like fruits. The phlegmatic tendency is discernable in this figure's facial expression—and also in its link to a container, which we have seen previously in the forms of a tankard (Dürer), a barrel (Picasso), and a coffee cup (van Gogh). Slightly to the right of this "phlegmatic" figure is a shorter figure with uplifted arms, dressed in blue and red. This one emanates the sanguine inclination, in certain ways likening the personification in Picasso's *Saltimbanques*. The choleric aspect appears in the form of an antenna-like eye hovering far above the horizon, its gaze radiating from the heavens. The walking bird with the fire blazing in its belly represents the melancholic bent. The archetypal, primordial feminine element takes shape on the right side of the picture, in the complex figure with the large head, uplifted arms, and striding gait. From here we can proceed to explore each of the figures in detail.

The figure on the left personifying the phlegmatic tendency displays a quality of dignity with the aura of a celebrant or magician. The large empty eye suggests an attitude of inward concentration, a preparation for a celebration of some kind. The importance of the figure's function and task is emphasized by the top hat, a traditional accouterment of the carnival master. On the whole it is clear that someone or something is in charge here, to ensure the fulfillment of a task and calling.

It is not entirely clear whether this figure portrays a man or rather a woman. The hourglass contour of the body suggests a woman, while the disproportionate and dominant head suggests a man. What we see here, then, is a hermaphroditic emanance underscoring the man/woman duality that often belongs to the physique and garb of magicians and priests. In a number of different contexts, such bisexuality or exceeding-of-gender expresses a status that exceeds all ordinary distinctions between man and woman. Going beyond ordinary human reality, the hermaphrodite can embody the position of a sublime intermediary to a transcendent realm.

In Klee's *Carnival* the hieratic figure holds five pieces of fruit in a bowl or basket, as if presenting an offering or even a sacrifice. Customarily in sacrificial rites, human labor can be expressed in the gift of fruit, which is accepted and transformed by the entity to which the offer is made. This applies for instance in the transformation rite of the Roman Catholic mass, where the gifts of bread and wine are offered as expressions of human labor and then returned to the supplicants, transformed as body and blood of Christ.

In a similar vein, Klee's picture resonates the sense of a sacrificial offering. The offered gift consists of the five fruits, which could have the symbolic meaning of sensory experience associated with the five senses. Yet this gift appears to be already transformed and returned, for the fruits have assumed the more essential shape of the sphere. The motif as such alludes to the artist, who as the master of color, form, line, and proportion, experiences himself as the re-creator of nature and her essences. For Klee in particular, this means that sensuous objects stand no longer as random, stimulating motifs, but they are transformed as archaic images and signs that reveal nature's *a priori* structures. This idea characterizes Klee's artistic self-understanding, which led him to say often that he worked "*ab ovo*," that is, from the egg, from the primordial origin of life's genesis.

Similar symbolic meaning seems to be conveyed in the container that holds the gift. Its undulating, hollow form corresponds with a feminine vessel that both contains and brings forth. On one hand it recalls a basin, a womb, or a boat that have the meaning of a container—and on the other hand a seashell, a mouth, a vagina, from which something emerges. So it could be said that what is held up and called into existence here is the reality of nature, distilled to the most elemental form of five spheres contained in an artifactual vessel. In the sense of a condensation symbol, we could say that nature appears here in its core essence, contained in a womb, that is, in the gestational medium of art. The gestalt as such points to soulful beginnings and metamorphoses that transpire in the making and beholding of art. For Klee, the transformational power of art lies in the emergence of "changed, transmuted image[s] of nature."[56] "Art," he says, "imitates creation."[57] These ideas belong to the metaphysical task, which for Klee inheres essentially in "the rebirth of nature [in art]."[58]

The making visible of inner essences, purging things of their outer layers to reveal their abstract *a priori* forms, bespeaks Klee's central credo that, "Art does not reproduce the visible but makes visible;" or as he puts it otherwise, in the creative process, the artist moves "from prototype to archetype."[59] Carola Giedion-Welcker in her monograph on Klee recognizes the artist as "an intermediary 'gathering and passing on what arises from the depths below.'"[60] She amplifies,

> Again and again it is not the forms of the visible world, which are crucial but those discoveries we make of deeper life and broader regions of being when we return to the ultimate sources and formative powers of nature. And it is from this deeper perception that the artist derives the inspiration for his interpretive language of symbols. In the process he turns his back on finished, "terminal forms," replacing them by original or initial forms.[61]

Giedion-Welcker's perspective well captures the phlegmatic contribution to this gestalt of creativity. It also makes clear that if Klee considered himself to be a depth artist, a metaphysician, and a basic researcher with artistic resources, it does not mean that such understanding is limited to his person. The same set of traits manifests in other artists, in whom it abides as a fundamental creative potentiality. It characterizes painters, thinkers, musicians, and creative people in general who are concerned essentially with discovering and reflecting the primordial structures of nature, the soul, or creativity itself.

Returning now to Klee's *Carnival*, we can consider the little gestalt on the left-hand side, the one with up-raised arms, which we have associated with the creative potential of the sanguine tendency. A number of antithetical characteristics join in this figure. It emanates a quality of girlishness and at the same time it has an old face, recalling the renowned 1918 self-portrait, in which Klee appears with the inward expression of a hermit. This figure thus alludes to a child-like state of genesis-and-becoming, contrasting a riper and more enduring state of being. A further pair of opposites appears on one side in the closed eyes and sealed lips, and on the other side in the attached feline ears. With these elements we have the mystic and the cat, suggesting the juxtaposition of transcendent spirituality and natural instinctuality. Opposites appear as well where the figure's colorful attire and nearly colorless face allude to a vivacious earthly life contrasting a spiritual orientation to the beyond. The opposites of blue and red in the figure's dress stand for the antitheses of spirit and emotion. Finally and most strikingly, the free high-reaching movement of the arms contrasts the massive cuboid belt or corset, which seems to bind the figure to the earth and worldly materiality (symbolism of the number four).

All of these antithetical "moments" bespeak Klee's intention to reflect in this ambiguous figure the tension that exists between earthly anchoring and transcendent yearnings. It is such tension that essentially characterized Klee's artistic self-understanding and creative individuality. The small figure with uplifted arms represents these polarities with a remarkable quality of formal condensation and simplicity. Upward spiritual striving is counterposed by the downward pull of an earthly reality that corsets, limits, and binds, and that at the same time provides fundamental groundedness. The colorful world of child-like play and futurity counterposes the yearning for eternal being and unalterable mystical experience.

This existential tension, which is an important aspect of Paul Klee's creative activity and self-understanding, belongs also of course to artists of similar ilk. These are artists whose creativity springs directly from experience of the fundamental gap between limiting finitude and the yearning for transcendence and eternity. For them, creativity is ignited by the irreconcilable conflict of the animal/earthly condition of life and determination by a spiritual/transcendent force. Their creative activity is the bridge between the two hostile realms of being, and it offers the only possibility to endure, to move beyond, and to somehow heal the experienced brokenness. Indeed these people are compelled to creative activity as a means of surviving the threat of sinking into the despair of "nothing but" concrete being, or of becoming prey to the force of the spirit and ending up in the beyond like homeless vagabonds. For these people, creative activity is the only way out of the either/or dilemma.

Returning to Klee's *Carnival in the Mountains*, we have already noted the motif of the antenna-like eye. We can now delve more deeply into its symbolization of the choleric perspective in the creative process.

What we see here is one single eye, hovering far above the horizon. It suggests no ordinary two-eyed visual capacity. Far more, it alludes to the mystical vision associated with the third eye, which apprehends the unity and deeper being of things. This "third" kind of vision is not trapped in surfaces, but can see through and more deeply, observing things and people as if from a distant watchtower. For this reason the choleric perspective can seem to be lost in reverie, but it is seeing things that escape the foreground view. It penetrates to the inside and therefore apprehends more than do the five senses that are fixed on the surface of things. It is the creative transcendent gaze, seeing the essences of things. It corresponds with the Platonic recognition of "ideas," that is, the apprehension of the constitutive, spiritual fundaments that make things what they are.

The quality of vision symbolized in the antenna-eye evidences the artist's self-understanding, which Klee himself expressed among other ways as follows: "The artist's power should be spiritual. But the power of the majority is material. When these worlds meet occasionally, it is pure coincidence."[62] Elsewhere Klee explains, "[M]y human faces are truer than the real ones... . I am not here to reflect the surface ... but must penetrate inside."[63] In the true Platonic sense Klee does not reproduce only accidental, visually perceptible, and fleeting surfaces, but rather, he reflects the very essence and the spiritual and inner being of things.

Paul Klee was fully aware that his perspective was demanding for his audience. His resignation to this reality comes across in his above quoted sense of "two worlds meeting but occasionally" and "only by pure coincidence." In a later passage, it is more pointedly so:

> Do I radiate warmth? Coolness? ... [F]ew [people] will be touched by me. There is no sensuous relationship, not even the noblest, between myself and the many. In my work I do not belong to the species, but am a cosmic point of reference. My earthly eye is too farsighted and sees through and beyond the most beautiful things.[64]

The antenna eye, lifted to the heavens, expresses precisely Klee's experience of himself as a "cosmic point of reference." However, this quality of vision is not a free-flying one fully absolved of earthly bonds. To the contrary, its linkage to the earth is likened to a stem, a cord, or a canal. These pictorial elements throw light on some facts about Klee: Despite his emphasis on *a priori* and abstract dimensions, he never surrendered entirely a figurative style of depiction; that is, he never completely gave up the recognizable portrayal of humans, animals, and things. A basic graphicness always sustained. Klee described himself as being "abstract with memories."[65] Meaning that, as an abstract artist, he found himself both drawn to life's primordial dimensions, and also echoing memories of the sensuously perceptible world.

Moreover, Klee saw creative activity to mediate between a spiritual spark and the world of material realization. As he wrote in his notebook,

> The history of the [creative] work, which is chiefly genesis [human action], may be briefly characterized as a secret spark from somewhere, which kindles the spirit of man with its glow and moves through his hand, and the spark moves through his hand, and the movement is translated into matter.[66]

The artist in this process, Klee emphasizes, "neither serves nor commands, but only acts as a go-between. His position is humble. He himself is not the beauty ...; it has merely passed through him."[67]

The motif of the stemmed cosmic eye beautifully symbolizes Klee's ability to absorb and transmit higher and essential meanings into the here-and-now. But again, this is not Klee's ability alone. It is the expression of one of the fundamental ways that a creative task and purpose can be experienced. Indeed, creative individuals are characterized in general by their tendency to be seized by a transcendent force, which has the feel of some Other that compels their mission to convey new standpoints, new ways of understanding, and novel modes of expression.

We can now continue with Klee's *Carnival* and a fourth figure, the gestalt that we associated briefly with the melancholic outlook, namely the walking bird with the fire in its belly. How might this creature express a further dimension of the creative individual's experience? On the whole, the walking, fire-bearing bird points symbolically to the reality of the spirit. Insofar as it is a ratite or flightless bird, it symbolizes a spirit that connects with and shows itself in earthly reality. So we can speak here of an empirical, phenomenological spirit that manifests itself step-by-step in conscious experience. In contrast to the previously mentioned Platonic view, this would correspond with the Aristotelian premise of a form-giving spirit that abides in nature itself.

The fire glowing like an interior lantern within the center of the bird's body suggests the inner fire of creativity. It proposes a quality of insight that goes beyond all rational foreknowledge, and that presents itself imagistically to the inner eye, and that is meaningful in the immediate here-and-now. Just beneath the ball of fire in the bird's belly, there is a lens-shaped object that mirrors the mouth of the small figure to the left with uplifted arms. Taking this object, too, to be a mouth, we can speculate that it symbolizes a voice that always co-determines inward vision, apparently seeming to know what is important in the creative process and which new insights or new shapes are to come. More specifically, it could be the inner voice of Logos, which comes into play with inward vision to enable and compel the steps of creative discovery.

The bird is surrounded by five prominent objects. Observed from the tip of its tail, to the tip of its toe on the lower right, they include: a cuboid beam; an uncoiling, climbing snake; an egg-like object: a gabled house; and finally, a dark, oblique borderline suggesting the top edge of a wall that separates this scene from the complex figure on the right. These five objects can be understood to signify various aspects of reality in which creative fantasy locates its points of departure.

The cuboid beam could stand for primal being and concrete things, to be transformed into symbols by the fire of creative imagination. The uncoiling snake could represent evolving life and the potentiality of spiritual meaning obtained by the transformative power of fantasy. The perfectly formed egg-like object would epitomize creation as such, to be taken up and built upon by creative fantasy. The house symbolizes perhaps the humanly constructed world of culture and history, which also provides creative fantasy with fundaments and points of departure. The oblique wall could suggest the point at which creativity rubs up against the limits of reality, or a cold wall of non-imagining, non-change, non-transformation, or even anti-creativity. Belonging as well to the creative process is the bird's forward strut, an expression of vehement revolt against the world's anti-creative forces.

These five objects can be understood differently, however. They could point to the ways and means by which an objective creative force manifests itself in inorganic nature (the cuboid beam), in the phenomenon of life (the uncoiling snake) within the cosmos (the egg), within history (the house), and within reality's given limits (the wall). Going with this interpretation, it is not so much the artist's personal creativity that transforms reality into pictures and works of art. Far more, it is the objective force of creation itself that engenders creative and sublime works filled with beauty and meaning. It is the artist's task to apprehend the larger transcendent force of creation and reproduce it in his or her own creative work.

The non-human hand in the force of creation is evident in the overwhelming beauty and variety of crystals and metals, in the abundant array of landscapes, and in the rich diversity of the seasons. Paul Klee grasped nature's bounteous and creative offer of forms and contents, and transformed them into his own aesthetic vocabulary. An entry in Klee's diary describing an experience at the Lake of Thun in Switzerland reveals his nearly mystical connection with nature's grandiosity and beauty: "A good moment … . No intellect, no ethics. An observer above the world or a child in the world's totality. The first unsplit instant in my life."[68]

Life manifests itself in the staggering variety of animals and plants, and in its astonishing ways of evolving and embedding itself in the surrounding world. Here, too, the force of creation is visible, a force that does not always follow the principles of utility and expediency. It seems as well to follow the playful intentions of an artistic fantasy attuned to beauty. In this sense, too, Paul Klee availed himself of the repertory of forms provided by the creative spirit of nature. In the whole cosmos as well as in the world, the power of creation reveals itself as an entity that seems to possess a sense of beauty as well as a sense of the ugly and the abysmal—a kind of aesthetic intentionality, we could say, that far exceeds the basic requirements of material creation and its maintenance. Many of Paul Klee's pictures reflect his inspiration by this cosmic creativity.

An objective creative power is active also in culture, the spiritual realm represented in *Carnival* by the gabled house. The diversity of languages, cultures, religions, art forms, and histories document the presence of this creative fantasy. With its lavish abundance of forms and guises, it seems to relish in the creation of *l'art pour l'art*, art for art's sake.

In its bareness and confining character, the oblique wall could stand for an equally objective principle, namely that of anti-creation, which manifests itself as unimaginativeness, or the absolute absence of symbolic life, beauty, and meaning. Like most creative individuals, Paul Klee, too, experienced such phases and was thus confronted with laming evidence of the anti-creative force.

The awareness of nature's impact as an objective creative force or spirit, which characterizes the specific type of creative experience expressed in this picture, can be called alchemical consciousness. It encompasses the artist's sense of involvement with an autonomous creative power that is present *in matter*, in nature, in the world, and in history, and that engenders formation and transformation in all of these areas.

Such alchemical consciousness characterizes Paul Klee's attitude, and also the attitudes and creative approaches of many other artists. Albrecht Dürer himself asserted that, "[A]rt standeth truly in nature, and whoso can rend her forth thence, he only posseseth her."[69] Dürer reminds us of the contemporary movement embracing what is called land art, earthworks, or earth art. In this movement art is not placed in nature, but is created in and of nature. The artist employs creative possibilities that nature offers or insinuates. Indeed, the artist follows nature's own creative intentionality. Accordingly, the previously mentioned British exponent, Andy Goldsworthy (born 1956), creates wonderful sculptures of branches, leaves, stones, and snow. For him, there is an important interplay between the hidden mysticism of places and his own spiritually orientated perception, whereby the natural surroundings influence him and he makes visible the art of the landscape itself. Art created by the artist's sensitivity to the things given in nature thus amounts to the exploration of nature's own creative force and potentiality.

In a similar vein, the Fluxus art movement evidences the artist's redeployment to creative nature or to creative being as such. The exponents of this movement work on the premises of fluid transitions existing between art and life, and the unity of art and life, whereby things are always indeterminate, always in "flux." Life is viewed as art and art is viewed as life. In this context, an object or landscape may be declared a piece of art, as Wolf Vostell (1932–1998) did with a stretch of land in Malpartida, in the Spanish Extremadura. These are but a few of the artists who illustrate the idea of an objective, creative force that manifests itself in reality.

Our discussion of Paul Klee's *Carnival* brings us finally to the complex gestalt that appears just to the right of the center. Earlier I suggested that this figure symbolizes an underlying feminine reality that belongs to the picture as whole and its theme of creativity. Let us now explore her more closely, seeing her as a symbol-making factor in the unconscious that corresponds with the four-fold pattern of creative consciousness.

What we see here is a strange archaic being with a large head, uplifted arms, peculiar eyes, and body parts that are assembled in a cubist-like style. Obviously this figure portrays not a real woman with personal features, but an archetypal phenomenon. Recalling a similar gesture known from the Minoan snake goddess in Crete, here both arms are uplifted in the manner of a liturgical gesture of worship or veneration. The ritualistically raised arms, together with the elevated gaze, express movement upward into the dimension of the numinous and transcendent. This figure thus makes visible a factor that leads to the higher realms of sense and meaning. Insofar as this factor has a certain divine quality, it could be said, psychologically speaking, that it holds a fascinating power of influence.

This complex and strange figure pictures a mighty underlying symbol-making factor that inspires creative individuals and engenders in their perception of the world not only as factual being, but also image and potentiality. This factor transforms sensorially perceived things into spiritually meaningful images and gestalts. In other words, it is not solely by the gift of imagination that the creative individual transforms things into images and symbols. Rather, due to this factor—the creativity that is inherent to being—the world speaks to the individual from the very start in the language of images. Always from the start creative individuals find themselves being approached and addressed by inner and outer images, out of which their own images and works are created.

We note that from this figure's eyes there extend two differently shaped lines of vision that reach in two different directions. The trajectory of the right eye, pictured in the shape of a mountain range, has in its scope the picture's whole middle realm. Following Paul Klee's poem, "The Two Mountains," this would be the realm that describes the specifically human condition of existing in-between the two fixed orders of nature and spirit. It appears that the symbol-making factor itself gives shape to the reality of this in-between condition.

In *Carnival*, Klee describes the in-between realm both as an imagistically and symbolically formed world, which emanates from the creative eye of a great imagination. Insofar as the contour of the in-between follows reality, or actually gives reality its shape, it can be said in a symbolic sense that the outward appearance of the world itself is shaped by this greater, form-giving power of imagination. This is the case not only for nature, represented by the mountain, but also for humanly built culture, represented by the double gabled house standing at the picture's horizon. In both manifestations, nature and culture, the world is subject to a creative principle that springs forth from a great creative fantasy.

From the figure's left eye, there emanates another aspect of the creative impulse, the trajectory of which appears in the form of a tube slanting downward, toward the center of the picture. Whereas the right eye symbolizes creation in the outer world, the left eye symbolizes creation in the analogous dimension of inner reality. The impulse as such flows forth from an eye, a quality of vision, the essence of which Klee portrays to be nocturnal and moon-like, and with a centeredness that characterizes and emphasizes the symbol of the Self. So it can be said that the creative dynamic pictured by the left eye springs ultimately from the inwardness of the soul and the autonomy of the Self.

The line or trajectory of *this* vision appears in the form of a tube that is oriented toward a square yellowish surface, which itself appears nearly at the center, of both the strange figure and the picture as a whole. This surface could symbolize inner reality as such, insofar as the square per se stands for reality, and the inward dimension of reality is suggested by the small square within this square. More precisely, the square could symbolize the inner reality of image or imagination as such. This aspect of image is suggested by the square's position in front of the feminine figure's body, which makes of the square itself a kind of projection surface. Furthermore the detail of a small square in the right upper corner of the larger one defines *pars pro toto* the whole square as a picture.

To review in summary, we can say that the two lines of vision point to two interconnecting principles, which belong to the transpersonal power of creation that both shapes the appearance of the outer world and also engenders the inner realm of ideas. This objective power of creation or symbol-making factor works both within and outside of us in many ways: to engender outward appearances and inward perception; to shape physical and psychic realities; and to engender gestalts and their corresponding images. The creative force thus works at two different levels and in two different directions: at the levels of objective being and psychic apperception; and in the directions of outward existence, and toward inner processing. All such aspects belong together, just as do two eyes to one head, with their fundament in the one primal reality of imagination. This idea follows the renowned Jungian analyst Erich Neumann (1905-1960), whose thought on the matter is expressed in his essay, "Experience of the Unitary Reality."[70] What Neumann describes here is an archaic all-encompassing world, in which inner and outer realities correspond with each other, and which is the world experienced intimately by "primitive man," children, mystics, and also creative people.

The complex feminine figure of Klee's *Carnival* shows a torso that consists of several layered parts, which appear as two containers or vessels. The first takes the form of a brightly hued, narrow vase or vial that contains the figure's large head. This container is held within a larger shape that resembles an ancient amphora or jug. Its contours run parallel to the figure's upper thighs, to just below her bent knees. The second, more widely encompassing than the other two, takes shape as a contour that emanates from her hips.

Just as containers serve in everyday life to store foods and liquids, they can be understood symbolically as the containers of images and forms that are stored in the unconscious, from which creative individuals derive their ideas. In the image at hand, the widest container stands for the collective unconscious, the storage place of archetypal ideas, which creative individuals access more readily than do other people. The slimmer vessel likening an amphora would represent the storage place of cultural ideas and experiences. In his letter to Erich Neumann dated December 22, 1935, C.G. Jung gives an example of such cultural foundation of creative ideas: "Analytical Psychology ... is deeply rooted in Europe, in the Christian Middle Ages and, in the last analysis, in Greek philosophy."[71] The narrow vessel containing the figure's head can be understood as the storage place of personal memories and history. Both such larger and smaller vessels bring into play both deeper and closer layers of the unconscious that provide the creative individual with a special reservoir of ideas and gestalts emanating from the depths. It is thanks to the fundament of a greater, transpersonal ground that the individual's works, reaching beyond the time of their creation, speak to and remain understandable by others.

With her evidently striding gait, Klee's curious feminine gestalt presents an expression of powerful movement. This dynamic element appears in stark contrast to her aspect as a static container of bygone experiences and memories. The antitheses are portrayed so pointedly as to raise the questions, do the active steps and the passive containment have anything to do with each other, and if yes, what? Might it be implied that individual and collective human steps and experiences are stored in history and in the depths of the unconscious? Or could it be meant that the creative individual transposes the well of foregoing experience into the here-and-now? The horizontally splayed legs suggest that both interpretations could hold: There is on one side the archiving of experiences and on the other side, their transposition into the here-and-now.

For our continuing excursion into the symbolic meaning of this figure, it remains to discuss her arms. As we see, her right and left arms are portrayed differently. Her right arm, the one with red hues, has in place of a hand a sort of eye. Her left arm, turbidly colored and composed in a cubist style, has a small circle in place of a hand. Her right hand appears to perform a constructive gesture, an act of building-up. This impression is enhanced by the arm's color, the dawn-red that bespeaks auspicious beginnings—and also by the dawn-red eye, shimmering in the picture's center like a morning star and signaling a new day. In contrast, her left arm makes us think of division and destruction, the breaking up of things into pointed parts. And here, a bloodless grey dominates the arm's yellow hue, while the hand itself consists of a compressed circle, closed into itself, and emitting a murky light. In the motif as such, the movements of reduction, closing, and ending are in opposition to augmentation, opening, and beginning. The contrast symbolized in the two arms thus characterizes the underlying force of creation in its double sense of being both constructive and destructive, both initiating and limiting, working toward both beginnings and ends—in short, a creative and anti-creative phenomenon.

The creative principle works in the world and in the creative individual not only through its bounty of potential gestalts and its overflowing wealth of beauty.[72] But the same reality engenders also negation, transforming creativity into its opposite, when out of its depths the autonomous symbol-making factor conjures up evidence of a non-creative void, and life, robbed of its stimulating abundance, is experienced only in its limits and finiteness. Such a problematic worldview is expressed perhaps by the block-like buildings in the picture's far right background, defined only by their external geometric shapes and seeming to be void of life.

The peculiar, rake-shaped object in the lower right-hand corner might also have something to do with this world of anti-creativity. The object has no self-evident pragmatic function, but it does make visible the existence of mechanical repetition. In this sense the motif could stand for the experience of rigid, senseless iteration that leads to no works, no birth, no goal oriented action. This is when sequences of action without grounds or aims, series of things, tribulations, and obstacles are at cross-purposes with fruitful creativity. The experience of total stagnation and chronic block is the quintessence of the anti-creative spirit.

In the psychotherapy consulting room one encounters often the accomplished novelist, actor, painter, or musician who at a certain point in life flips suddenly to the shadow side and finds him- or herself vegetating in a state of non-productivity and triviality. In such cases it is helpful to be conscious of the fact that the gift of creativity encompasses inherently the downside, a condition of paralysis, inflicted by the creative force itself. This perspective can help avert a guilt-inducing diversion of the painful situation into questionable behavior and unconsciousness. Even while the process of personal consciousness-raising and clarification can be therapeutic, one should not lose sight of the fact that a sudden depression can occur for no other reason than its belonging to the puzzling creative force itself. This kind of approach creates the better preconditions for healing.

We may do well to end this chapter with Rainer Maria Rilke's familiar words. In a stanza from his *Duino Elegies*, they express well the close proximity of constructive creativity and its destructive counterpart: "... beauty is nothing but / the beginning of terror, / that we are still able to bear, / and we revere it so, because it calmly disdains / to destroy us."[73]

5.5. Missionary Individuality

5.5.1. In Albrecht Dürer's The Four Apostles

(Fig. 15): Albrecht Dürer, *The Four Apostles*

The underlying intention to reflect the artist's creative task and special individual charisma shows up again in Albrecht Dürer's *The Four Apostles*, an oil painting on two panels (Fig. 15). It shows the four gestalts that stand for the four temperamental perspectives that appear in the creative personality—but it is the only one of the discussed pictures of this kind that lacks the feminine image. What has become of the feminine gestalt? We will try to answer the question in the course of the coming discussion.

The Four Apostles is titled somewhat imprecisely in that Mark, the second figure from the right, was not an apostle but an evangelist. Dürer completed this non-commissioned work in 1526, and bequeathed it to his native city of Nuremberg "as a remembrance [of himself and his art];" his letter to the Nuremberg City Council explains further, "Now … that I have just painted a panel upon which I have bestowed more trouble than on any other painting, I considered none more worthy to keep it as a remembrance than your Wisdoms."[74]

As Dürer's last known oil painting, *The Four Apostles* presents a kind of summation of his complete life's work. It can be understood as a symbolic representation of his personal artistic calling per se, and beyond this, as a general representation of the nature of creative individuality. In this basic sense the painting is of interest and belongs to the present discussion.

Dürer's chosen motif, the four apostles, is meaningful in itself. Apostles are witnesses to and disseminators of the Christian faith, but from a symbolic perspective they can stand as witnesses to and disseminators of spiritual experience in general. They can express, so to speak, the "apostolic" calling of all artists and creative individuals who find themselves compelled to represent, translate, and transmit their inner experiences. Such a calling need not involve an explicit religion. Even atheistic artists respond to some inner creative force that exceeds the ego's intentions and goals and that demands the open expression of ever newer and greater ideas. What wants to realize itself in the creative individual's work is the power of creation as such. In this sense we can understand Dürer's *Four Apostles* not only as a masterly interpretation of the pictorial motif of four holy figures. Even if not consciously intended, it is just as much a picture of Dürer's own artistic calling, and beyond this, a picture that can be understood to express symbolically a "mission" that characterizes the creative individual in general.

Before we undertake to explore the four figures in depth, it should help to observe certain aspects of the surrounding framework. The floor in this painting is illuminated so as to imply special meaning of the ground upon which the figures stand. It is neither the abysmal ground that we see in Dürer's *Desperate Man*, nor is it the pathless desert of Picasso's *Saltimbanques*. It is also not the ground of elemental life as in van Gogh's *Potato Eaters*, nor is it the ground of the uncertain existence portrayed in Paul Klee's *Carnival in the Mountains*. It is the concrete if also empty ground of this world. When Dürer donated *The Four Apostles* to his native Nuremberg, it was hung in the upper Regiments Chamber of the city hall. His accompanying letter addressed the government that in the previous year had committed Nuremberg to join the Protestant Reformation. Texts inscribed at the bottom of each panel and belonging to the work as whole emphasize the creative individual's felt mission to take a stand with respect to the social and political situation of the day. Understandably, the inscriptions were sawed off in 1627, when the panels were acquired by the Bavarian Duke Maximillian I and whisked to the Catholic city of Munich. From the Duke's standpoint, the inscriptions were inopportune because they reflected Dürer's support of the Reformation and constituted his Apocalypse-inspired warning to the secular powers of the day:

> All worldly rulers in these times of danger should beware
> that they receive not false Teaching for the Word of God.
> For God will have nothing added to His Word nor yet taken
> away. Hear, therefore, these four excellent men, Peter,
> John, Paul, and Mark, their warning.[75]

When the creative force expresses itself on the ground of an existing socio-political reality, it does so often in the form of written opinions and manifestos. Thus in Dürer's painting, the Bible around which the apostles gather could signify more generally the creative individual's tendency to convey in writing those existential concerns that are apprehended as intuitive visions. For example, we think of Martin Luther (1483-1546) and his Wittenberg Theses, and again Ignatius von Loyola (1491-1556) with the "Foundation" chapter in his *Spiritual Exercises*. There is as well André Breton (1896-1966) with his Dadaist manifesto of surrealism (1924), and C.G. Jung with his "*Septem Sermones*." Underlying the obvious variety of personalities and situations there is always the common ground of an individual creative mission evolving from a primary, intuitively perceived text.

Dürer's biographer and contemporary Johann Neudörffer, who painted the inscriptions at the bottom of the panels, emphasized *The*

Four Apostles' reflection of the four classic temperaments. On the left-hand panel, Peter in the background stands for the phlegmatic, and John in the foreground, the sanguine. On the right-hand panel Paul in the foreground stands for the melancholic, and Mark in the background, the choleric. Dürer's incorporation of the temperaments goes beyond the importance that this motif held for him personally. He represented it often in his works, and we encountered it earlier in his *Desperate Man*. The appearance of the motif represents even more than the worldview of Dürer's time, which was oriented generally to the idea of the temperaments. It expresses as well the more fundamental meaning and fact that the temperaments present a primal or archetypal pattern for creative work and creative individuality as such. The temperaments represent four object-related perspectives, which, taken together, play a role in the creative process and in the composition of creative works. They also represent four modalities of subjective experience that constitute the creative Self, and that, in interplay with each other, spawn the great creative individual.

Let us now examine each of the four apostles. Taking them in the sequence indicated in Dürer's inscription, Peter in the background of the left panel represents the phlegmatic. The characteristic pensiveness is expressed in Peter's slightly bowed head and in his rapt immersion in the text before him. There is an air of deliberation but also of restrained sadness and nostalgic yearning. For his depiction of such qualities Dürer relied on Hippocrates's guidelines, whereby the predominance of phlegm determines the phlegmatic's slow pace and tendency to a depressive worldview.

Peter's gaze lingers in the here-and-now of the presented word. He is the embodiment of attention to that which reveals itself with sensuous immediacy, in empirical reality. His finely modeled skin and fluffy beard bespeak a person with sensibilities for the tactile dimensions and orientation by the sensorium of the body in general. His rather pyknic or round head, emphasized by the blue shawl encircling his neck and shoulders, alludes to the phlegmatic's typical all-encompassing or holistic thinking.

The Christian Bible here deserves a side remark. As is well known, the accounts of Christ's works, the four gospels, differ according to the perspectives of the apostles who wrote them. Surprisingly, the four perspectives mirror those that belong to each of the four temperaments. The phlegmatic view personified by Dürer's Peter corresponds with the perspective of the apostle Luke, who conveys the Christ story above all in its warm-hearted and corporal aspects. Luke provides a full account of Christ's works, but among the four apostles, he is the most emotionally palpable and so to speak most human.

In his papal function as Christ's representative on earth, Peter holds the golden key to the heavenly kingdom, an attribute that necessarily belongs to his pictorial depiction. Perhaps, though, in this iconographic sign of the papal office we can discern the symbolization of a gift belonging to the phlegmatic temperament. The gift could consist of the capacities to advance new ways of understanding, to open new dimensions of meaning, and to tap into its higher horizons. These are abilities that evidence one's possession of the key of symbolic understanding. The key, that is the symbolic view, transforms empirically experienced things into outward signs of otherwise hidden or underlying meanings. Belonging to the phlegmatic temperament is indeed the special ability to recognize in sensuous materials spiritual forms, ideas, and symbolic gestalts, or to see through and beyond, to grasp the added symbolic value of things. In this sense it opens the way to a higher reality, to a heaven of spiritual meaning, as it were. Peter's association with this key thus characterizes poignantly the phlegmatic gestalt and charisma, symbolizing its gifts of sublimation, symbol-making, and grasp of the symbolic dimension in general.

Standing next to Peter is the tall figure, the young John, whose red cape and red hair signify his representation of the sanguine view. The young man is equipped with harmonious features. Compared with the other three characters, his face seems almost strikingly unremarkable. He reads the open Bible with apparent level headedness, with a nearly undercooled objectivity—signs of the sanguine type that we have noted repeatedly in our discussion of other pictures. However, in contrast to John's discrete, matter-of-fact bearing, a certain playfulness comes across in his curly red hair and in his sweeping red cape, slung around his shoulders in a nearly casual fashion. These features, too, allude to the sanguine bent and aspects we have already observed to be characteristic, namely, the aesthetic sense, the formal aptitude, and the importance of personal appearances.

Using the language of Ernst Kretschmer (1888–1964), we can say that John is depicted with an athletic body type, which shows especially in his wide obliquely sloping shoulders, his muscular neck, his strong arm, and his square hand.[76] According

to Kretschmer there exists a relationship of the athletic constitution
and the sanguine temperament.

As John holds the open Bible, he is reading the opening verses of
his own gospel, which the legible text allows us to discern as follows:

> In the beginning was the Word, and the Word was with
> God, and the Word was God. The same was in the
> beginning with God. (John, 1:2-3) … . There was a man
> sent from God, whose name was John. The same came
> for witness, to bear the witness of the Light, that all men
> through him might believe. (John, 1:6-7)

Going beyond the attribution of John as an apostle and the author of
the fourth gospel, the symbolic value of the above verses lies in their
expression of a specifically sanguine mindset. They refer, first, to a
beginning and John's bearing witness to it. This kind of thinking is
characteristic of the sanguine perspective. We saw it for instance in *The
Jew in Red*, where Chagall inscribed the names of his predecessors, his
artistic lineage. Accordingly, spiritual beginnings, lines and traditions
of thought, and origins and history are all especially important for
the individual's creative thought and activity. The sanguine view sees
personal creativity as part of a process and historical progression. The
author of the gospel according to St. Matthew is a typical representative
of such sanguine thought. In distinction to the other three apostles,
Matthew begins his gospel with an extensive genealogical account of
Jesus's predecessors. Where beginnings receive special observance,
there is particular interest in the genesis of the world and humanity, in
archaic fundaments, and in early childhood.

John's above cited verses refer as well to "the Word," or, we can
say, to Logos: "In the beginning was the Word, and the Word was with
God, and the Word was God." God as "word" is an image that in itself
bespeaks a sanguine-inspired worldview, which sees in the word or
Logos a rational and meaningful world, and this as the first and last
reality. For sanguine types, the ultimately binding and transcendent
powers are reason, meaning, and the medium in which they manifest
themselves, the word.

John's verses mention also the bearing of witness: "[John] came
for witness, to bear the witness of the Light, that all men through him
might believe." The ethical testimony on truth, and the revelation and
dissemination of the truth by the witness's existential example, correspond
as well with the typically value-oriented sanguine perspective.

In Dürer's depiction of John, we can detect a further detail and symbolic expression of the sanguine character. The Bible in John's hands features a striking pair of latches. As with Peter's key, the rendering in gold emphasizes the object's absolute value and transcendent meaning. Described purely formally, the latches function to hold the book closed by joining the front and back covers. The motif as such readily brings to mind the idea of a pair of opposites that function in tandem to connect two different dimensions. Thus the pair of latches might be understood as a symbol of relationship—perhaps even the pattern of relationship in Jung's sense of the marriage quaternity, whereby the two relational poles on the conscious side connect with one another also by their relational poles on the unconscious side. Obviously such meanings are not explicit in Dürer's use of the motif, but they are possible or implicit in that the autonomous world of meaning is built into the artist's pictorial reality and its symbols. In fact, thinking in relational categories is indeed an essential trait, a part of the charisma, and a favored key to understanding in the sanguine-based relationship to the world.

Another style of thinking typical of the sanguine way of thinking can be deduced also from the two sides, the "front-and-back" or the latch-like way of emphasizing opposites: The sanguine thinker thinks often in terms of antithetical sides or conditions, taking into account aspects such as the state of maturity and the original state of things; the ideal norm and the diverging factual reality; the civilized world of the spirit and the world of animal-like instinct; and contrary moments of meaning and meaninglessness, consciousness and unconsciousness, the real and illusory, the positive and the negative.

Now, Dürer personifies the *"Cholericum"* in Mark, who stands in the background of the right panel. This figure shows especially vividly Dürer's intention to distinguish the different temperaments. Mark's volatile facial expression is striking and suggests a generally irascible, emotion-laden character. He corresponds with the common use of "choleric" to mean quick-temperedness. In his piercing gaze one senses the qualities of fiery enthusiasm, explorative curiosity, passionate questioning, and unsparing bluntness. His face expresses something of the explorer and conqueror, the pioneer and the prophet, the revolutionary. The impression is conveyed that this "head" gives rise to promising new deeds, as if it were the source of fundamentally new vision, *ex nihilo*. These are again all assets that spring specifically from the choleric perspective.

Mark's slightly parted lips emphasized by his surrounding beard are visual elements that point to the choleric gift of rhetoric and general capacity to express and formulate things. It is the choleric perspective that holds the special ability to transmit inwardly perceived vision in the form of lively language and in this way to make it immediately viable.

Mark's figure is reduced almost entirely to his *head*. While one foot and one hand are visible, his head is so prominently featured, nearly floating in the dark background, that it appears to represent the whole personality. The isolated head prompted some scholars, such as Erwin Panofsky, to conjecture that Dürer added it as a compositional afterthought. Later photographic investigation disproved such theories by verifying Dürer's original plan for this panel's display of two figures. Nevertheless, the conjecture speaks for the impact of such an unusually depicted head. Considered *pars pro toto*, the isolated head shows the choleric's characteristic relationship to the world. It is, namely, the very tendency to work from the head, to be led by ideas that arise and develop from the creative.

We can see that Mark is holding a scroll, a mere piece of paper that comes across as a rather modest thing in comparison with the objects held by the other figures. The humble scroll alludes to a first draft, an initial sketch, an apparently incidental and preliminary attempt to peg down in writing an emerging thought. But it contains the larger meaning of a document that marks a beginning and testifies to a new idea or perspective. Mark's own gospel exemplifies this characteristic choleric tendency to initiate things. His is the shortest and most dramatic of the four gospels and at the same time the oldest, i.e. the first one. Its prototypical character typifies the forerunner's role, which is generally inherent to the choleric temperament personified in Dürer's Mark.

In the image of Paul, appearing in the foreground of the right-hand panel, Dürer represents the melancholic temperament. The apostle's dark, sidelong, and distancing glance evidences the melancholic black bile. His gaze recalls that of the angel in Dürer's renowned engraving of 1514, *Melencolia I*. But we think as well of sketched self-portraits in which Dürer depicted himself recognizably as the melancholic. In itself profound, Paul's gaze is of the kind that penetrates beneath surfaces and gets to the depths of things. It is the look of the skeptic who is familiar with the dubious nature of existence, who recognizes the limits of knowledge, and who has experienced failure personally. Disillusioned by disappointments and self-delusions, and yet still affirmative and dedicated to life.

Paul's remarkable *nose* alludes in a figurative sense to the subtle and precise perception of infinitesimal realms that surpass everyday reality. It suggests an instinctual sense of trails that lie off the beaten path, there to be taken when the signposts of general conventional norms no longer offer guidance.

Paul's is the only *ear* that Dürer portrays distinctly. It could symbolize the melancholic capacity for spiritual internalization. Speaking both literally and figuratively, the melancholic ear is a musical one, the ear that registers and comprehends inner meanings and inner melodies, the living essences of people and things. It is the gift of hearing, listening, and listening-into—the gift of sympathy and empathy. Paul's renowned conception of love, articulated in his Corinthians I, 13:1 and 4, is indeed melancholically inspired:

> Though I speak with the tongues of men and angels, and have not charity, I am become as sounding brass, or a tinkling cymbal... . Charity suffereth long, and is kind; charity envieth not; charity vaunteth not itself, is not puffed up.

For the melancholic ear, in other words, when loving listening fails, there are merely sounds without tone or melody; and by contrast, love is understood to be a putting-aside of one's self and an empathic entering-into-the-Other.

Paul's long full *beard* underscores the gravity of his character and his priestly authority. It emblemizes a superordinate function that belongs to the melancholic type, both literally and figuratively. Nearly covering the mouth, the beard emphasizes as well the enigmatic style of the melancholic temperament, which is concerned less with clearly articulated and communicable thoughts than with suggestive ideas and intuitions emerging, as it were, from the thicket of such a beard.

In Dürer's rendering, Paul's *skull* is distinguished by a remarkable surface profile, the outer shape of which seems to enhance the inner realities of the brain and the person. A unique quality of inwardness becomes visible in the physical gestalt, or said otherwise, an inward being can be read in the outward appearance. This aspect of the work that Dürer undertook with his *Four Apostles*—and the aspect that we are at pains to re-trace—corresponds with the melancholic approach that discerns inner from outer reality and makes visible its soulful and spiritual dimensions.

Paul is wrapped in a grey *cloak*. The light pouring in from the right is of such intensity that the cloak's back side appears to be nearly white. The strong illumination gives rise to an image of opposites or near contradictions that range from the nearly white, to the grey, to the black. A kind of antithesis is thus established symbolically, which encompasses the poles of the light and dark, day and night, good and evil, abundance and nothingness. Melancholic thinking thinks often in terms of such existential dichotomies. They are not only theoretical formulas, but also expressions of painful experience.

With their often sharp contours, the folds in Paul's mantle display manifold, complex, and dramatic contrasts that readily suggest a dialectic quality of consciousness. The folds appear most intensively where the mantle is draped across Paul's arm. This fact, too, has its symbolic implication: It is in relationship to the individual's arm, that is, in relationship to the standpoint of the acting ego, that the folds of successive gestalts appear in the fabric of an experiential process. It belongs to the melancholic approach to experience and creatively design such a process in its completeness. Or said metaphorically, the melancholic characteristically wraps himself in the mantle of a phenomenological spirit that is personally experienceable, and manifests itself as a differentiated whole. Among the apostles we have been considering, it is John who most poignantly carries this perspective. He is the apostle who most thoroughly dedicates his gospel to the experience of the spirit in all of its aspects and sequential gestalts.

Returning now to Dürer's Paul, we notice two attributes: a folio-sized book and a sword. We can assume that in addition to the writings of the other apostles, the *folios* include the complete body of Paul's work, that is, his many letters to the Romans, the Corinthians, the Galatians, the Philippians, the Colossians, the Thessalonians, and his letters to Timothy, Titus, and Philemon. The work is all-encompassing and in its complete aim, universal. This quality belongs to Paul's own writing and serves here as an emblematic marker of the historical figure—but also in a general sense it points, amazingly, to a characteristic feature of melancholic thinking. It is the particular tendency to systematic completeness and the use of universal references. Even the four ribs on the bookbinding correspond with four binding sites that could have meaning beyond the merely anecdotal: They could stand for the melancholic thinker's special proclivity for the logical ordering of things in fourfold structures, exemplified for instance in the four temperaments themselves. Like a bookbinding, this kind of structure gives the written experience a quality of inner hold and cohesion.

The *sword* in Paul's right hand traditionally signifies the martyrdom he suffered by beheading at the hands of the Romans. The sword is thus a reminder of absolute loyalty to a mission, and of an unerringly authentic and radical personality that will not be deterred by the prospect of martyrdom. The melancholic is characterized by this kind of straightforward adherence to a task and uncompromising engagement in a creative calling. An example of such existential earnestness is found in Dürer's remark, "Life is either a tightrope or a feather bed. Give me the tightrope."

Figuratively speaking, the sword is a weapon wielded in the fight for one's convictions or truest beliefs. It represents the mental ability to cut and divide. It stands thus for judgment and in this aspect corresponds with the executioner's sword, or allegorically, the sense of justice. In Paul's hand the sword has the meaning of the melancholic gifts of appraisal and discrimination, differentiating intellect, and the certain sense of what is timely and needs to be done in the here and now. It symbolizes this temperament's inherent and special sensorium for the creative moment in which a general and eternal essence incarnates itself.

With these four holy men Dürer undertakes no mere allegorical or artistic portrayal of the temperaments as such. He conveys as well the variety of creative perspectives that correspond with the temperaments. He was obviously aware that he had created not only the images of four holy figures and representatives of the temperaments, but that with them, he established an expression of his own creative being, and an expression of the innermost nature of creativity as such. Without this understanding, Dürer's reason for donating the painting to his native city would be little apparent. He evidently knew the painting was connected with his own artistic personality and that, beyond this, it brought to expression something about the good of the creative force itself. It was certainly Dürer's deep respect for his artistic gift and his appreciation for the divine force that manifested itself therein that led him to dedicate this, his last great work, to Nuremberg.

If we can claim accurately that this painting of the four apostles with their corresponding temperaments says something about Dürer's artistic nature and the reality of the creative force, then the question arises, why are all four temperaments portrayed rather than the particular one that the artist recognized in himself? The answer could be that Dürer did not aim to immortalize himself with a psychological self-portrait, as it were. For this, it would have sufficed to represent the melancholic, the temperament with which Dürer felt identified. He was far more concerned to portray the creative force as it was recognizable in the four-fold gestalt of the four temperaments and their creative perspectives.

Creativity per se, that is, creativity experienced as a divine, transcendent force, manifests itself in the mandala-like constellation of the four temperaments. In the five painters discussed in this chapter we have seen that the creative force empowers and enables individuals to enter into the experiential horizon of all four temperaments. Under the sway of the creative force individuals can surpass the conditions of their own temperament, to experience and create out of the perspective of the others. This is the prerogative of great creative individuals. It explains their multidimensional giftedness and their broad and enduring influence. Yet a single, specific temperament by all means remains as the primary shaping force of the individual's personality, experience, and manner of thought. In relationship to the primary one, the other three temperaments open up complementary horizons above all at the level of creative work.

We have yet to answer the question that arose at the beginning of our discussion of *The Four Apostles*. How are we to understand the difference between this picture and the other four discussed pictures of this kind, in which we discerned not only the four temperamental perspectives but also always a corollary feminine gestalt? How can we explain the absence of the feminine gestalt that otherwise appears to correspond with the fourfold masculine pattern? Could it be that in *The Four Apostles* the fundamental creative force is reduced to the aspect of a masculine consciousness or spirit at the expense of the feminine aspect of the creative unconscious and soul?

The absence of the feminine gestalt in Dürer's *Four Apostles* has troubled art historians, too. Not because they have proceeded as we have to compare artistic renditions of a primary creative pattern, but because iconographic study raises the expectation that the image of the four apostles should appear with a corollary depiction of the central figure of the Virgin Mary. It seems that the unusual composition here can be explained only with reference to the "sacra conversazione," the motif of the holy conversation, which ordinarily depicts a group of holy men gathered around the Virgin Mary and baby Jesus. Dürer's early sketches show that he had in fact intended to create such a picture but never followed through on it. But modern research technology established that, from the start, Dürer had conceived the four apostles here without a central image of the Madonna.[77]

An explanation for the missing feminine element could lie in the dramatically shifting religious situation in Nuremberg at the time. As previously mentioned, in the year prior to Dürer's completion of *The Four Apostles*, the rulers of Nuremberg decided to make the transition from the Catholic faith to the Protestant Reformation. Corresponding with the new theological conviction, the imagistic depiction of religious themes was thrown into question, and the status of the Mother of God and her visual depiction became especially problematic. In his monograph on Dürer, Peter Strieder mentions this historical possibility.[78] If such an explanation holds, then we can say that, psychologically, the feminine lacuna in Dürer's painting points to the reformist repression of the veneration and depiction of Mary. This in itself would bespeak a collective devaluation of the feminine element of the creative force and a suppression of the image as a voice of the unconscious.

5.5.2. In Albrecht Dürer's Madonna and Child with the Pear

Independently of the official art history, and despite immediate appearances, I am of the opinion that the masculine personification of the four temperaments in *The Four Apostles* does indeed incorporate a feminine element. Granted, it appears not as a complete feminine gestalt but in subtle ways that I will note later, as we explore a different but related painting, *Madonna and Child with the Pear* (Fig. 16). The *Madonna* unquestionably demonstrates Dürer's parallel occupation with the feminine and for a number of reasons can be seen in complementary relationship to *The Four Apostles*.

Speaking in favor of a coupled reading of the two independently composed paintings is the fact that both works were completed in 1526—and both of them represent the end of Dürer's painterly work. *The Four Apostles* is Dürer's very last masterly painting, and *Madonna*

(Fig. 16): Albrecht Dürer, *Madonna and Child with the Pear*

and Child with the Pear is the last of his long series that portrays the Virgin Mary. Furthermore, the two paintings have in common a smooth and flowing style. Both of them also display a dark background that sets the portrayed figures in high relief. In both paintings, the year of completion and Durer's monogram appear in the upper right-hand frame. And finally, in *Madonna and Child with the Pear*, Mary appears with half-closed eyes. This motif makes her unlike the Virgin in Dürer's earlier portrayals, but it corresponds with the pattern of the great feminine force as we have seen it rendered in *The Desperate Man* (Fig. 11) *and The Potato Eaters* (Fig. 13). Based on such observations, I would consider *this* Madonna to be a counterpart and equivalent to Dürer's four apostles and their representation of the temperaments. This *Madonna* at any rate corresponds with Dürer's activity and will, at age fifty-eight, two years before his death, to continue testifying to his experience of a primal force that manifests itself in the double aspect of a creative spirit and an image-mediating soul.

In *Madonna and Child with the Pear*, Dürer acquiesced to the spirit of religious reform by omitting the blue veil and halo that traditionally signified Mary's holy nature. Her transpersonal status as the Mother of God is thus sacrificed in favor of a more human and empathic quality of motherhood. Nevertheless, her face and bodily bearing emanate a feeling of the sublime and mysterious. And despite her apparent youth, her half-closed eyes, her nobly arched eyebrows, her flawless skin, her high forehead, her discretely tilted head, and her graceful neck convey an impression of dignity and sheer greatness.

In this image of a young and noble Mother Mary, we might discern symbolically something about the mysterious fascination of the mother archetype and its link to the creative unconscious. It has manifested itself through the ages in a treasury of images, and expresses itself in artistic works in ever-new forms. From this creative unconscious we receive an inexhaustible fount of imagination, ideas, intuitions, images and forms. As Dürer so often did in his portrayals of the Virgin Mary, he surely here too expresses the wonder of this inspiring source coming from the depths of the soul. The picture at hand is a realization of the creative force that (in the truest sense) underlies and supports the creative process with unexpected contents and autonomous impulses.

A careful look at the portrait shows Mary's facial expression to differ on the right and left sides. Covering each side in succession along the centerline, we find on the right (from the onlooker's perspective) a somewhat austere countenance; and on the left side the look is that of the sweet, tender mother. These qualities could reflect the feminine archetype in its contrasting aspects of the containing archaic Great

Mother and the animating young anima. In *Virgin and Child with St. Anne* (1519, Metropolitan Museum of Art, New York), Dürer in the traditional way attributed these aspects to two different figures, namely St. Anne, Mary's mother, and Mary herself, the daughter. Using Erich Neumann's terms, the two aspects would correspond respectively with the archetypally feminine "elementary" and "transformative" characters.[79] In *Madonna and Child with the Pear* the qualities appear together, in somewhat attenuated form, as two different aspects of one and the same person. Mary's two-foldness could point to the fact that the creative unconscious stores a treasure of archaic images, but it is at the same time an eternally renewing source, and thus brings forth also new images. The creative unconscious appearing in one person and specifically in the figure of Mary points symbolically to the autonomous activity and transpersonal nature of the creative force. In both aspects—the autonomous and the transpersonal—creative individuals experience the special fascination of being led by a mysterious inner force and being overpowered by meaningful archetypal contents.

Mary's face emanates also a kind of sibylline enigma, an air of mystery and wisdom. Her half-closed eyes watch over the baby Jesus but just as much seem to gaze inward. In the same vein her lightly closed lips suggest the mystic or the *mystai*, as the ancient Greeks called the "closed-mouth ones" whose practice of silence deepened their inward listening. Accordingly, the apostle Luke in his Gospel, 2:19, writes, "But Mary kept all these things, and pondered them in her heart." In Mary's silence holds the mystery and the ultimately ineffable nature of something that has been seen or witnessed. "'What Beauty is,'" said Dürer, "'I know not,'" and to this he could have added that the creative force itself is ultimately ineffable.[80]

Dürer frames Mary's face with a mane of ringleted, chestnut hair shimmering with red and gold highlights. It contrasts the hairstyles of the four apostles, who are indeed partly bald. By comparison, Mary's ringleted locks point to an associative, dance-like, and non-linear manner of thinking. In other words, her hair symbolizes a feminine mindset that can be described as spring-like, watery, flowing, inexhaustible, brimming with suggestive fantasy and playful imagination, and embellished with surprising ideas that come like light flashes. C.G. Jung offers an example of the fact that this modus is not limited to women but can appear in men as an expression of the inner feminine. In testimony to his student Erich Neumann Jung wrote to the members of the Zürich Institute,

> [Neumann's] intellectual achievement is outstanding. You are all a bit spoiled by my anima, which is capable of switching between light and dark—nothing is entirely dark and—thank God—completely light! That is why I am accused of contradictions! With Neumann it is different. One needs to think with him, otherwise one is lost.[81]

In this writing Jung acknowledges his own anima or Mary-like iridescent thinking, a thinking of the kind that admits dialectic polarities. As an aspect of the creative feminine, it is especially associative and symphonic. By contrast, Neumann's modality of thought belongs to the creative masculine and its proclivity for systematic structure and linearity.

The contrasts we observed in Mary's facial expression can be seen also in her hair. Again from the onlooker's perspective, on the left side, the side of the sweet young mother, it clings to her cheek and flows over her shoulder, where two neatly bunched ringlets spill around her child, as if embracing him. On the other side, three ringlets disperse themselves loosely over her right shoulder, on the side of the averted, less graspable and archaic St. Anne-like mother. Moreover, on this same side Mary's hair is pulled back, gathered tightly away from her face. Her ear is thus especially exposed, as if to make of it symbolically an open listening funnel that detects signals in a great dark realm—in the shadowy world of the unknown, in a Hades-like place, like the kind Persephone sometimes inhabits. Likewise on this side Mary's hair partly disappears, blending into the dark background, and then pours from her own shadow into the light cast on her shoulder. This flow of her hair seems to belong to the inherently sibylline aspect of the mother archetype, which bestows the gift of feminine intuition or the ability to transmit messages heard from the beyond. This gift includes openness to subliminal and parapsychological phenomena— an archaic ability that Jung, for instance, both feared and admired in his own mother. His doctoral dissertation dealt with the occult world that he experienced in séances conducted together with his cousin Helene Preiswerk. In the *Red Book*, under the rubric of the "*Septem Sermones ad Mortuos*," the "Seven Sermons to the Dead," Jung describes his own, later encounter with the world of the deceased. All of this testifies to Jung's feel for the creative feminine force, its relatedness to the beyond, and the close proximity of his own anima to its archaic, St. Anne-like aspect.

The child in Dürer's painting is imbued with a look of wonder and expectant curiosity. We are reminded of the child within in each of us, the one that marvels, poses questions with wide-open eyes, wants to know about things. *Thaumazein*, the gift of wonder, is not only the beginning of all philosophy, but also the driving force of all creativity. It is the capability and thirst for knowledge that we encounter as well in the *puer aeternus*, the archetypal eternal boy. The boy here clutches earnestly what appears to be a meaningless clover-like sprig. Yet his gesture recalls the creative individual's playful experiment, the process of discovery in seemingly useless things, *art pour art*—art for art's sake. We find the same child-like attitude in the fairy tail Thumbling who never searches but stumbles on things—and in creative individuals who discover ideas by chance. Mary's child symbolizes a basic process of becoming, a child-like essence of new and developing life, which is underscored in his green garb. In a certain sense, creative individuals are always child-like greenhorns, or "green behind the ears," as the saying goes.

The sleeves of the Madonna's gown are green, like the Christ child's garb. But there are other colors in this painting that point to beginnings. The salmon-like red of Mary's smock stands symbolically for the sunrise, for new creative beginnings, for the appearance of a new day, the dawning of a new time. It is the expression of creative energy in the sense of pointing to the coming of something primarily new and entirely other. A brilliant white collar or neckline contrasts with the dark background. And this white is also a symbol of beginnings, for it is the sum of all colors and emerging potentials. By contrast, the black background itself denotes the end of all possibilities.

This contrast between white and black envisions the feminine standing in between beginnings and ends, day and night, being and nothingness, life and death. In this chapter we have encountered other pictures that express the feminine archetype's borderline or bi-polar potential to spring forth from the darkness as a creative spark, or to lead into completely dark realms of paralysis. The spectrum of possibilities corresponds with the individual experience of surrender to an astonishing creative force that animates but that can just as much destroy. It is in this duality that the creative force asserts its inviolable, absolute autonomy. It is responsible for enthusiasm and aversion, inspiration and spiritual paralysis, creativity and illness, discovery and the mere treading of water.

It is worth noting that in this painting Dürer's colors correspond with colors that mark stages of an alchemical process of transformation: The background corresponds with the *nigredo*, the blackening. The Madonna's green gown and her child's garb bespeak the *veriditas*, the greening. Her pear points to the *citrinitas*, the yellowing, and her smock to the *rubedo*, the reddening. And finally, her white collar corresponds with the *albedo*, the whitening. While I do not know the extent of Dürer's familiarity with alchemical symbolism, a woodcut of his on the title page of an alchemical work suggests that he had some knowledge of it. Even if his choice of color in *Madonna* was without conscious reference to alchemy, it can be said to contain an inner logic. Because in any event, the color scheme symbolizes a dynamic creative transformation—be likened to processes of creation, or to the stages of an alchemical process of individuation. In both dimensions the symbolism is the same: white and black stand for beginnings and endings; green for the moment of becoming; yellow for new beginnings; and red for the dawn of a new day. One might argue, however, that it boils down to nothing more than the resource of the complete color spectrum, and that the particular choices of color have no particular significance. Against this argument it must be noted that the demarcation of the alchemical stages does not include the color blue, and as if by analogy, blue is missing in the *Madonna's* palette. Had Dürer intended a traditional portrait of the Virgin, blue would have been an indispensable color. The remarkable absence of blue readily suggests that Dürer chose not to portray a spiritual dynamic that belongs to the heavenly spheres—and that he did in fact mean to visualize a more elemental creativity, perhaps with conscious reference to an alchemical process.

In this context it should be emphasized that all great painters are alchemists by nature, in that they intend far more than a random coloring of their pictures. Color has essential existential meaning as it appears, for example, in the alchemical re-creation of the world (Paul Klee) and in the individual's inner creative process. Pablo Picasso speaks for the fact that certain periods of the creative life can be dominated by particular color schemes, and that color is thus fundamentally of existential significance in the artist's work. To take a famous example, his Blue Period with its dark colors can be said to correspond with the alchemical *nigredo* stage, and his Pink Period with the *rubedo*. C.G. Jung's work illustrates the phasic impact of color for other creative individuals: His so-called "Black Books" and his subsequent *Red Book* record the decisive inner experience through which Jung discovered the fundamental understanding of the soul that he would come to apply to himself and others. Granted, the colors may be only coincidental, as the earlier work was recorded in notebooks of the kind that are typically bound with black wax covers. However, Jung chose to have the later work bound in a red leather cover, and his conscious choice of red seems to have been at play even in the name *Red Book*, which is actually the subtitle to the main title that never caught on, *Liber Novus*. In "Chapter I, The Red One," we learn how Jung, in his practice of active imagination, encountered color with the alchemist's understanding of its powers of meaning and transformation.

Let us now explore the meaning of the pear, the motif that endows this particular portrait of the Madonna its distinctive title. The pear is a feminine counterpart to the sphere that typically appears in the hand of the Pantocrator, the masculine god of creation and ruler over the universe. The motif appears elsewhere as the imperial orb denoting the emperor's power. By analogy, the pear is a symbol of the numinous feminine force of creation and its autonomous creative power within the realms of the unconscious and the soul. This is the creative force that neither wants to dominate in worldly horizons, nor to create from within the upper domains of the spirit. Thus the symbolism of the pear diametrically opposes the four temperaments, which incarnate masculine creative modalities that derive from above, from the element of ether or the spirit as such. As made visible in Mary's beautifully rendered fingers, the feminine touch entails a quality of creativity that grasps things sensuously, through the organs of the senses.[82] Masculine creativity as personified by Dürer in the four temperaments articulates itself through the spirit, that is, in writing and by means of other masculine attributes symbolized by the scroll, the books, the sword, and the key. In contrast, feminine creativity is distinguished by its relationship to the reality of the unconscious and the soul, symbolized here by the pear.

Shaped like a feminine body, the pear very well symbolizes the sensorium of the human body, the primary vessel through which the feminine creative force conveys itself. However this is not the body as an object seen and defined from the outside, as it can be by the male gaze that perceives in the real sense of the German *wahrnehmen*, "to take a truth." Rather, this body consists of an organic and holistic interplay of all five senses, whereby sensuality and spirituality come together, as in the ecstasy of immediately perceived beauty. This subjectively resonating body is an organ of experience, perception, and activity that participates in a feminine modality of creative expression.

A man, too, can experience a Mary-like feminine creativity with its origin in the body, its sensuous and poetic qualities, its ecstasy, its holistic inclusiveness, its cyclic rhythms, and its sweet beauty. It is a man's experience insofar as a developed anima allows him to enter into the amorphous wholeness of inward sensuous creativity. It is a creativity that manifests itself not in active and aimful gestures, but that befalls one and completes itself in the way that ripe fruits fall from the trees. It is a non-linear, non-intentional, receptive, and birth-giving kind of creativity. As opposed to the books held by the apostles, Mary's pear has to do with a sensuous tasting and absorbing of soulful contents, with natural and instinctual reactions, with nurture and fulfillment, with flavor and feeling. The pear symbolizes an experiential logic based on the biology of bodily evidence, as it were. Moreover, the pear in its roundness alludes to the unified multi-facetedness of feminine creativity. It contrasts the book, the word, the sword, and the key, the symbols that point to a masculine creativity that relies on theories, theses, distinctions, hierarchical principles, exclusionary demands, and claims to absoluteness. The masculine style follows a linguistically explicit and documentable logic.

There is a telling set of details in the two paintings: each of the four apostles carry their objects to display, but the Madonna clasps the pear close to her heart. Her gesture suggests a creative feminine power that is embedded in and bound to the whole body, its cyclic rhythms, its sensuous perceptions, and a nurturing Eros that both depends on and begets vibrant relatedness. Contrarily, masculine creativity relies on an objective Logos that stands alone for itself and is independent from immediate experiencing.

Masculine and feminine creativity differ in ways we have underlined several times. The questions now arise, are the two related? Are men and women necessarily consigned respectively to the masculine and feminine modes of creativity? Might the two paintings discussed in this chapter hold the answers?

(Fig. 15, left): Albrecht Dürer, *The Four Apostles*
(Fig. 16, right): Albrecht Dürer, *Madonna and Child with the Pear*

Dürer's intention to strictly separate his portrayals of masculine and feminine creativity is underscored by their staging as the central subjects of the two respectively different paintings. I would think this radical division must have deeply contradicted Dürer's artistic personality. It can be explained perhaps as a reflection of his great struggle and ultimate acquiescence to the mighty force of the Reformation. With enormous exertion the Reformation determined a new religious order that favored a primarily masculine, spirit orientated creativity—and this, with historical consequences that would endure for centuries to come. Among the results was a substantial collective departure from the prevailingly soulful, feminine creativity that had existed in Catholic Christianity.

Wherever the Reformation prevailed, the Word as transmitted in the Bible came to stand as the sole guiding principle for all individuals. St. Peter's key to the heavenly kingdom was taken from the pope and the priests, and handed over to the "priesthood of all believers." Papal supremacy and the Catholic Church hierarchy gave way to the community of believers, who are represented by the four apostles in Dürer's painting. Ethical uprightness and strong faith became the guiding moral principles. Or said imagistically, Paul's sword became the instrument of the radical separation of good and evil, the godly and the sinful—and accordingly, it stood as well for the individual's responsibility to lead the worthy life. By analogy to Mark with his holy scroll, all individuals were now empowered to either knock on the church door, as did Luther with his Wittenberg Theses, or to testify their faith by inward listening. Such developments led to the Protestant Gnosis and the battlefields of the Peasant Wars. The central power of the Catholic Church that ruled in the world and mediated the hereafter was deposed in favor of governance by temporal, political, regional authorities of the kind in Nuremberg who received Dürer's gift of *The Four Apostles*.

This was the end of a Catholic system of belief with its feminine-oriented mindset and creativity. Countless churches and cathedrals were purged of pictures and statues. Representations of the Madonna were among the sacred images that became casualties of the fanatical uproar and fate that befell all materiality, sensuousness, and beauty. In the reformists' hands, churches became gathering places, devoid of imagery that allegedly stood to distract attention from the pure Word or to seduce the faithful into the dangerous realm of the reified icon. Pictures and other visual arts were no longer seen as mediators of divine and transcendent powers, but as golden calves that obfuscated the true faith. The realm of sensuously perceivable signs and gestures was sacrificed in the name of a faith mediated by the word. And thus also diminished was a feminine creativity mediated in concrete practices of the Catholic faith—such as in its symbolic rituals, sacraments, prayers and indulgences, festive celebrations with incense, candles, and liturgical garments in an array of colors. A heroic mode of masculine creativity was on the rise, one that corresponded with the inward ideals of asceticism and radical personal authenticity.

Wherever the Reformation held sway, the decline of feminine creativity with its sensibility for thingness and sensuous corporeality manifested itself as well in the theological debate. Among the casualties in this sense were the Catholic mass and its underlying doctrine, which holds that Christ's sacrifice is re-lived *in concreto* by the divine mystery and miraculous transubstantiation of bread and wine into his body and blood. This conviction was supplanted by Protestant understanding, which in its most bared-boned form holds that the Communion service serves *simply* to commemorate Christ's redeeming sacrifice.

From now on, revelation was considered to have come to a full and final end in the biblical text. The Reformation doctrine, *sola scriptura*, "by Scripture alone," decreed not only the supreme authority of the Bible in all matters of faith, but also that no further development should ever take place. Dürer denotes this one, absolutely self-sufficient, immutable, and binding Scripture in the apostles' demonstratively displayed, thick, and lockable Bibles. With the key and the sword, he points to the opening interpretation and missionary dissemination of the binding revelation. The situation as such corresponds very much with the masculine patriarchal spirit and creativity.

The Reformation caused the obsoleteness of new revelation of the kind suggested in *Madonna and Child with the Pear*, where the Christ Child embodies the emergence of a new spirit and signals the opening of new experiences. Considering that the boy's green garb is the color of the inspiratory Holy Ghost, and that the boy's clover is mandala-shaped, we have on the whole the image of an immanent incarnation of the Self. The gestalt as such points to the opening up of a feminine creativity that could inspire growth and change. And accordingly divine revelation cannot be encased in a four-corned book, nor can it be considered closed. Quite to the contrary, the Madonna's flowing hair symbolizes an inexhaustible wellspring of imagination that is by nature both archaic and eternally young, and thus provides ever-renewing impulses and archetypally orientating ideas. The tapping of this source leads to never-ending renewal, change, and transformation led by an anima quality of relatedness to life itself. The opposing patriarchal position thinks from within the horizon of finitude and death.

Let us again underscore Protestantism's rational masculine spirit. In *The Four Apostles* it is made visible in a number of ways that we have not yet marked, for instance in the emphasis on the four highly attentive men obtaining spiritual vision by their eyesight and intellect. Their powerful hands suggest the modus of energetic action that later was to become the Calvinistic performance ideal. This kind of rational stance could do little other than to abnegate the more irrational feminine relationship to the world, typical aspects of which are implicit in Dürer's *Madonna and Child with the Pear*. As we mentioned earlier, Mary's soft skin, her delicate fingers, and her pear suggest the non-rational mode of perception by sensation, feeling, and taste.

The abnegation of such creative feminine potential entailed also the devaluing of other non-rational attributes. As symbolized in Mary's open ear, we can speak of the faculty to listen-in-to the darkness or the unknown, and the related gifts of intuition and extrasensory perception. Being components of a matriarchal heritage, all such abilities were decried. In their place came the incisive clarity of intellect and the pragmatic treatment of the worldly here-and-now. In *The Four Apostles*, the masculine stance as such is visible in the clear emphasis on the apostles' heads, in their alert and directed gazes, and as well, in the brilliant stream of light illuminating the far right-hand side of the painting.

Collective transformations brought about by the Reformation were determined by grievances arising within the then matriarchal world of the Catholic Church. Many of them concerned perversions of feminine spirituality, whereby superstition and malpractices had come to express the materialistic objectification and mechanical treatment of religious belief. We think, for instance, of the dissolute lives of the popes who succumbed entirely to immoral sensuality. Such failure was bound to evoke demands of piety from above. In this context, the Reformation regarded with suspicion all allusions to the body and the embodied soul, such as the kind symbolized in Dürer's pear. The reformed faith was more inclined to adopt the very masculine and disembodied doctrine, "*sola fide, sola gratia,*" that is, salvation comes "by faith and God's grace alone."

To further consider the characterization of the difference between masculine and feminine mentality, it is worth noting Dürer's portrayal of the four apostles in two narrow upright frames that constrict the four men to a relatively narrow space. Mary on the other hand is given more room, and her figure occupies it in a circular expansion that originates at her own center. Taking the composition symbolically, we could say that masculine mentality belongs to the vertical dimension of lofty ideals, intellectual principles, pioneering ideas, and transcendent goals. Also, it submits as if self-evidently to externally determined frameworks like those of performance standards, social norms and rules, and to the pragmatic conditions of reality. In contrast, feminine mentality obtains its fundamental orientation from the center of the individual personality. Out of this center evolve aesthetic preferences, ethical valuations, instinctual appraisals, and spiritual interests that unfold unmistakably from within a personal Self and realm of being.

In the Occident the war between the two worlds was waged brutally during the times of Reformation and the Counter-Reformation. However, it continues to be a worldwide archetypal battle. Events in today's Islamic world illustrate poignantly how a masculine-inspired spirituality, turning to the absolute, does not hesitate to abrade precious monuments and raze other cultural assets to the ground. This is not to mention its cold resolve to wipe out the lives of all supposed non-believers. This kind of development makes it difficult if not impossible to conceive of religious change and renewal.

We can imagine the drama posed for Dürer by the Reformation war on images, sensuality, and beauty. To whatever extent he acquiesced, Dürer cut himself off from his own matriarchal world, the primal ground of his creativity and artistic engagement. It is little wonder that he died at the age of fifty-eight, just two years after he completed the two separate paintings that allude to his pain or at least to his tragic sense of self-division engendered by his exit from the feminine form of creativity that had been nourished by the matriarchal Catholic Church.

Earlier in this chapter we raised the questions: Does a relationship exist between the masculine and feminine modes of creativity? Are men and women consigned respectively to the masculine and feminine modes of creativity? Without doubt, a relationship exists. It can precisely be discerned in a comparison of Dürer's two paintings, *The Four Apostles* and *Madonna and Child with the Pear*. Here we see that the qualities that are characteristic for one side are *mutatis mutandis* present also on the other. This shows indirectly a connecting similarity.

For example, the typically feminine, irrational creative spirit expressed in the Madonna's ringleted and free-flowing hair finds analogy in the free-falling folds of John's and Paul's robes. The latter beautiful compositional detail is one of the subtle feminine elements Dürer employs, now to attribute the otherwise stringent heady apostles with a feminine creative joy that has no practical purpose except that of following the natural laws of rhythmic motion. In this sense, the biblically transmitted Apollonian revelation from above is balanced by a Dionysian revelation from below. (See Nietzsche's characterization of the two in *The Birth of Tragedy from the Spirit of Music*, 1872). As intimated in the two apostles' robes, the Dionysian element conveys feminine spiritual experience through movement, rhythm, and mood. That a typically feminine creativity can abide within a man shows also in the intense coloring of John's and Paul's robes, for color in general stands for feeling and emotion. Thus the two creative modalities, the masculine and the feminine, intermingle and co-relate in the realm of emotion. Emotion is the base substance of creativity, its point of departure, its vehicle, and its effect.

VI

CREATIVE EXISTENCE

Artists' reflections on the essence and mystery of creative power are especially palpable in their self-portraits. A self-portrait does not simply reflect outer appearances. It is more than a photographic reproduction of visible surfaces, and more than a factual record of sensory data. It is an interpretation that captures the artist's very being. It is an answer to the question of the specific thing that makes up the artist's personality. It is moreover an answer to a more basic question, namely, what is this mysterious creative force that asserts itself in one's life under the specific conditions of one's origin, one's time, one's particular surroundings, and one's personal destiny? The self-portrait is an expression of the creative force revealing itself in the life circumstances that are specific to the individual.

With this in mind, we will now undertake the discussion of four artists' self-portraits. These pictures should evidence the need to understand the creative force as something that incarnates itself most essentially in the circumstances of an individual's life. We will mark this, then, to be another basic attribute of the creative force: It necessarily concretizes and embodies itself in the *particular* person— in *this* unique life and personality, in *this* biography and existence. It does not float in the sheer ether of potentialities, ideas, random creative impulses, or abstract hypotheses.

The existential dimension of the creative force is not easy to envision on the basis of artistic examples. Not that examples would be lacking. To the contrary, the challenge lies in the plenitude, for the self-portrait belongs as a basic task to every artist. Given the conspicuous abundance, how shall we reasonably choose? Choices can be made on the basis that some self-portraits and the respective artists' experience of creativity reveal especially poignantly the four temperamental modalities that have been much under discussion here. So we will look at self-portraits that provide outstanding examples of creativity as it is experienced specifically in this way.

This approach assumes that the creative force realizes itself in the life of the individual artist, according to one of the four temperaments, that is, either the choleric, the sanguine, the phlegmatic, or the melancholic. Yet creativity is not reserved to artists. It is an inherent and core reality in everyone, meaning that each one of us embodies prevailingly one of the four temperaments that influence our creative relationship to the world. Unfortunately limits of space constrain me in the enticing temptation to develop a detailed typology of the individual based on the temperaments and their respective creative styles and potentialities. So I shall limit myself here to a description of four painters whose lives and works correspond respectively to a typical temperament-based style of creative experience.

6.1. The Choleric Mode in Vincent van Gogh's Self-Portrait with the Bandaged Ear

Self-Portrait with Bandaged Ear (Fig. 17) is one of two self-portraits in which van Gogh points to the hideous event of his severed ear. As the well-known story goes, van Gogh in fit of madness sliced off his own ear lobe and presented it to a prostitute. However, according to Hans Kaufmann and Rita Wildegans this story was conceivably a cover-up construed by van Gogh and his painter friend Paul Gauguin to conceal the truth that it was Gauguin himself who had performed the massacre.[83]

6.1.1. Existential Truth

The portrait pictures van Gogh with a resolute look, showing no trace of the agony suffered on the dismemberment of his ear. Despite his difficult life circumstances, he looks forward with brave optimism, the line of his gaze extending beyond his own right-hand side, that is, into the future. The yellow and orange hues of his face, recalling his landscapes of fertile wheat fields, oppose the misery and express instead his fundamental confidence and decided focus on his inner task. It appears that nothing can hold van Gogh back from his innermost concerns and personal artistic calling.

(Fig. 17): Vincent van Gogh, *Self-Portrait with Bandaged Ear*

The vitality sustaining despite the accomplished mutilation shows as well in the intensive color of van Gogh's coat, a vigorous elemental green that bespeaks a strong, imperturbable nature and fresh developmental potential. The gift of steadfastness in the face of setback and tribulation is characteristic of the choleric/hysteroid personality. People of this inclination re-orient continuously to new horizons, although they often suffer painful adversity. Other people suffering in smaller portions would fall apart, but the choleric moves on, apparently unfazed. This impression of an almost soldierly resolve comes across in van Gogh's blue fur-rimmed winter cap, the brim pulled down over his forehead in the manner of a helmet. An attitude of fierce self-protection and resilience comes to light here.

Portrayed in the affirmative bearing that conceives of no abuse, van Gogh stands before an open window or door, as if he were turning with determination toward some felt destiny. The composition as such symbolizes a situation of transition—in the truest sense an existential situation that entails a crossing and transcending of borders and passing from a known reality to an unknown one. Characteristic of van Gogh's life, this is an image of the transitory life as such, one that is constantly in flux, in crisis, in a permanent ecstasy of decampment. It is characteristic not only of van Gogh, but of the choleric/hysteroid type of life in general.

6.1.2. Binding of Nature and the Person

Van Gogh's transitory life takes shape in-between the before and the after, in-between the now-known and the yet-to-be-known. However, his transitions unfold not only in temporal terms, but also in-between outside and inside, in-between nature and the artist, and in-between outer reality and the inner world. As a creating artist, van Gogh sojourns the interstices lying between nature's sensuous phenomena and their inner spiritual meanings. The painting is the mediating reality between reproducible nature and the artist's creative vision of it.

This binding of nature and the person is especially intensive in van Gogh's works, which carry unmistakably his subjective painterly signature. His landscapes in particular are imprinted with the stamp of his person, revealing it in the strong, thick, and rhythmic brush strokes that come directly from his inner kinetic center. The other way around, the self-portrait very well makes visible the presence of nature in the person, van Gogh. We have already noted the yellow and orange facial hues. More than simply recalling, these colors also visualize the indwelling of the wheat fields in the man; to these we can add the scenes of golden harvest sheaves and the famous sunflowers. And in the color of his coat we encounter the inward presence of his beloved green groves, shrubbery, and cypresses.

Let us have a closer look at this reciprocity between the artist's subjective relationship to nature, and the objective presence of nature in the artist. Van Gogh's works communicate on one hand his very personal view of nature and the world. His artistic view does not pretend to be factual, nor does it imply a perception of the world that is devoid of subjective wishes and preferences. It is not a scientific view. Far more, it is an expressive view led by personal concerns, preferences, and imaginings. Accordingly, the unique composition of landscapes and objects follows van Gogh's personal preferences of color, form, and rhythm. It is with such unique creative accents that his subjectivity as a painter comes to life.

The other way around, van Gogh envisions his individuality to be a piece of nature. His very personhood is felt to be designed in co-participation with nature's objective reality. How shall we understand this? We can think of the objective facts of every person's individual constitution, and conditions that determine his or her personal nature from the start. In this sense, nature is the sum of all factors that compose the person independently of his or her biding or consent. Given elements that contribute already at birth include, for instance, astrological constellations, bodily constitution, the family's social and economic standing, and other conditions deriving from the society, the country, and the environmental surroundings. Such factors set the frame for individual development, for the influences of health and illness, and for the predisposition to a particular psychological type or temperament. As inherent pre-givens that largely determine our lives, we experience them as objective, quasi natural forces over which we have little or no control.

People of the choleric/hysteroid bent hold in common the subjective trait of enthralled binding to the world, a state of being that they tend to conceive poetically. The world is the cipher of their inner state or soul. On the other hand these people are especially subject to the above-mentioned pre-conditioning factors, or to the influence of nature in its broadest determinative sense. And it can go in both directions: They might succumb often to any number of ailments, or they might enjoy generally robust health. They might suffer many blows of fate, or they might be swept into happenstances that charm their lives with beauty, success, charisma, and other gifts. Their families, communities, or cultures may be hard to bear—or they may feel well supported and nurtured in such surroundings. And finally, choleric individuals feel either basically anchored and safe in the world, or they suffer feelings of being adrift and homeless. As concerns van Gogh, there is no doubt that the negative determinants stood in the foreground. His physical constitution was rather unbalanced and weak. In his professional life he experienced little support from his family and community, except that from his deeply trusted brother Theo. And he carried an abysmal feeling of homelessness that accompanied him to the grave.

Now some delicate questions arise: Is van Gogh's kind of creativity caused by negative life factors? To better understand, might we refer by analogy to the wounded healer that is well known in the realm of psychotherapy? Might we envision a wounded creator? Or, can we imagine the same creativity emerging in a van Gogh, embedded in a family that nurtured unconditionally his artistic ambitions and supported his attendance of an art academy? A van Gogh who with his handsome appeal found success with women, got married, and established a proper family? What if his art had found resonance with the collective taste of the time and brought the corresponding financial success? And on top of this, what if he had lived with a balanced soul and feelings of harmony and reward at home and in the art world? What if he had felt at home anywhere, for that matter? The same artistic achievement of this van Gogh is hardly imaginable. However, history contains examples of happily existing artists, musicians, and painters, so it would be mistaken to claim that comfortable lives and creativity cannot go hand-in-hand. But we very often find tragic individuals within the framework of this creative gestalt that we are calling the choleric/hysteroid life. They are the ones whose difficult lives are inimical to a happy existence but conducive to vital creative work.

6.1.3. The Soul in Nature

In the background of van Gogh's self-portrait, there is a Japanese woodblock print that portrays several women and Mount Fuji. As many of his paintings indicate, van Gogh was a great lover of Japanese art. Besides taking it as clue to his avid liking, what meaning might we find in this woodblock print motif? To begin with, it alludes to the sudden appearance of Japan's art in the western world, which occurred during van Gogh's lifetime. It points as well to van Gogh's participation in the resultant opening up of a general interest in exoticism and wholly new conceptions of art. This could partly explain van Gogh's use of the woodblock motif.

But more than this, the exotic Japanese world proffered a new kind of transcendence, that is, a horizontal or earthly and temporal one. It invited the observer to set aside familiar convention and habits for a step into wholly new, unknown, and intriguing territory. A hereafter existing in the inner world offered an alternative to the Christian ideal of vertical transcendence. This greatly appealed to van Gogh, whose traditional Christian orientation got lost as a result of his failed aspiration to become a preacher—a job for which he had applied and been rejected several times. With the image of Mount Fuji itself, the woodblock print portrays one of Japan's most sacred and revered places, and it thus emanates an animist religiosity that was in tune with van Gogh's loving celebration of numinous nature. Similarly, the brightly clad geishas in the midst of the vast natural landscape can be interpreted as a symbolic expression of an anima-like soul dwelling in nature. The Japanese values well accommodated van Gogh's spirituality and need for an alternative to traditional Christian belief with its emphasis on the spirit in the vertical dimension. Containing such meanings, the woodblock print itself documents some of the biographical determinants underlying van Gogh's self-portrait. In particular, it highlights his personal credo in terms of a new animistic religiosity rooted in the earthly here-and-now and inspired by the feminine soul.

Van Gogh's discovery of the Japanese color woodblock was important also in that he would come to adopt elements of the aesthetic and technique. For instance, it was here that he encountered the flat, purely colorful surface and simple bold line. And here, too, he found the possibility of dispensing with contour based on shading and shadows. Assimilating such approaches, he gained more creative autonomy in his use of form and color, and he was freed of Realism's dictate that required the painter's illusionistic depiction of three-dimensionality. In Japanese art van Gogh certainly also recognized a principle of his own, namely, the absolute benchmark of self-sufficient beauty. Thus with the background motif of the woodblock print, van Gogh affirms both his soul kinship with the Japanese world, and his close proximity to the Japanese understanding of art.

6.1.4. The Destined Life

To the left of the Japanese woodblock print there is a portrayal of van Gogh's wooden easel displaying a canvas. With this motif, van Gogh underscores his understanding of himself as a working painter. With the placement of the easel and canvas at his back, van Gogh emphasizes the reality that the creative task is his existential backing and the primal ground and spine of his selfhood. He shows himself through and through as a destined painter—even though his art at the time lacked the confirmation of external success.

The background canvas itself shows no completed picture or obvious sign of a solid work-in-progress. The coloring is mainly white, with faint yellow and blue strokes offering fleeting hints of something happening. The image as such suggests a creative process in *statu nascendi*, in a nascent state. It likewise evokes the sense of primal creation and the mystery of a coming-to-being ex nihilo or out of the hazy mists. Just as the canvas seems to emerge in *statu nascendi* from the surrounding green background, so might we understand that the image emerging on it is a nascent realization of surrounding nature. As the color white can symbolize all at once purification, potentiality, transformation and transcendence, we could say that this background canvas pre-sages van Gogh's transformation of nature's offerings into sublime, symbolically resonant images. We can only speculate: With the canvas motif, might van Gogh describe his experience of recovery from the episode of his severed ear? Or might he hint more broadly about his experience of the choleric life and his creative handling of it? Or perhaps both?

Where van Gogh's portrayed easel protrudes above the white canvas, the intersection of the central support beam and crossbeam forms a cross. With the two side beams cut short by the narrow pictorial space, the easel top appears as an abstract human gestalt with uplifted arms. Although the shape may be coincidental due to spatial limits, it still has symbolic impact. Before we explore the meaning of it, we should recall that a picture's symbolic value does not necessarily entail the artist's conscious intention. Independently of the ego as the conscious director, coincidence and accident play their own roles in meaning-making led by a variety of unconscious factors. This phenomenon can be seen well in psychotherapy, where therapeutic painting is usually done by patients who lack the skills of the professional artist. Perhaps all the more because of their limited control of the composition, we encounter very often in their paintings the autonomous meaning-making factor. Akin to the Freudian slip, it manifests itself typically in the compositional flaw or accident.

Intended or not, the cross motif formed by the easel top can appear to portray a person performing a gesture of supplication or sacrifice. It could as well picture a crucified human being. The meaning could be that van Gogh's creativity is born like a cross—as a burden and fate. The creative life is indeed an inescapable destiny. It is all at once one's central axis and one's way of individuation. For the choleric artist in particular it entails sacrifice, abdication, and spiritual death, as the cross motif can imply. But as the motif can just as much portray the performance of an uplifting gesture of triumph or celebration, it points to the reality that this creative life also gives rise to spiritual resurrection and transcendence.

6.2. The Sanguine Mode in Nicolas Poussin's Self-Portrait

6.2.1. Exacting Factuality

Poussin's canvases, often filled with abundant contents, display structure and balance, and his plentiful motifs are integrated in a rational order. Likewise in Poussin's self-portrait (Fig. 18) we encounter a man dedicated fully to ideas of proportion and exacting factuality. So factual is the portrayal of the man that it reveals next to nothing of his subjective emotional register. The dry rendition of the painter's outward appearance creates the impression of a rather impersonal character, as if the main concern would be the depiction of an official persona. In service to this task and the completion of the work, the palpable man seems absent, making of the portrait a kind of monument. Nevertheless the picture fascinates us, drawing our attention to Poussin's technically accomplished rendition of reality. Such will to achieve factual objectivity, such dedication to objective truth, and such serious effort to realize both factors in the execution of a task—these attributes fundamentally characterize the sanguine/compulsive orientation.

It is also telling of the sanguine character that Poussin created his self-portrait following not his own spontaneous desire, but acquiescing to the will of his friend and patron Paul Fréart de Chantelou. Motivated at first only by an uninspired sense of duty, Poussin ultimately poured all of his available strength and artistic skill into his completion of the portrait. Just as Poussin did, people of the sanguine bent in general derive the basic motivation to act from feelings of obligation, moral duty, and ethical responsibility. If the sanguine character seems to lack personal inner drive, its outwardly determined actions and creative activity nevertheless bespeak the existence of genuine inner demands and values. For instance, the background canvases in Poussin's portrait point to the sanguine's inner drive to live within the framework of general norms, to internalize given laws and ethical standards. Except

(Fig. 18): Nicolas Poussin, *Self-Portrait*

for the one portrayal of the muse, the canvases show no pictorial contents. Consisting essentially of frames, these images underscore the existential importance of frameworks or framing norms and conditions as such. Thus it comes as no surprise that Poussin dedicated himself intensively to epistemological study, focusing especially on ethical questions pertaining to his calling as a *peintre philosophe*, a "painter-philosopher." In other words, his immediate concern was not only to produce paintings, but also to philosophize about the general conditions of painting.

As we have already noted, the sanguine tendency comes through in Poussin's emphatically factual self-representation, in lieu of a painting that emanates his subjective life conditions. In line with this choice, the portrait provides no clue that Poussin was suffering from Parkinson's disease. With enormous artistic discipline he overcame a symptomatic handicap, such that the hindering tremor of his hand is undetectable in his execution of this painting. Indeed, Poussin's will to portray the objectively accomplished and enduring artist prevails—especially so in the immediate background, where the depicted canvas prominently displays in Latin his name and other key identifying features. Appearing like an effigy set in stone, the text defines and commemorates the artist for all posterity: *Effigie Nicolai Poussini Andelyensis Pictoris, Anno Etatis 56. Roma Anno Jubilei 1650*—"Portrait of the Painter Nicolas Poussin of Les Andelys at Rome during the Jubilee Year 1650, age 56 years."

6.2.2. Layers of Lightness and Darkness, Foreground and Background

Poussin's works typically display strongly contrasting lightness and darkness and foregrounds and backgrounds. In the self-portrait, his use of these design elements makes of the depicted man a large and imposing presence, both corporeally and in his occupation of the three-dimensional space. The composition as such lends itself well to symbolic understanding.

To begin with, contrast is given by the light source that pours in from the upper left corner, largely illuminating the painter's figure and leaving a part immersed in shadow. At the same time his presence is doubled by the distinct silhouette appearing in front of the commemorative Latin inscription. The impression is furthered of a man staunchly possessed of an exacting quality of mind, one that differentiates the dark and the light, good and evil, and consciousness and unconsciousness. As the light streams in from the upper left-hand corner, it symbolizes in Jungian parlance the active influence of the father archetype. The father archetype's domain of spiritual values and ideals corresponds with Poussin's study of ethics as well as with his adherence to a Stoic way of life. The Stoic framing-of-the-world in terms of clashing opposites is inclined to favor the pole of lightness and consciousness over darkness and unconsciousness. The same inclination belongs to a specifically sanguine way of being. Symbolically in line with the painter's face illuminated on the right-hand side, the sanguine character highly values the paternal qualities of moral rectitude and uprightness. Poussin's brightly lit, ring-adorned right hand comes across as the man's demonstrative signal of the virtue of righteousness.

Multiple depths take shape in the picture's layered dimensions: The foreground is demarcated by the image of the painter himself. The three stacked canvases delineate the middle ground. Finally, a door on the right-hand side marks the background and increases the impression of depth with its outer and inner frames. Perhaps with this distinct composition Poussin expressed his knowledge of the psyche's own layers, which encompass foreground and surface, and background and the deepest depths. The faculty of introspective self-reflection is implied, a capacity that characterizes the sanguine personality to a high degree.

6.2.3. The Meaning of Myth and the Muse

On the left-hand side of the canvas, the painting within the painting depicts a muse. She faces a pair of arms that reach into the frame, apparently ready to enfold her in a loving embrace. Her typically Greek facial contours may well reflect Poussin's inspiration by antiquity. Functioning like a meta-level of his soul, the mythology of this time transcended and widened his ego perspective with symbolic material. Earlier we noted a similar function for van Gogh, where the Japanese woodcut mediated an exotic and transcendent "other," thus expanding and enriching his Occidental view and imagination. The specifically *mythological* imagination, however, characterizes the creative perspective of the sanguine inclination. Sigmund Freund illustrates the point with his use of Greek myth to understand by analogy the decisive Oedipus complex. Indeed Freud called the entirety of his drive theory a mythology. The important mythical background principles were Eros and Thanatos, the drives toward life and death.

In the self-portrait, the lovely gesture of embrace alludes to Poussin's intimate dialogue with an inner muse. If we associate the outreaching arms with the artist's ego, then it can be said that they symbolize his active desire for his muse's inspiration. To move beyond the horizon of his own thoughts, he welcomes her soulful insight and outlook. As much as the self-sovereign artist and his painterly abilities dominate the foreground, Poussin portrays himself as well to be reliant on the gifts of a stimulating background soul. With this he suggests the interplay of a masculine mastery of reason, order, and technical design—and a feminine counterpart that transmits a wealth of fascinating ideas and images drawn from the wellspring of the unconscious. The creative potency of the sanguine approach is marked especially by this kind of dialogue between form and content, between artistic or linguistic brilliance and inspired imagination. Again, Sigmund Freud is an outstanding example.

6.2.4. The Sketch and the Final Work

In the painting Poussin's right hand rests on the upper edge of a sketchbook. Yet the portrait as whole emanates the accomplished artist posing before his achieved works and declaring his definitive artistic identity. And yet again, speaking both literally and figuratively, Poussin's sketchbook suggests the existence of germinal ideas and works-in-progress. The sanguine character typically carries both aspects, bearing the tension of child-like beginnings and adult maturity. Other painters of this bent represent themselves similarly in their self-portraits, depicting an intriguing juxtaposition of sketchy gestalts and adult ideals. It is this kind of creative mind that thinks in developmental categories, proceeding from adult conditions of maturity or ripeness to uncover undeveloped or developing forms. A good example of this quality of understanding lies in Freud's ideas about the sexual development of the child.

Our consideration should go to one last pictorial element, a motif that may be difficult to decipher but nevertheless holds significant meaning. It is part of the red brocade-like fabric appearing directly at Poussin's back. The brocade incorporates the image of a strong, lush tree emerging from the background silhouette of another tree. Imaginably, this is Poussin's symbolic tribute to nature as the background and primary ground of his oeuvre. In his view, untouched nature was the highest expression of human self-realization. Original nature, which his paintings represent so idealistically, reflected for him the essential nature of humanity itself, its origin, and its goal. In this image of the tree, Poussin might point symbolically to the individual's natural developmental potential—or to the natural way for each individual to develop, like a flourishing tree. Poussin's underlying philosophy and prerequisite for his self-understanding as a creative artist was deeply embedded in his respect for nature. For him, nature was no stranger but his familiar guide to self-recognition and development. He was very much characterized by his relationship to objective nature and to individual reality, which, by analogy to the lush tree, he saw as holding the capacity for developing consciousness. His stance as such characterizes generally the sanguine constitution and view of things, which we have recognized several times in Freud's maxim, "Where it was, I shall become."

6.3. The Phlegmatic Mode in Paul Gauguin's The Artist with the Yellow Christ

(Fig. 19): Paul Gauguin, *Portrait of the Artist with the Yellow Christ*

Paul Gauguin's famous self-portrait, *The Artist with the Yellow Christ* of 1890 (Fig. 19), serves as the basis for our exploration of a phlegmatic artistic existence.

6.3.1. Natural Authenticity, Visceral Presence
Gauguin's very close, authentic, and visceral corporeal presence comes across in his self-portrait in a number of ways: in the palpable

quality of his skin; in his simple pullover and shirt; and in the bearing of his head, such that it almost merges with the silhouette of his rounded shoulders and compact body. Together with his alert eyes, the gestalt on the whole suggests a natural, experiential way of thinking and it furthers the onlooker's impression of the painter's imminent proximity and bodily presence.

The highly tactile quality of the portrait is enhanced by Gauguin's pasty application of color within distinctly defined fields, a technique that characterizes his Cloisonnist painting style. His colored surfaces appeal to the onlooker's sense of touch and exert an immediately touching effect. What Gauguin conveys here is the phlegmatic's essential being-in-and-with-the-world through the sense of touch and the other bodily senses. In his eventful life Gauguin searched continuously for this primal quality of sensuousness and discovered it in particular places, landscapes, and people, for example, in Port-Aven in Brittany, and in Tahiti and other islands of the South Seas.

6.3.2. The Art Work and the Depths

The portrait background incorporates two of Gauguin's earlier works. One portrays his famous painting, The Yellow Christ (1889). The other pictures an anthropomorphic container, in reality one of Gauguin's several earthenware or ceramic pots that were inspired by a pre-Columbian face urn encountered in Peru. With the two large parallel images forming the entire background, Gauguin refers to his double occupation as painter and sculptor, and he moreover identifies himself fundamentally as a creator and a working artist. Quite evidently, just as important to him as his self-representation are the things he produces with his own hands. Here Gauguin defines himself essentially as a creative individual, not just as someone with a more or less coincidental biography. For with the background images he places himself in the midst of the collective Christian myth and an imagined primeval pagan world, suggesting his awareness of his grounding in mythological depths. He reveals, as it were, deeper layers of his consciousness.

It is in fact the case that phlegmatic creativity typically involves an awareness of the ego's fundament in a collective mythological reality. Another representative of this inclination is C.G. Jung, with his sensuous work on the *Red Book* and his later theory of the archetypes and discovery of the collective unconscious. Illustrating here with Jung, I of course do not intend the colloquial and erroneous understanding of the phlegmatic as the sluggish brooder, for in reality Jung as well as Gauguin possessed extraordinary energy and vibrancy.

Jung's own phlegmatic tendency comes across generally in his research and thinking, where his primary interest and creative curiosity are directed toward archetypal backgrounds, collective structures, mythological contents, ethnological factors, and the original great shapers of spiritual reality such as religion, philosophy, art, and alchemy. Also in a characteristically phlegmatic spirit, Jung attends equally to symbols and symbolic expression in general—for instance, where he encourages painting, sculpting, and dancing as activities that further the direct sensuous experience of unconscious dimensions of the psyche. From his standpoint, the especially significant question is that of the therapeutic effect of working along such lines. Whatever works, what ever is effective, is psychologically real. A typically phlegmatic existence and creative approach are embodied in Jung's aim to uncover archetypal layers of the psyche and their concrete manifestations, and to weigh the criteria of effect and effectiveness.

My reference to other examples, such as that of Jung, assumes fundamentally the determinative influence of the four temperamental types. Which is to say, the temperaments take shape in psychologists, scientists, philosophers, artists, and all other individuals, regardless of their field of engagement. And a particular temperamental predisposition configures one's main interests and creative way of seeing and exploring them. In other words, I take for granted that the individual's creative perspective is pre-conditioned by an innate temperament that antecedes consciousness.

6.3.3. Proximity to the Archaic Source

Let us now return to Gauguin's self-portrait and its portrayal of the pot fashioned after a Peruvian pre-Colombian urn. Now, in reality, Gauguin was especially proud of his own Peruvian origin, given by his Peruvian mother and his early childhood in Peru. However, the image of the archaic pot does far more than denote this family background and Gauguin's sculptural work.

Viewed symbolically, a pot is a maternal container. More specifically, it symbolically mediates the mysterious aspect of the Great Mother as the night and dark source—the uterus, as it were—

from which unfathomable things emerge and manifest themselves as present and visible realities. In this sense, the pot could stand as a symbol of the mystery of creativity *per se*. Accordingly, in its primitive gestalt Gauguin's pot alludes to the age-old wisdom that new creative forms emerge *ex nihilo*, undergirded by elemental, archaic imaginings and archetypal ideas.

It is after all characteristic of the creative force to manifest itself suddenly, wondrously, like a living partner who reveals and asserts from the darkness of indefinite potentiality a visible form or idea. In the case of Gauguin's pot, the realized inner vision even has a human face. It conveys very well the sense of a mysterious creative partner that wanted to be visibly revealed, seen, and accepted. On close examination, we see that the pot has also a hand, complete with a thumb and four fingers. It can be understood symbolically as the hand of the creative force itself. Or, said slightly differently, it could be the Great Mother's hand, which holds and bestows the primary impulse to create and the faculty to bring forth artistic form and reality.

In summary, the pot with its Pre-Colombian design symbolizes Gauguin's underlying experience of the primal creative force, its enduring original source, and its fount of ideas and creative impulses that spontaneously seek artistic realization. The experience as such corresponds with the phlegmatic mode of existence and its characteristic creative embrace of archaic and archetypal energies.

6.3.4. Experienceable Transcendence

With the background image of *The Yellow Christ*, Gauguin might signal the great artistic significance of his original painting and also his personal, felt link to the portrayed motif. The latter proposition is strengthened by the fact that there is some correspondence between the Christ figure's facial features and Gauguin's own.

The Yellow Christ is an unconventional portrayal of the Calvary crucifixion scene. The bright yellow tone of the Christ figure at the moment of death anticipates the hopeful event of the resurrection on Easter day. Two remarkable green surfaces on Christ's breast herald new life and growth. The orange-toned cross, almost seeming to lift up the crucified body, conveys the impression of a mighty tree of life and vital energy. The Breton landscape setting with its orange bushes and green trees expands the joyful atmosphere. Evoking the sense of a nearly peaceful scene in the light of high noon, the image as a whole emanates the paradoxes of death and resurrection, death and new life, death in the midst of life, and death as both an end and a beginning.

Gauguin's choice of *The Yellow Christ* as a background motif testifies to his valuing of the paradoxical archetype of crucifixion and resurrection. Indeed the archetype manifested itself pronouncedly during his life, when he many times bore the cross of hopelessness and despair that gave way to his great new works. He resurrected from crucifying life circumstances with ingenious creative accomplishments. It is as if some life force had intentionally summoned existential crises in such guises as financial crisis, illness, alcoholism, separation from his wife and children, his daughter's death, his own attempted suicide, and unrest and uncertainty with respect to the location of his home and workplace. And just as much summoned on the other side, paradoxically, was his creation of unique artistic works.

Gauguin's itinerant life is marked to an excessive degree by the reciprocal relationship of destructiveness and creative ingenuity, yet it manifests fundamentally a general mode of creative existence. It naturally entails recurring encounters with the paradoxical archetype of crucifixion—that is, one spiritual death after another followed by geneses or new beginnings and experienceable transcendence. It is phlegmatic creativity that is most characterized by co-existing death and resurrection, or by processes of transformation in which personal suffering resolves with the creation of universally valid works. And it is in phlegmatic individuals especially that the bi-polar creative force and transformational process resonates as immediate and vivid sensuous experience.

6.4. The Melancholic Mode in Edvard Munch's Self-Portrait: Between the Clock and the Bed

In his self-portrait (Fig. 20) Edvard Munch (1863 - 1944) stands in a room, surrounded by pieces of furniture and other objects, including a number of pictures hanging on the walls of a background room. The staging as such seems to relativize the artist, making of him one among many other objects. The other way around, his presence expands, as it were, on the stage of a larger reality.

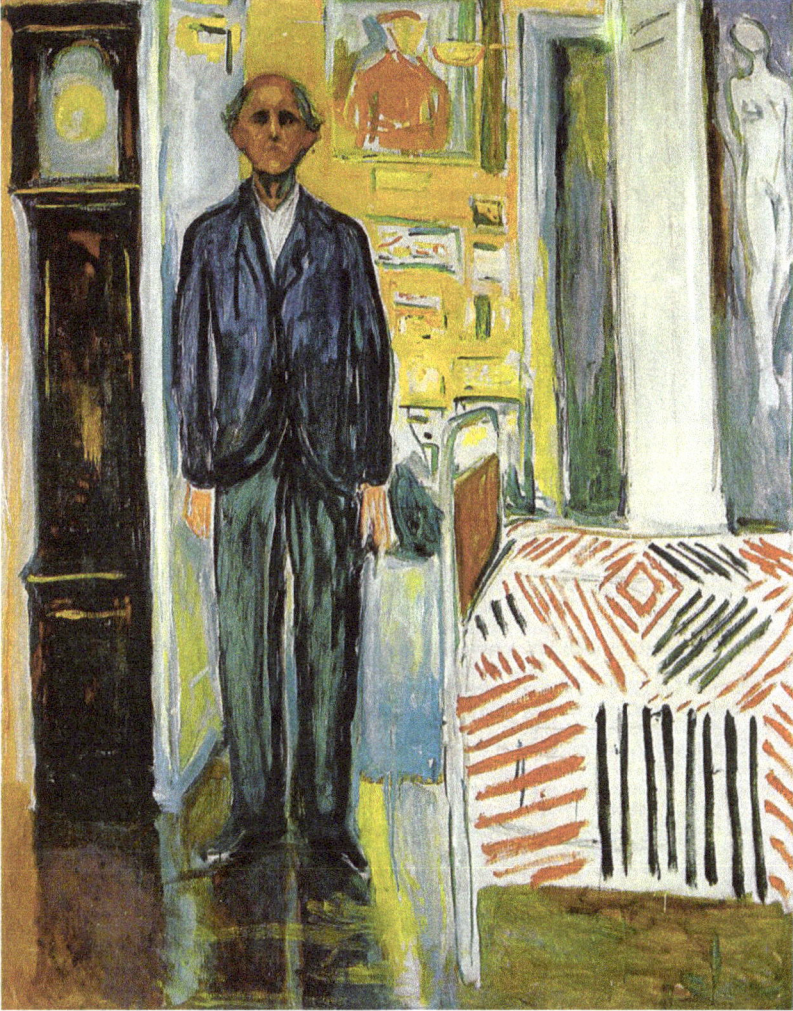

(Fig. 20): Edvard Munch, *Self-Portrait: Between the Clock and the Bed*

6.4.1. The Gaunt Introspective Gestalt

With his gaunt body, asymmetrically drooping shoulders, dangling hands, and slightly bowed legs, Munch comes across as a rather awkward misplaced figure. Yet his facial expression emanates the aura of a deliberating person, someone who is full of life experience and wisdom. His figure on the whole conjures up a Don Quixote, the image of an introspective individual who is led by ideals, by often unrealistic but also true principles. Munch's self-portrait in this sense well represents a melancholic/schizoid perception of the world and creative approach to it.

6.4.2 Depressive Character, Bright Background

The deep blue and green hues of Munch's suit recall the nocturnal melancholic scenes that often characterize his paintings. The dark tones here, along with his generally disheveled look, evoke Munch's lifelong experiences of depression, illness, death, and loss. Indeed, his suit, contoured as it is with thick black lines, resembles a constraining straightjacket and suggests the loss of freedom caused by depression. This impression is strengthened by a perhaps unintended and yet telling small detail on Munch's right, where the contour lines of his jacket converge at the sleeve cuff and jacket hem. At this converging point, a black line seems to cut off his right hand—or seen another way, his hand seems to be held in a lasso noose. We might understand this detail as a further expression of a dark and laming depressive energy that crimps the artist's ability to handle and deal with things. However, behind the dark self-representation there is a light-drenched yellow room, where some ten pictures hang on the wall. The background as such symbolizes Munch's store of vital energy and wealth of ideas, in short, the rich imagination that stood to oppose his depressive loss of creative fantasy.

In such contrasting aspects, the portrait alludes to the bi-polar moods that determined Munch's life. Melancholy and joy came hand-in-hand. But speaking archetypally, we might recognize the dynamic interplay of the elder and the child, the senex and the puer. The opposing poles represent on one hand the capacity for sober reason, which is oriented toward reality, fact, temperance, and limits—and on the other hand, the faculty of emphatically enthused imagination, which explores and creates without bounds. In Munch's self-portrait the senex comes across in the artist's elderly gestalt, while the puer appears in the background portrait of a young man. Lacking sharp contour lines, his figure suggests fluid potentiality, an essential condition of being-in-formation. Likewise the vital and stimulating orange hue of his shirt directly opposes the subdued dark blue of the elderly man's suit. The contrasting colors themselves emanate the senex/puer dichotomy—age versus youth; restraint versus activity; reflection and soberness versus impulsivity and expansive potentiality.

Beyond expressing Munch's bi-polar condition, this self-portrait can be viewed as a portrayal of attitudes and moods that belong fundamentally to creative work and that belong all the more to the existence of the creative melancholic. Melancholic individuals in particular experience the inner conflict of the senex and puer, with their opposing principles of order and tempered design on the one side, and on the other side, unbounded imagination and expression.[84]

6.4.3. Origin of Creativity in the Antagonistic Unconscious

In the right-hand foreground of the self-portrait we see a simple bed draped with a red and white striped cover. Munch's awareness of the symbolic potential is evident in the painting's title, *Between the Clock and the Bed*. His concern was to portray not only an accurate scene of his bedroom with its incidental furnishings, but also, to convey symbolically a more essential message.

Setting his own figure at the foot of the bed, Munch envisions himself in a space where the upright world of the ego, conscious, awake, and commanding—surrenders to the horizontal and passive world of sleep, dream, unconsciousness, and unbridled fantasy. The bed in this sense symbolizes immersion in the depths where images supersede the dominance of thought, where undercurrents of yearning and anxiety come to the surface, and where disturbing intuitions materialize as visible gestalts. As implied in so many of Munch's titles, his lifelong artistic work drew largely on this phantasmagoric nocturnal world, the realm of the unconscious, which harbors passion, illness, angst, and other sufferings. To name but a few examples: *The Sick Child* (1886); *Melancholy* (1891); *The Scream* (1893); *Anxiety* (1894); *Jealousy* (1895); *Vampire* (1895); *Death in the Sickroom* (1895); *Madonna* (1895); *The Separation* (1896); *Kiss* (1897); *Child and Death* (1899); *Golgotha* (1900); *Self-Portrait in Hell* (1903); and *Crying Nude* (1907).

The bed cover, with its pattern of red and white stripes, seems to convey the basic opposites of the positive and negative, the affirming and negating. Considering other aspects of the color symbolism, red can stand for emotion, activity, vitality, and love—and black for distance, passivity, limitation, and death. The juxtaposed colors here suggest the conflicting impulses in the unconscious between an animating tendency and a distance-making one, or between the constructive and deconstructive effects of the unconscious in Freud's sense of opposition between Eros and Thanatos.

This basic pair of opposites takes shape again in the right-hand corner of the bedroom, just above the bed. Here we notice first a cropped off picture of a female nude. Emerging from a moonlight blue background, this feminine figure is a poignant embodiment of a boundlessly inspiring anima. To the left of this figure we see the undefined empty space formed by the doorframe. There is a door between these two areas, between the anima figure and the framed emptiness. It is not entirely clear where the door is hinged or anchored and how it functions. It suggests, nevertheless, an oscillation between two situations: that of an animating fantasy, which is represented by the feminine figure and that of a limited emptiness or withdrawal into a formless nothingness.

Thus far with its imagized polarities, the bedroom can be imagined to symbolize the dual unconscious as the point of origin of Munch's creativity. But again considered more broadly, the imagery can just as much symbolize in general the origin of the melancholic's creative existence. The melancholic's creativity essentially and painfully involves being subject to alternating impulses of the unconscious—its stimulation of creative activity, and opposing this, its creation of creative block, which itself arises from the natural tendency toward limits, abstraction, and negation. Creative individuals with a fundamentally melancholic/schizoid temperament find themselves to an especially large degree torn between phases of fruitful inspiration and unbearable sterility.

6.4.4. Chronological and Creative Time

Munch's self-portrait is highly characterized by "moments" of opposition. We have noted them among other ways in the senex/ puer dichotomy. The senex, we recall, is personified in Munch's own figure and represents the reality-oriented, shape-giving, limiting, and negating mind. Opposing this attitude the puer, pictured in the background portrait of a young man, stands for the urge to expansive, intuitive play in the world of sheer potentiality. We noted similar opposition between the daytime or ego consciousness embodied in the figure of the artist, and the nocturnal consciousness associated with the bed. The bed cover, also associated with nocturnal consciousness, evokes with its decorative pattern the sense of opposing tendencies in the unconscious: The red stripes point to an uplifting Eros—and the black stripes, contrarily, to a negating Thanatos. We mentioned as well a lively, anima-inspired imagination that can become blocked by the arbitrary reign of depressed emptiness. I noted that while such polarities characterized Munch's life and work to an extraordinary degree, they just as much characterize generally the melancholic/schizoid mode of experience and expression as such.

The motif of the longcase clock alludes to the same basic polarities, taking shape now in the realm of time: The clock symbolizes the passing and forward march of time, time enduring, time running out, and time coming to an end—and, just as much, it symbolizes timelessness in the present and timely force of creation. The latter is creative time, experienced not within the ordinary linear continuum, but as the fructifying moment of original creation, when something new is begotten. As the clock dial on Munch's clock displays no hands to mark the time, and no numbers to designate the hours, it does not make visible the on-going progression of time. Instead, the color of the dial, an egg-yolk yellow, evokes the idea of the ovum and the moment of fertilization, the instant when new life is conceived. Indeed, as this dial emerges from a virginal, sea-blue background, it is as if Munch's clock most essentially would mark the unique here-and-now-time when something new is born out of an original ocean of possibilities and premonitions. The clock dial, in other words, provides less an image of chronological time, but far more, an image of creative time.

This is the time of ever-recurring creativity, not the time that measures the duration and passing away of creative impulses and achievements. Creative time battles against chronological time, which threatens to devour all being in the name of incessant creative production. It was thanks to his impulse to create *ex nihilo* that Munch broke through the brutal aspect of objective time with its unrelenting threats of aging, demise, and oblivion. Thus, Munch countered the force of death with his spontaneous creation of new works and his recurring experiences of becoming; he opposed the gnawing force of objective and quantitative time with the subjective and qualitative experience of the present and timely force of creation. Individuals of the melancholic type in general experience intensely the urge to survive the pressure of time with creative activity. Another example is Pablo Picasso, who is well known to have worked until his death, producing one painting after another as if possessed to do it. In this way he resisted the impact of elapsing time and the process of aging.

Now, a closer look at Munch's longcase clock reveals its expression of further time-related pairs of opposites. This clock is quite evidently portrayed to be an old one, perhaps of heirloom quality, constructed of time-resistant wood. Yet the clock dial augurs the future, or the zero hour, the hour of new beginnings. The case has a rectangular structure with clearly defined fixed parts but the arch above the clock dial suggests a gateway and openness to things that are yet to come. The front of the case, depicted in dark wood, echoes a coffin and endings of things, but the clock dial rendered in a spring-like yellow offsets the portended ends with a premonition of the future. So we discern here the contrasts of the old and the new, the past and the future, ends and beginnings—all of which bring to mind and suggest an unfolding of creative imagination from the old, the dead and the end, which is so typical for the melancholic.

Munch's clock shows that astonishing creative beginnings can bloom within old casings or past time frames. The past provides fertile ground for the creative impulse. The new takes shape from the old; future possibilities are discovered in bygone things; new seeds are found in the traces of history. So, too, a creative point of departure can be found in finite or time-limited existence as it is suggested in the slim, coffin-like clock case front, with its pronounced cross lines. This reality appears in other of Munch's works, in particular those that thematize illness and death: *Death in the Sickroom* (1893); *Death and the Child* (1899); *The Death of Marat* (1906-07); *The Death of the Bohemian* (1915-17); and *The Sick Child* (1925). In the same vein, Munch often produced new versions of previous works, for instance, *Two Human Beings (The Lonely Ones)* (1892); *Vampire* (1893); *Madonna* (1895); *The Sick Child* (1896); and *The Scream* (1910). It is indeed generally characteristic of the melancholic to draw on earlier phases of his or her creative process, to take creative impulse from the themes of death and mortality, and to be nurtured by the certainty of life's transience and end.

In still another way Munch's clock alludes to opposing time dimensions. Whereas the clock case front is dark, its right-hand side is bright, with airy and cheerful color tones that call to mind the ideas of coming-to-being and growth. Time is thus not only identified with what has become but it also resonates with what is yet to be. The dark brown front, displaying the enclosed motionless pendulum, characterizes time in its aspect of an established, objective reality. But the bright right-hand panel, with its approximate contours and bright hues of white, light blue and green, and pale yellow, points to the potential emergence of new, imaginative ideas and forms. Factual time and imaginative time need not stand in irreconcilable opposition to one another, but rather—as suggested by Munch's clock case with these two different panels—they can work together constructively.

The interplay of the two sides is emphasized by the central, white vertical axis, the meeting line of the clock's front and right-hand panels. This axis, in its coloring and symbolic function, likens the door on the right hand side of the painting, in that it joins together two opposing meanings and holds them in reciprocal relationship to one another. The clock's front and side panels represent symbolically what we could call the objectively real, chronological dimension of time and creative time, the time of imagination. In its tri-partite vertical layering, the frontal clock casing symbolizes three aspects of chronological or linear time: the base alludes to the past; the middle part containing the pendulum stands for the present; and the clock face points to the future. Creative time is represented by the clock's lateral surface, with its fantasy-inviting colors. It is important to note again the connecting axis or hinge rendered in transparent shades of white, a color scheme that could symbolize a transcendent element that brings the two kinds of time into reciprocal relationship; this element would be a unifying thread of meaning.

The appearance of connecting meaning as a time-linked phenomenon is what Jung calls synchronicity. Synchronicity is, in other words, the experience of meaningful coincidence between events that take place in outer life, and/or between the events of outer life and inner life—such as dreams, thoughts, or some other conscious or unconscious contents. In such latter cases we speak of an autonomous meaning-making factor that aligns or synchronizes outer and inner life. The occurrence is experienced both as a moment in real objective time and also as the expression of the timeless and timely force of soul or creativity. Synchronistic phenomena manifest with great frequency in the lives of creative individuals. This fact shows the large extent to which these individuals are attuned to the very experiences and encounters that have the greatest bearing for their creative endeavors. Or seen slightly differently, it explains why their works express a particular Zeitgeist and cultural situation. A curious but meaningful correspondence occurs, whereby the creative individual's personal life events coincide with outer social circumstances.

In connection with the clock motif we can observe one last symbolically meaningful polarity: the one between the longcase clock and Munch's own figure. Both are set in remarkable parallel. Munch's right arm hangs parallel to the clock and with such striking proximity to it that it almost seems like the artist would be touching or even bound to the timepiece.

What meaning might we discover in this compositional element? There is on one hand the objective reality of time symbolized by the clock, and on the other hand the subjective reality of the individual embodied in Munch's figure. As different as the two realities are, the composition brings them into close relationship. The closeness of the two could point to the interconnectedness of collective Zeitgeist's history and the creative individual's intuitive knowledge. Or put a bit differently, the proximity here could symbolize an objective Zeitgeist mirroring, realizing, and developing itself in and through the creative individual. The melancholic mode characteristically involves the individual's keen awareness of the interdependence of creativity and time, and in particular, the mutual reliance between personal creative processes and timely happenings.

VII

CREATIVITY AND THE EXPERIENCE
OF TRANSCENDENCE

The creative person experiences being led by the power of the creative force itself. In other words, creativity is experienced not only as a willfully applied personal gift or ability, but also as an autonomous will *sui generis*, which radically reverses guiding relationships such that it is not the ego but a larger, ego transcending factor that has the say.

This larger influential factor delivers the themes that are to be processed. Just as much, it compels particular perspectives and designs that do not necessarily correspond with individual preferences and thinking or with public expectations and assumptions. It demands consistency and truthfulness toward the creative process and it punishes diversion and neglect with non-productivity and the loss of soul. It conveys the individual's consciousness of being involved in the emergent and continuously progressing creativity per se. Ultimately, this larger creative force imbues the creative individual with the basic certainty that it realizes and incarnates itself in his or her own creative activity and life.

In the parlance of C.G. Jung's analytical psychology, this transcendent force that knows, desires, demands, manifests, and incarnates itself, could be called the reality of the Self. In the experience of the creative individual, it is this Self that enters the scene as an autonomous force and generator of new insights and forms. The self-portraits of five different artists should help us to elucidate this aspect of the creative force.

7.1. Juan Miró: Self-Portrait

(Fig. 21): Joan Miró, *Self-Portrait*

Miró, known for his colorful, playful, and abstract surreal paintings, portrays himself in (Figure 21) in an unusually mysterious and metaphysical way. The cosmos, replete with the sun and stars, appears to be present in his face and body. It is as if the whole universe with its constellating energy would mirror or condense itself within the creative individual, Joan Miró.

In this portrait, Miró's sensory organs seem to connect him with the greater universe, so it is worth considering their symbolic meanings. His eyes, seer-like, emanate outward like heavenly bodies, and being also like burning points, they draw one in as well. The two directions, suggested in the ray-like eyelashes and the flaming pupils, symbolize respectively an outward and expansive cosmic view, and an inward view into the depths—both of which lead beyond the horizon of the ordinary ego. Described here is a will to metaphysical understanding, which itself belongs to creativity and which is not content with immediate and foreground aspects of things, but is interested in their wider connections and deeper grounds. Creative consciousness transcends the kind of perception that cleaves to surfaces and concreteness; rather, this consciousness investigates essentially the fundaments and the necessary connections of things. In this sense it is in the nature of creativity to be metaphysically oriented; it wants to get behind and beyond incidental singularities. It tends toward an ultimate ground and overall context.

Miró's remarkably protruding ears come across like cosmically attuned listening devices that detect, deal with, and internalize information with their snail-like whorls. The process taking place here is one that receives and filters timely things, things that are in the air. With these outstanding ears Miró attributes the creative individual with the ability to perceive within a given society and time the ego transcending realities of transpersonal events and to make them his or her own. The creative person is able, as if with special antennae, to register the time's superordinate dimensions, both as they manifested themselves in the past and as they present themselves in contemporary new form.

Likewise Miró's nose lends itself to symbolic interpretation. It stands for a special flair, a particular sensibility, an original instinct, for apprehending things that lie beneath the threshold of consciousness. It symbolizes an animal-like ability to sniff out subliminal, intuitively discernable realities. Thus we have another sensory organ marking an ability that exceeds the ordinary boundaries of perception and that describes the creative person's experience of the world, which transcends the ordinary, everyday perspective.

Miró's mouth with the curiously pursed lips appears to express the value of saying nothing over that of speaking. Rather than discussion with possible partners, what is suggested here is an inner dialogue with some mysterious depth. With such inward-turning, the deeper grounds of being come to discussion, just as with the mystic's silence. Insofar as the mouth contains the tongue, the taste organ, it suggests as well the spiritual striving to savor things inwardly.

Miró's reddish necktie could stand in place of his hands as a marker of the sense of touch. It is the sense of touch, or the skin, that conveys immediate bodily contact. Miró's necktie, representing the sense of touch, likens the other sensory organs portrayed here in that it displays the symbol of the star. The star motif could thus contain the thought that each sensory organ can be experienced as the agent of a higher mode of perception. This means that the sensory organs function not only to perceive the surface of things but also to apprehend the more fundamental aspects of being. With this idea, Miró describes both the personal background of his abstract surrealist approach to art, and also a general and essential pattern of creativity.

The pattern is characterized by the knowledge that the creative force is an all-encompassing reality, which creates everything that has existed, which manifests itself in the work of the creative individual, and which imbues the creative individual with the potential to transcend his or her limited perceptual horizon in favor of a more encompassing one that extends beyond existing things and toward things that are yet to be created.

7.2. Marc Chagall: Self-Portrait with Seven Fingers

In (Fig. 22), we see Marc Chagall's very first self-portrait, a painting that emerged shortly after his initial arrival in Paris (1912-13), and that clearly displays the Cubist influence he discovered there. He depicts his own body in flat primary shapes that join to form a complete figure. But despite this analytical reduction of the organic body—and despite the added poetic and fanciful elements—the painting allows our unmistakable recognition of Chagall's personality.

Indeed, the dissociated Cubist style conveys so to speak a higher status. Like the previously discussed painting by Joan Miró, Chagall's

(Fig. 22): Marc Chagall, *Self-Portrait with Seven Fingers*

self-portrait transcends a factual rendition of the artist's body. In Miró's portrait, we observed the five sensory organs to be metaphorical expressions of the creative individual's widened and deepened view of the world, and his or her work in service of the creative force of the world as such. In Chagall's dissociated and yet still recognizable self-image, the artist is elevated to the level of his essential meaning, which is that of a mana personality. The painting manifests Chagall's consciousness of a creative force that comes to expression in his artistic activity and that exceeds his own ego. It shows both his self-understanding and his experience of a superordinate creative power *par excellence*, incarnating itself in his life and work through his artistic skills and biographic conditions.

Chagall stages himself here within two worlds that provided the nurturing grounds for his artistic life and creative exchange, namely Russia and Paris, as can be read in Hebrew at the very top of the painting. The image depicted within, propped on an easel on the right-hand side, reproduces his work of 1911, *To Russia, to the Asses, and to Others*. In the upper left-hand corner we see a cropped view of his somewhat later painting, *Paris Through the Window* (1913). Besides these references to Russia and Paris, Chagall displays in the upper right-hand corner an image of Vitebsk, the ever vibrant and influential place of his birth.

Chagall's use of his own paintings to reference the great influences of Russia and Paris, and his portrayal of Vitebsk surrounded by a personal cloud of imagination, tell us that these places meant more to him than their factual existence. He seems to want to reveal how they appeared and formed themselves in his artistic experience and creative imagination. In other words, these biographically important places influenced Chagall's creativity with the images they engendered and called forth in him. His world was created by the images of these places and the amalgamated memories of them, which consisted of olfactory, visual, acoustic, tactile, and taste impressions. Or more radically: it was the imagery of these places that shaped Chagall's imaginative background and world. That is to say, the personal imagery of Russia, Paris, and Vitebsk expressed in Chagall's work, made of themselves specific reference points for his own creative imagination.

In Chagall's imagination, Russia becomes the land of wild fantasy, peasant authenticity, Dionysian irrationality, and the religious beyond. These elements appear in his self-portrait in the images of the headless milkmaid, the red ass with the human suckling, and the Orthodox Church building. Contrarily, Paris becomes the cipher for urbanity, "blue" rationality, technical achievement, progressing civilization, and upward movement—and these, as suggested in the background image: the blue pyramidal surfaces, the square building facades, the sky-diver (performing what was, at the time, a new sport), and the ascending Eiffel Tower.

If Russia and Paris represent places that were meaningful in Chagall's personal biography, might we come to understand the implicit opposites also in a more general way? Might we see them as a pair that determines other creative individuals' experience of creativity? Might this opposition be held generally as one of the typical conditions and manifestations of the creative force?

Chagall's self-portrait visualizes a basic polarity consisting of two opposing experiences or notions of the world. There is on one hand an original background world located in natural surroundings, close to the earth. As a world of origins, it awakens nostalgic feelings of belonging to a nation, to a community, to a tradition, and to a belief system—and all of this, accompanied by the idea of happy originating circumstances. It is an image of a maternally containing, archaic home occupying an earthly horizon and anchored in an unquestioned world of given values.

The former pole, standing for a priori origins and a basic home, is opposed by another one that stands for a new vivifying era and a changing, transforming world. This opposite pole involves openness to the new, an affirmation of technological advancement, and an optimistic alignment with revolutionary utopian visions and new goals for humanity. It is about a modern and critically challenging paternal reason, and a vertical upward movement toward the heights.

Creative consciousness contains both poles: the one oriented to the past, a regressive one, so to speak—and the other, a future-oriented, progressive one. The contents of each pole vary according to the individual. The polarity marked by Chagall's "Russia" and "Paris" appears differently in other artists' works. Yet it always boils down to the same basic pair of opposites: the archaic world versus the modern one; origins versus what is to come; present existence versus change; tradition versus the future.

Creativity plays decisively between these two antithetical poles, taking its energy from the tension between them, and opposing both in that it says "yes" to each. It admits the demands of both sides, although they contradict one another. It floats the contradictions, allowing something new to evolve. In this sense creativity is the transformative power that both conserves and changes old forms, aiming to discover within them something new.

Let us now return to Chagall's self-portrait (Fig. 22). His visions of Russia and Paris establish the two polarized imaginative worlds upon which creative work rests. But he does not decide between the two. Far more, he admits and recognizes the value of each of them, as creativity lives from the tension between the two.

The creative force chooses motifs that stem from personal history, as in the case of Chagall's portrayal of Russia. But it also orients to the present time, as shown so well in the influence of Parisian Cubism on Chagall's work. The creative spirit is drawn to origins and at the same time it searches for new gestalts. It relies on the natural, concrete appearance of things, on their sensuous surfaces, but it senses equally the necessity to simplify and abstract them. Ultimately it combines an empirical and a speculative attitude: it starts from empirically observable facts and existing experience and points at new ideas and possibilities of design.

Creative activity plays out in between these polarities of the old and the new, the primeval and the modern, the concrete and the abstract, the empirical and the speculative. We could consider such dichotomies to form the opposition between a primary and secondary dimension. Or, as we have done with Chagall's self-portrait, we could conceive this opposition as an energetic polarity between a regressive backward-looking tendency, and a progressive forward-reaching one.

The figure of the artist in Chagall's self-portrait clearly shows how these two aspects join to constitute a third element, namely, creative consciousness, which appears initially as a capacity to allow something new to emerge from the old, or to allow the old to emerge in a new form. Pointing in this direction is Chagall's use of the Cubist style, which transforms the natural body into a new artistic gestalt. The same inventive and transformative fantasy appears in the figure's wavy hair and coiling ringlets. It manifests as well in the green and white facial tones that symbolically allude to becoming and new beginnings.

Creative consciousness reveals itself further in the ability to connect the old and the new, to bring the past and the present into relationship with one another. It is evidenced as a creative Eros that values the old, lovingly receives the new, and allows the unknown to emerge. This dynamic is visible in the motif of Chagall's bow-tie, which, joining the right and left sides, joins also respectively the red pole associated with the emotionally toned past, and the white pole associated with the spirit of the future. In this paradigm the red pole corresponds with the red ass—and the white pole corresponds with the white Eiffel Tower. The emphasized twist of Chagall's bow-tie recalls a coupling device that links two sides and uses them to generate energy by rotational motion. The rose with a pair of spiraling leafy twigs adorning Chagall's lapel points to a similar symbolism, in particular, that of a connecting Eros.

Creative consciousness is further characterized by the ability to generate entirely new material from archaic or primary sources. This idea is pictured in Chagall's palette, itself placenta-shaped and displaying many circular and triangle-shaped dabs of color. The artist's right hand with the five fingers, holding both the palette and five brushes, symbolizes according to the physical meaning of the number five the practical act of transforming primary materials and imagined ideas into a concrete new work.

Creative consciousness reveals itself also in the ability to internalize the past and allow it to gain a new lease of life in contemporary gestalts. It is the capacity to vitalize, update, and refresh archetypal experience, be it collective or personal. This gift appears to be symbolized in the image that lends Chagall's self-portrait its title, the seven-fingered left hand. In the Jewish tradition, to do something "with seven fingers" is to do it with special care and religious devotion. We think as well of the seven days of creation. The number seven was especially important to Chagall in that he was born in 1877 on the seventh day of the seventh month of the year. Putting these elements of meaning together, we could say that Chagall's seven-fingered hand expresses his own meticulous treatment, personalization, and recreation of a collective stock of traditional ideas and images.

Ultimately a creative consciousness amounts to the intriguing ability to give rise to a great fantasy, a new piece of art, or a creative idea, stemming from an individual's actually limited reality. Such bringing-forth is expressed symbolically in Chagall's portrayal of his own right leg, which appears to function like a lever that heaves something into being. Here he sets into being what the easel and the painting of Russia suggest: the realm of art, designed fantasy, and symbolic reality.

In this image of Chagall's, the artist—or more generally the creative person—is portrayed as the vehicle of a greater creative force that instigates transformation, connection, renewal, enlivening and creation. In this sense Chagall portrays an organ or function of a transcendent creative reality. This reality is transcendent insofar as it surpasses that which exists, and introduces something new, and insofar as it creates higher, soulful, or artistically sublime meaning.

Chagall's portrait describes the great individual who stands in service of this creative, transcendent power. A closer look leads us to see in Chagall the typological differentiation according to the four temperaments that we discussed in Chapter 5, "The Creative Individual." The round head with the fanciful locks of hair, the visionary eyes, and the intuitive nose all point to the visionary sense and the openness to the surprisingly new that typify the choleric character. The sanguine character is expressed in the bow-tie that joins the two jacket sides, and in the rose, both of which stand for the binding element of Eros. The phlegmatic character comes across in the palette of colors held by the one firm hand, an image which evokes the impression of emotional sensitivity joined with energetic pragmatism and the ability to draw on a wealth of fundamental ideas and energies. The melancholic type takes shape in the hand with seven fingers that respectfully wants to capture and internalize the image on the canvas propped on the easel.

In Chapter 5 we discussed several paintings, saying that in each one of them, one of the four depicted individuals personifies one of the four temperaments and patterns through which the creative force expresses itself. In the chapter at hand, we have seen how the same four temperaments and patterns can express themselves and function organically as parts of a whole in one person. As they take shape in this way, we can say that, as little as the body can be separated from its parts, so little can the four temperaments be separated from the one individual. Thus in one person, the choleric bent is represented by the head, the sanguine by the heart, the phlegmatic by the belly, and the melancholic by the hand. The interplay of these four creative functions within one person characterizes the individual as the bodily location and realization of the fourfold creative force of transcendence. The creative force as such thus becomes effective and visible in such an individual. It is the great creative individual in whom the creative force finds a container and realizes its mysterious aims.

7.3. Paula Modersohn-Becker: Self-Portrait with Amber Necklace

Figure 23 is a self-portrait by the German expressionist painter Paula Modersohn-Becker, who lived from 1876-1907. The painting was completed in 1906, one year before her premature death. With a first glance of the plain and yet moving image, we might notice the qualities of roundness and centeredness. An impression of an

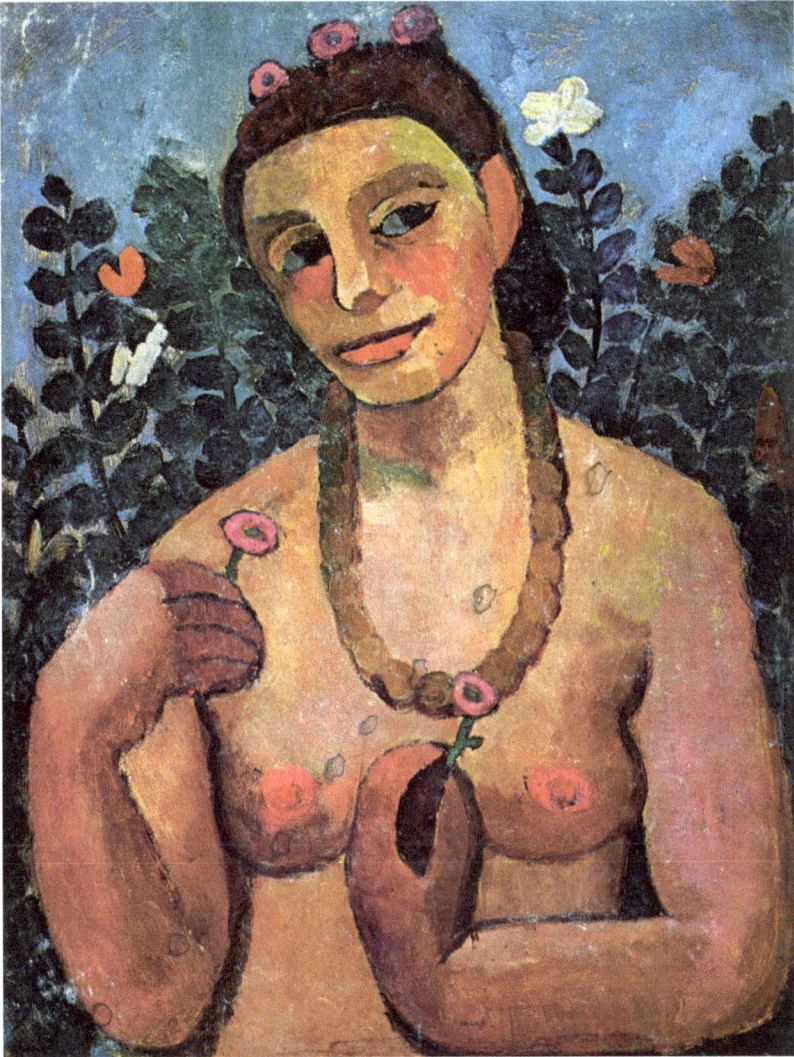

(Fig. 23): Paula Modersohn-Becker, *Self-Portrait with Amber Necklace*

encircling totality is conveyed in the artist's curved shoulders and round necklace. Her arms, rather than reaching out, seem poised in a self-embrace or a gathering-into her own center. All of this points to the phlegmatic experience of an all-encompassing containment in personal and bodily being.

Nature's strong presence in this portrait takes shape in the artist's unabashed nakedness, in the flowers in her hands and hair, and in the dense backdrop of flowering branches. It would appear to be the self-portrait of an artist who experiences nature intimately and feels contained in its cycles.[85]

However, our first impression alters with a second glance, when the warm, thirty-year-old artist appears in stark contrast to the dark background foliage springing forth ominously from an evening sky. The questions arise: Do the two white blossoms in the background suggest a cemetery decoration—or do the pink blossoms in the artist's hands and hair hint of marriage nuptials? We begin to discern strains of the motifs of "the maiden and death," death and resurrection, youth and mortality. The artist's large eyes with deep, dark pupils express yearning and sad wanderlust. Likewise in her slightly tilted head we sense a floating melancholy, or mixed expectation, hope, and surrender.

The portrait, suggesting the artist's proximity to nature and echoing the motifs of death and resurrection, calls to mind Persephone, the archetypal figure of Greek myth. This daughter of the goddess Demeter was picking flowers in a meadow when Hades, Lord of the Underworld abducted her. Thereafter Persephone was destined to spend one third of each year in the Underworld, where, by the Orphic account, she always wore a crown of poppies. She spent the rest of each year on earth, when nature again came into full bloom.

In the self-portrait a trace of Persephone's emblematic pomegranate could appear in what seems to be a flower bulb or rhizome cupped in the artist's left hand. The pomegranate, associated with the mythical Underworld, and also the rhizome, point to a nourishing substrate of the earth. From this substrate arises new life, here depicted as a pink blossom, bearing the color of a new day's dawning. Such gestalts allude symbolically to a new sense of self-emerging from a dark depressive mood. Born out of experienced ineptitude, awakening feelings of self-esteem can be gathered like the beads on the artist's amber necklace. As moments or pearls of serendipity, they add to the valuable experiences that build up the sense of continuity and confidence in life as whole.

As the portrayed artist appears to display the blossom in her elevated right hand, Modersohn-Becker might be showing us the nature of her own creative process, at least insofar as it brings forth and artistically depicts new life. Perhaps, too, this blossom is meant to be added to the crown of flowers resting in the artist's hair. If this is the case, then these flowers would symbolically contribute to the artist's transcendent status, that is, her being as an individual who is crowned or attributed with enduring significance and who holds the charisma of a special calling.

Modersohn-Becker's self-portrait points to two parallel strands of development: a personal meaning-making and individuation process, expressed symbolically by her amber necklace—and a transpersonal work process, symbolized by her crown of flowers. It is worth noting, by the way, that the necklace consists of about thirty beads: some twenty-three visible ones and an estimated seven that would be hidden, completing the circle at the back. The number thirty would appear again if we would allow each of the three "crown" flowers to stand for ten years. Paula Modersohn-Becker painted this portrait at the age of thirty, in the year before she died from an embolism following the birth of her passionately desired first child. The renowned researcher Susan Bach, in her seminal book, *Life Paints its Own Span: On the Significance of Spontaneous Pictures by Severely Ill Children*, evidenced the fact that paintings can express a painter's inner or unconscious knowledge of his or her remaining life span.[86] Accordingly, it is well possible that while painting this moving self-portrait, Paula Modersohn-Becker somehow intuited that she had little more than one year of life to live.

Can this portrait tell us something more about the basic experience of the creative force? What specific dimensions of creativity might the painting express? It perhaps symbolizes the creative individual's experience of creativity as a superordinate force of nature, which manifests itself with typical properties and processes. Five such properties can be pinned down here:

There is first the natural phenomenon of *things and beings coming-to-being and dying away in the course of time*, expressing miraculous beginnings and inescapable ends. Nothing remains forever. Everything is in flux, pivoting on birth and death. Nature intends dissolution and decay, but also creation and new life. This ambivalent trend is reflected where Modersohn-Becker illuminates nature's two sides, with the flourishing and eerie plants in the background. It shows as well in her depiction of the youthful body and the dark eyes, reminiscent of the Persephone motif with its resonances of dying and becoming. The creative individual experiences this cyclic aspect of nature in the unexplainable emergence and disappearance of motifs and interests— and more so, perhaps, in the ebb and flow of creative potency in the course of a lifetime.

Secondly, there is the characteristic phenomenon of nature *whereby all forms of life develop in a step-wise manner*. Nothing manifests itself from the start in its final gestalt all at once, *en bloc*. There is always a history. Everything harbors nature's aim of developing and ripening, blossoming or bearing fruit, or living on in new ways. This reality is expressed in Modersohn-Becker's backdrop of lush vegetation yielding four blossoms. Creative individuals realize it concretely in the natural, phasic development of their works. This includes the natural progression from a dazzling idea, to the gestation of thought, to the initial experiments with drafts and variations, and to fruition in the form of a final work.

Thirdly, *nature creates organisms equipped with unique bodies, instincts, and senses*. It is part of nature's design to ensure that bodily beings are capable of surviving in particular environments and preserving their species. Modersohn-Becker illuminates this decisive meaning in the image of her right hand, which points toward and emphasizes the body and its significance. It is as if this hand's touch would conjure up the blossom, or would allow a creative reality to come to being. This natural aspect of the body comes to bear in the sensuous perception that always guides the creative process. The body always comes to play with each choice of theme or motif, and with the sensitivity for certain colors, lines, light, proportion, material, and rhythm. Also the sense of beauty and harmony is subject to an instinctual judgment grounded in bodily perception, that is, in a nature-given sensibility. Even the appetite for creative activity is mediated through the body. The body is a perceptual organ and organic vessel of judgment *sui generis*, involving approaches that differ from those of the conscious mind. For creative individuals the body functions as the organ of nature's vital spirit.

A fourth element of nature with relevance for creative experience is *it's principle of transformation and qualitative increase of life*. It is, in a manner of speaking, a vertical dynamic, with the textbook example being the metamorphosis of the caterpillar to the chrysalis, to the winged butterfly. The tendency of life to advance ever higher forms shows itself in grander style in the evolution of mammals. In Modersohn-Becker's portrait this natural dynamic of transformation and rise is made visible in the image of the artist's left hand cupping the bulb or rhizome from which the blossom springs. In this vertical dynamic, underscored by the artist's upwardly striving right hand, a primal or elemental condition gives way to a sublime goal. We have here an especially striking image of dynamic increase and growth transpiring from bottom to top, from elemental to subtle and differentiated life. This natural transformational dynamic mirrors itself in the creative individual's recurrent experiences of impotence, chaos, and doubt giving way to the birth of creative ideas. It is completely in line with Friedrich Nietzsche's thought that, "one must have chaos within one still, in order to give birth to a dancing star." Personal experiences of impotence prove to contain the birth of new discoveries. Painful non-productivity is overcome by the enormous experience of being carried on a tide of creative thought. Such reversals represent above all nature's special capability to generate transformational processes.

A fifth and final aspect of nature that can express itself in experienced creativity is the fact that *all elements of life are connected in larger unifying contexts or wholes*. In Modersohn-Becker's painting this truth takes shape symbolically in the circular necklace, which can have a variety of meanings. For instance, that of the symbolic circle itself; that of a containing totality; that of a goal, and conversely, an archaic beginning. These are the basic ways in which nature's own wholeness manifests itself as a condition of life: in cycles such as the procession of the seasons, and day and night; in the vital cosmos that contains and balances all of life; in the goal that enables the development of life; in the primordial origin that transmits life's fundamental conditions. The creativity of creative people embodies such forms of wholeness that are available to nature and by which she herself is creative. Their work is not linear or one-dimensional, but is rather subject to natural rhythms that swing back-and-forth between oppositional positions. It is characterized by a natural "penchant for the total artwork,"[87] insofar as they choose different techniques (painting, woodcutting, drawing, etc.), genres (illustration, format, series, etc.), themes (landscape, self-portrait, still life, etc.), and media (pigment, wood, writing, etc.). In the creative process, the diverse means of expression combine to realize nature's own tendency to maximize the complexity of design. When artists follow nature's creative modus, their work is often imprinted with a goal-oriented pull toward the ideal, the utopic, and/or the prophetic. (See Friedrich Schiller's "naïve" poet contrasting the "sentimental" one.) In this approach the larger whole is envisaged as the long-term unifying objective. The paleontologist and Jesuit Pierre Teilhard de Chardin typifies this nature-bound creative activity with his vision of the Omega Point, the maximum level of complexity toward which all natural and spiritual development strives. The other way around, nature as the guide leads also to creative work characterized by a pull toward the archaic and the primitive. This kind of work reveals the greater whole in forms that express primordial beginnings and archetypal realities. It is beautifully exemplified in Paula Modersohn-Becker's unpretentious and primitive expressionist style.

In summary it can be said that Modersohn-Becker's self-portrait points to the fact that creativity can be experienced as a phenomenon that stems from creative nature herself, whose specific dynamic properties determine the evolution of the single artistic work as well as the evolution of an artist's entire oeuvre. Nature's agency is thus not simply a lovely metaphor for human creativity, but far more, it manifests the actual presence of an objective force of creation.

7.4. Albrecht Dürer: Self-Portrait with Landscape

At the age of twenty-six Albrecht Dürer completed the magnificent self-portrait reproduced in (Fig. 24a), which hangs today in Madrid's Prado Museum. The portrait emanates a majestic quietude, which is rather astonishing, considering the artist's youth. Here Dürer portrays himself in the bearing of a master cognizant of the meaning of his artistic task. He projects both his elevated social role as a now recognized artist, and also his consciousness of his inner vocation. The portrait as such points to Dürer's freshly gained self-awareness as an artist—and it reveals his coming to terms with deeper questions about painting and creativity per se.

7.4.1. The Balance of Opposites

With a closer look we notice Dürer's masterful, indeed ingenious depiction of sensuous properties, in both the human figure and the landscape. Rendered with inimitable exactitude, Dürer's skin, hair, cap, and clothing are immediately palpable. Bearing in mind the portrait's date of 1498, the marvelous background landscape demonstrates a quality of observation and reproduction that comes to blossom in later centuries. Despite the superlative precision, the painting is not static or rigid. Rather, it radiates light and vitality. It holds the paradox of balance between the many precise details and a generous whole—between the sensibilities for both the material dimensions and the superordinate idea. In terms of Jung's psychological types

(Fig. 24a): Albrecht Dürer, *Self-Portrait with Landscape*

what we recognize here is the equal play of exacting sensation and far-seeing intuition.

The balanced opposing tendencies carry through, too, in Dürer's ambiguous position within the pictorial space. All at once he is both near and faraway. His right arm, resting on a parapet ledge, is so close to the onlooker as to create the impression it could be touched. Yet distance is expressed in his figure's contiguity with the dark, recessed background niche and the far-off landscape. The ambiguity here gives rise to an enigmatic blend of nearness and remoteness, a dual quality found also in Leonardo da Vinci's Mona Lisa, whose figure has intrigued viewers for centuries. In the qualities of the palpably near and the unattainably remote we encounter the paradox and mystery of Dürer being both an ordinary human in flesh-and-blood and a man enthralled by a higher spirit. Still borrowing from Jung, we can speak here of the interplay of opposing functions: that of feeling, which facilitates relationship—and that of thinking, which affords overview.

Dürer intrigues us as well with his "both/and" approach to another pair of opposites, namely, exteriority and interiority. Going by his elegant dress, gloves, and cap, he staked great value in outer appearances. At the same time his inward visage and almost shy gaze express his authenticity and inner depths. Outer appearance and inner being seem to complement one another effortlessly. To again employ Jungian terms, extraverted exchange with the outer world and an introverted relationship to inner reality can exist equally, side-by-side.

Dürer paints himself as a man who occupies a threshold between the outer objective world of nature and the inner subjective world of consciousness. His partial congruence with nature is suggested by his pose in a three-quarter profile. Had he depicted himself in a frontal view, with the landscape at his back, he would have marked his full belonging to it and his role as nature's representative. The other way around, a half-profile would have evoked the sense of man whose unalloyed consciousness is at odds with nature. However, the three-quarter profile intends the portrayal of Dürer's integral vision, for it allows his gaze that seems just to have turned from a view of the landscape to look pensively into the foreground of the picture. In other words, his viewpoint conjoins both nature's background realities and the angle of a reflecting consciousness. In a certain sense, Dürer's orientation constitutes a third way of seeing things, and as such it bespeaks the transcendent function. It is artistic vision. As realized in art—or at least in figurative art—it clings to nature as its blueprint, but it relies on the perspective of consciousness to fashion from nature the image of a symbolic reality. With this midway "product" of the creative work, the givenness of nature and the formative function of consciousness play together to contribute to the emergence of the concrete transcendent third, the work of art. In a certain sense, artists habitually embody the transcendent function's autonomous symbol-generating force. And then, too, guided by the lens of consciousness, they re-shape objective natural reality into aesthetically satisfying and symbolically meaningful works of art.

Dürer's self-portrait presents the antitheses of painstaking detail and grand vision—or, the dichotomous worlds of sensation and intuition. Although the two are in principle mutually exclusive, they appear here in exquisite equilibrium. As we have already observed, the painting blends into a wondrous whole other apparently irreconcilable opposites, such as nearness and distance, and feeling and thinking. Also, too, vital balance appears in the portrayal of extraverted and introverted attitudes. Ultimately, Dürer's vision links the worlds of exterior nature and inner consciousness, or objective being and subjective perception.

The balance of all such polarities in this portrait creates the characteristic impression of Dürer's vibrant presence. It is the vibrancy of transcendent experience, obtained only through the suspension and reconciliation of seemingly irreconcilable antitheses. It entails the vital, sensuous experience of an alchemical *complexio oppositorum*—a union of opposites, giving rise to the encounter with a living spirit, or the effect of an autonomous symbol-making factor.

7.4.2. Spatial Symbolism

Dürer's self-portrait can be considered as well for the symbolic meaning of its pictorial space, and in this sense four things in particular deserve attention. To begin with, Dürer's figure poses in a space delineated by two parapets. One is in the background, displaying the window, and forming the threshold to the outside world. The foreground parapet, with Dürer poised behind it, forms the threshold to the onlooker's world. These two thresholds within the pictorial space create other imaginal spaces. The background parapet opens up a perspectival view of a landscape, while the foreground parapet allows Dürer to appear as if taking his place onstage.

In the composition as such, the landscape outside becomes the image of some other level of reality, imagined and conveyed through Dürer's use of a depth perspective. (See also the emphasized, deep windowsill.) With the depth view we see, as it were, through Dürer's gaze—or said otherwise, the landscape enters the picture through his eyes and visual field. Historically speaking, Dürer's depth perspective reflects his participation in the dawning of the Renaissance and its fascination with the artistic possibility to render objective things according to the visual conditions of the beholding eye. In this approach the creating subject and the given object become joined, allowing symbolic reality to take shape in the artistic product. Dürer himself was explicitly occupied with this possibility. We can assume, however, that his perspectival studies harbor more than mere technical interest. Far more, they reflect the enthused discovery that the creative individual is able both to perceive the world through his subjective view and to recreate it as a pictorial reality in its objective being.

Dürer portrays also himself as a person belonging to some other realm of reality. The other realm is implied by the foreground parapet or the imagined space behind it. Likening a theater stage that elevates and separates the actors from their audience, this space lends Dürer the status of a role-bearer enacting a symbolically meaningful event. He is thus portrayed as being something more than a true-to-life, ordinary citizen of Nuremberg. He is distinguished by his artistic role and his task of making visible the artist's view of things. He "represents." His job serves less the purpose of vain self-representation than to realize a higher, priest-like service dedicated to both his own and future times. It was the realization of this calling that changed Dürer's self-perception. No longer seeing himself as a mere craftsman, familiar with the métier of painting and laboring in a workshop, he became an author in service to a higher power.

A second symbolically meaningful aspect of the spatial composition is the setting of Dürer's figure at the intersection of two streams of light, one emanating from the background and the other from the foreground. The presence of the two is evident in the details. The light of the sky washes the landscape, spills through the window onto the windowsill, spreads along the supporting window column, reflects in Dürer's left eye, and outlines the contour of his left cheek. Implicitly, it shines on his back. The opposing light emanating from the foreground is more concentrated and intense. Streaming at angle from the upper left side of the canvas, it illuminates Dürer's right side—his face, his bare chest, his pleated white blouse, and the outer surface of his right sleeve. It also casts shadows on the areas turned away from the light source. The light flowing simultaneously from two opposite directions increases the three-dimensionality, the plasticity, and the volume of Dürer's figure—and so too, it magnifies the artist's presence in this stage-like space.

The light reflects symbolically Dürer's recognition that he is the recipient of two kinds of spiritual illumination. The one comes from nature as the alchemical *lumen naturae*. The other comes from the mind, as the inner revelatory flash of insight. In this sense, Dürer acknowledges nature's offerings in his rendering of beauty and meaning, and he acknowledges the influence of the mind in his rendering of structure and truth. He is open to the creative force in both of these emanations. The two cohere in his creative task, which consists of producing images that are both sensuously beautiful and spiritually meaningful. And he accomplishes his task thanks to his precise observation of natural phenomena and his meticulous attention to the inner principles of design.

Thirdly, the spatial composition gives us pause to consider the symbolism of the background from which Dürer's figure seems to emerge. It consists of two parts—the dimly lit interior, and the bright outdoor landscape. The dim interior evokes the sense of religious seclusion. Indeed, a dark arched beam on the left points symbolically to some higher reality. Simultaneous movement into the depths is implied by the three gradations of shadow reaching from the window area to the interior's darkest recess. Taken together, these motifs express Dürer's containment in a world of mystery, faith and transcendence. It is this spiritual world that provided his backing—a still medieval world, with a vertically oriented view. Many of his depicted religious motifs are indebted to this vital background and heritage.

Beyond the window, the bright outdoor landscape represents the dawning of a new spiritual world, the world of the Renaissance with its interest in the here and now, with its sense for nature and its horizontal orientation. Dürer became acquainted with this new outlook on the occasion of his two journeys to Italy. He took his first trip just shortly before he started to work on this painting. Many travel sketches in the manner of this landscape section document Dürer's initiatory passing the Alps.

Dürer's spiritual fundament, we can say, consists not of one but two worlds, standing side-by-side: that of the Middle Ages, steeped in the piety of the beyond and the here-after, and that of the Renaissance, steeped in the earthly here-and-now. He held the tension of the two throughout his lifetime, being both deeply devout and also devoted to corporeal pleasures and interests. With different accents, the same phenomenon realizes itself in other creative individuals: the holding of the tension of opposites in traditional and new worldviews, in long-held ideals and uncustomary ideas.

A fourth and final spatial component deserves our attention, namely Dürer's emphasis of the vertical and horizontal dimensions. The massive illuminated window column accentuates the vertical, while the column's supporting base, the windowsill, underscores the horizontal.

The window column forms a central axis within the image as a whole, extending the vertical space infinitely upward. In this and its illuminated quality, it points to an invisible upper realm that lies beyond the immediately graspable and that yet exists and exerts its impact. It alludes to the heavenly realm, the realm of a transpersonal and universal spirit that encompasses phenomena like the embedding cultural canons, which predetermine and permeate the personal perceptual modalities of creative individuals. Erich Neumann puts it this way:

> With the development and systematization of conscious-
> ness and the individual ego there arises a collective con-
> sciousness, a cultural canon characteristic for each culture
> and cultural epoch. There arises, in other words, a config-
> uration of archetypes, symbols, values and attitudes, upon
> which the unconscious archetypal contents are projected
> and which, fixed as myth and cult, becomes the dogmatic
> heritage of the group.[88]

The transpersonal spirit encompasses also the world of the archetypes, the font of universal human imaginings from which creative individuals draw their ideas. There is, further, the superordinate Zeitgeist, a powerful collective force that influences individual perspectives. We could count as well the zodiac constellations that have bearing on the conditions of personal biography. Like the dark shading that flows down along the window column, this higher transpersonal spirit imbues creative individuals with particular contours and depth. It invests them with universally meaningful tasks, directs them to function specifically in their own eras, and defines their destinies.

The window column places the determination of creative individuals within the context of a larger whole: Their human conditions and purposes beneath the heavenly firmament are lived *sub specie aeternitatis*, that is, under the aspect of eternity or outside of time. This column, then, is symbolically akin to the mythological motif of the axis mundi, the world axis or the celestial axis that joins heaven and earth. It symbolizes the understanding that earthly events are determined by a higher power of design and meaning-making, and that one's self-awareness is measured by one's consciousness of such a transcendent reality. The close proximity of the column to Dürer's visage marks his consciousness and valuing of this vertical worldview.

The opposing horizontal dimension is stressed by the windowsill, the base upon which the window column stands. Symbolically speaking, the horizontal dimension encompasses earthly reality or the realm of empirical phenomena, concrete things. It includes everything that a creative process can gain from real, observable, measurable, and limited being. Contrasting with the realm of infinite spirit, it is the finite world. In creative experience it is encountered in all kinds of confinement—be they one's limited materials and abilities, the difficulty of a theme, a rejecting audience, the struggle for financial survival, the pressure of collective norms, uncreative repetition and boredom, the feeling of one's normality or averageness—or any of the like. In the parlance of Jungian psychology, such apparitions of limit and finitude bespeak certain aspects of the archetypal *senex* or the wise old man. The senex diametrically opposes the *puer aeternus*, the image of eternal youth.

People aligned with the archetypal puer tend to live in ways that correspond with the vertical axis, the axis mundi. But their creativity strives one-sidedly for transcendence, demonstrating emphatically a lop-sided identification with the upper spiritual realms. They become enthralled by the world of archetypal ideas. They are prone to an exaggerated sense of their own uniqueness and high calling, knowing or believing themselves to be led by divine powers. They are disinclined to accept the contrary world of the senex and its alternative perspective. They can seem to deny entirely the implications of existence in the horizontal dimension, such as the need for boundaries, effort, labor, and perseverance. Their "vertical" lifestyle, indulging absolute heights of energy and unending creativity, bears the shadow consequences of nagging fears, self-doubt, and compulsions in which the repressed senex obsessively asserts itself. Creativity oriented predominantly by the puer breeds its own opposite, namely, disturbing symptoms and the painful experience of disabled creativity. Fear blocks the needed courage and optimism; self-doubt cripples the ability to step beyond one's self—the prerequisite for creativity per se; and the anti-creative force enacts itself in meaningless, unrelenting compulsions.

Dürer's painting, however, portrays a sublime balance between the vertical orientation and its counterpart, the horizontal plane. The balance appears most poignantly, perhaps, at the conjunction of the two opposing motifs: the upward rising window column, pointing to the heights of spiritual illumination and transcendence—and the massively solid, brightly lit column base, the windowsill, symbolizing the grounding dimension of earthly reality, yet with its own illuminating effects. It is the creative person who can, in the truest sense, accomplish the difficult task of honoring and reconciling such deeply contrary directions. The creative individual carries the paradox, remaining true to both the higher and greater creative spirit, and real human being.

7.4.3. Symbolism of the Body and Its Attire

Our study of Dürer's portrait now turns to a self-evident theme and yet one we have only briefly touched on, namely, the artist's portrayal of his bodily appearance. We will observe in detail a variety of motifs, continuing on the assumption that they not only depict facts, but also express symbolically other meanings. If such interpretive study seems objectionable, it would bespeak the expectation that Dürer's self-portrait aims at nothing more than the best possible, most naturalistic representation of outer appearances. It could be said that the exploration of symbolic meaning in such portraits amounts at best to conjecture. On the other hand, it need be recognized that in Dürer's vision, the body always carries symbolic meaning. Beyond this we recall the Jungian premise that, thanks to the inherent symbolic value of images, meaning can be discovered precisely where it was not intended. The search for meaning in this sense is not the same as conjecturing. Speculative interpretation forces preconceived ideas upon an image, while symbolic interpretation extracts meaning that abides in image as such.

That said, let us return to the idea that Dürer's depicted body captures something more than his factual appearance and being. The portrayal attempts as well to grasp his depths, as both a man and an artist. His successful effort to precisely reproduce his outer appearance and to authentically reflect his true personality expands into a description of the artistic personality as such. In other words, in our reading of the body motifs and their symbolism in Dürer's particular figure, we recognize the characteristics of the creative individual in general. These are revealed in Dürer's particular attitudes about himself as a creator, about his creative process, his creative experience, his creative designing in space and time, and about the creative gesture as such.

Following Dürer's pyramidal framing of the body, I will begin with the base corresponding with his arms and both hands, which "handle things," and thus correspond symbolically with the creative gesture per se. This aspect of the composition evokes certain questions about the basis of creativity. What kind of activity has the quality of creative activity? What attitudes do creative individuals hold when they work creatively? Dürer's two very differently depicted arms and his folded hands suggest that creative activity combines two contrary ways of grasping and understanding things. His right forearm rests on the parapet ledge to form the base of a ninety-degree angle in relationship to his upper arm. This pose alludes to an in-the-box, straight-forward empirical approach. It suggests Dürer's sober, fact-based vision and pragmatic relationship to reality, a rational orientation that corresponds with Jung's earlier mentioned concept of "directed thinking."[89]

Contrarily, in the perspectival view, Dürer's left forearm is virtually hidden behind the parapet and beneath the folds of his brown cloak. Implied here is a more diffuse approach that is perhaps less understandable to the rational mind, for it essentially is an irrational attitude. It gives rise to activity from within the dark and mysterious crevices of subjective perception, recalling Jung's idea of "non-directed thinking" or "fantasy-thinking."

Dürer's folded hands unite the dichotomous situation, suggesting that his creative approach conjoins the two opposing attitudes and brings about the interplay of a goal-oriented quality of consciousness (symbolized by his visible right arm) and the inner influence of the unconscious (symbolized by his hidden left arm). Such an attitude unifies two seemingly irreconcilable poles. We think, for instance, of directionality versus non-directionality; active relatedness to the outer world versus a receptive relatedness to one's inner life; consciousness versus self-consciousness (in Hegel's sense); and practical action versus passive experience.

Creativity is characterized precisely by the individual's extravagant juggling and noble expression of such opposites, that is, by the capacity to hold the "this-and-that" perspective. Oriented by "directed thinking," creative individuals follow a plan. But they are equally led by spontaneous ideas, which arise from "non-directed thinking." Creative activity transpires within the space of the improbable and seemingly impossible third approach, that is, in a balancing blend of methodological precision and spontaneous imagination or in the admixture of external facts and inner images. Creative activity, thinking, and designing inhere in the sublime and energetic interplay of all such antitheses.

Let us now return to Dürer's folded hands, which we noted to symbolize a union of opposites that comes to play as a third force in creative activity. On closer inspection, we notice that his left hand clasps his right hand such that his thumbs are crossed, and only his four left fingers are visible. His crossed thumbs, pointing in two different directions, represent two opposing attitudes involved in a fruitful dialectical discourse. Creative activity is in fact often characterized by systematic procedure alternating with chance inspiration. The process is enlivened and progresses as a dialectical counterpointed endeavor, whereby consciousness shifts from one modality to the other—from spontaneous imagination (left thumb) to logical deliberation (right thumb). Yet the four left fingers suggest a differentiation according to a four-part structure offered by the unconscious. This recalls the four temperaments that we have considered to constitute a basic Gestalt or pattern of the creative force.

Let us now focus on Dürer's attire, which conveys his attitude about his creative activity in the realm of his personal world and epoch. We can distinguish here two garments: the elegant ivory doublet or close-fitting jacket and the understated brown cloak with a prominently displayed twisted cord that seems to fasten to the doublet shoulder. What meanings might these garments have?

To begin with, the doublet and cloak should be considered as elements of a cultural language that overtly signal Dürer's intended self-image, showing how he wanted to appear in 1498 at the age of twenty-six, in the public life and interpersonal space of his European world. In this context, Dürer's fashionable doublet casts him as an artist who is conscious of appearances and who possesses the personal qualities of independence, self-awareness, elegance, and nobility. But as implied by his brown cloak, he also holds the traits of plainness, earthy simplicity, a workman's naturalness.

If we want to see in Dürer's attire something more than a description of his personality, culture, and epoch, we can consider its expression of an essential aspect of creativity. From this standpoint, we have on one hand Dürer's cloak, which largely covers and obscures the left side of his body. On the other hand, his doublet markedly reveals the contours on the right side of his body. In particular, along with the lighting effect, the doublet emphasizes his shoulder's convex shape and healthy volume. Moreover, the doublet is adorned with darkly hued bands or ribbons, which accentuate the basic opposition of black and white and the contrasting functions and shapes of his upper arm and forearm. Taken all together, these elements express Dürer's gifts of active differentiation, accentuating design, and spatial composition of the body in particular.

In contrast to Dürer's right shoulder, his left shoulder, draped by the brown cloak, displays a less convex shape and a diminished volume. His left shoulder thus seems to slope downward, and into himself and toward the center of his inner being, enhancing the impression of Dürer's withdrawal into the shadowy depths. Here, it is not outer contour that is emphasized, but inner structure and depth, which are even more accentuated by the enfolding cloak. And on this left side, in place of the stark contrast of black and white we have the one color, brown, in modulated tones that accent the undulating cloak. So, in place of a visible arm with clearly delineated parts, we have a mysterious phantom, shaped only by the play of the cloak's folds. The compositional elements on this left side express symbolically Dürer's more hidden, interior world; they imply his capacity for inner differentiation and nuance, and a wealth of forms that unfold from within his unconscious and innermost being.

Considered together, the two garments point to a pair of diametrically opposed creative principles. The shapely doublet suggests the active principle, or the handling of ideas by purposeful drafting, follow-through, production, and the drive to be publically represented in and by the final product. The active principle lies behind rational perception, and it ushers ideas into the outer world by giving them concrete form. It compels willful design, or the drafting of lines and the creation of boundaries. It provides the differentiating attitude that distinguishes opposites and achieves logical order.

Conversely, the loosely shaped cloak represents the more passive principle of receptivity and permeability. It underlies diffuse perception, or the ability to apprehend and value sensuous qualities, and the inner world of ideas and spontaneous imagination. It also allows the co-existence of antitheses, and by all such means enables playful diversity.

In the creative personality both principles come to bear, and ideally, they play equally, hand-in-hand. However, when they sustain in opposition to one another, each can become autonomous and create ill effects. Among them are empty activism and soulless agitation, or unlimited suggestibility and vulnerability to crippling moods. To use Jungian terms, these conditions resemble states of possession by a negative animus or a negative anima. The negative animus refers to the unconscious compulsion to act out unrelated behaviors and judgments. The negative anima refers to a state in which sound relationships and actions are threatened by overbearing moods and emotions. Creative individuals are extraordinarily liable to suffer from such compulsive activity and/or overwhelming emotion, from excessive decisiveness, and/or from exaggerated sensitivity.

Genuine creativity, then, comes to bear only when oppositional poles give rise to a sublime third. We have already observed symbolizations of this third in Dürer's self-portrait. It can be seen again in the twisted cord that spans Dürer's chest, seeming to fasten the left side of his cloak to the right side of his doublet shoulder. This cord makes it clear that the creative force brings forth symbolic creations by joining antithetical purposes—the receptiveness to inner visions and the search for forms that express them.

Closer examination of the cloak cord allows us to distinguish four further features: First of all, it connects the two opposing dimensions symbolized by the ivory doublet and the brown cape—respectively, the public space of active expression and the inner space of receptive or passive experience. So, symbolically speaking, the cord appears to stand for the midway or third attitude that links antithetical approaches. The "third" can be understood as a symbolic attitude per se—that is, the capacity to unify and hold in one intermediary image such diverse realities as the inner and outer worlds, one's self and the world, and intellect and sensuality.

Furthermore, Dürer renders the cord as twisted a loop without beginning and end, such that it resembles the number eight, the mathematical sign of infinity and an image of self-enclosed perpetual motion. In this aspect, the cord highlights the value of ongoing, self-satisfying movement and playful self-expression, as opposed to goal-oriented, purposeful activity. Dürer's cord thus alludes to the typical dynamic of the creative process that entails the continuous, playful circumambulation of ideas.

We note further that the cord consists of a pair of twisted strands, each of which consists of many twined threads. We can understand the cord in this sense to symbolize the intertwining or conjoining of multifaceted meanings derived from the outside world and inner life. In other words, a creative approach tends to yield connections—or better said, it tends to recognize connecting points within opposing tendencies and to gather their many threads of meaning into one image. Creativity is by nature interdisciplinary and prone to seemingly impossible syntheses and paradoxical constructions. Also belonging to this inclination is the perception of deeper meaning and astonishing beauty in what would appear to be useless materials and random motifs.

Finally, the two twisting cord strands are depicted in two different colors, green and white. The color green symbolizes experience related to nature, and white symbolizes spiritual understanding. As the colors intertwine, the cord resonates the sensuous and spiritual realities of images that emerge from the creative intertwining of the strands of empirical observation and practical procedure, and the sensibilities for symbolic meaning and spiritual understanding. This interlacing of sensuous and spiritual dimensions is what allows the particular sensuous gestalt to give rise to a spiritual discovery.

Returning to our study of the symbolism of the body, we can now focus on Dürer's torso, clothed beneath the doublet in a white pleated, low-necked shirt. The shirt's open neck, trimmed with a golden ribbon, exposes the upper part of Dürer's breast, revealing a strong youthful body. Rendered with subtle color tones and surface modulation, his skin obtains an inimitable true-to-life quality, again creating the impression of palpable nearness and sensitivity. This depiction of Dürer's breast reveals him in his essential nature, the sensitive man who is equally strong and tangibly open. Coming to expression here is the whole truth and nothing but the truth, or Dürer's inherent natural being, his undisguised naked reality.

If the picture as such can reveal something about the experience of creative individuals in general, we may observe the following: Creative individuals are existentially compelled to live authentic lives. Their points of departure, the contents of their works, and indeed their creative grounds inhere in the person—in the givens of personal abilities and limits, bodily and psychological constitution and personal and collective history, and the place and time in the world. Their creativity draws precisely from such unique and unshakeable realities. In this case, to step into someone else's shoes would be to sever oneself from one's own true being. It would constitute a flight into non-creative quasi-being, in which creativity would be no longer possible, but also no longer a necessity. Creativity is genuine only when it is felt as an unavoidable need and impulse to surpass one's inborn conditions. We can speak of a determining creative force only when the creative life proves to be the one way to realize something larger than and beyond one's self. We understand this "beyond one's self" in the sense of Nietzsche's Übermensch or "Superman." We do not mean, however, the grandiose, but the realistic and humble efforts to transcend one's self in service to a creative task. Dürer's portrayal of his true being, in body and soul, reveals as well his own sense of being destined by the creative force. His testimony to this effect appears as an inscription on the background parapet, just beneath the windowsill: "I have painted this from my own appearance. I was twenty-six years old. Albrecht Dürer." (*"Das malt Ich nach meiner gestalt/Ich war sex und zwanzig Jor alt/Albrecht Dürer."*)

Let us now return to Dürer's white shirt. With its sensuous loose folds, and the light shining as if from within the garment, the shirt displays a quality of playfulness that contrasts the straight forward depiction of his exposed breast. Dürer's liking for playfully composed surfaces shows in the shirt's many tiny tight pleats and loose folds, rendered in minute detail and apparently with great relish. Dürer makes of this surface an expressive and animated medium that contains interiority and depth.

The surface that Dürer celebrates in his wonderful shirt is all else but a superficial one. Rather, this surface is appearance *par excellence*. It manifests what art is—a bringing of invisible essences into appearance. The artwork relies on the medium of appearance to give form and shape to being, to manifest being in a sensuous and perceptible gestalt. In this revelatory function, art stands in service to beauty, which perforce manifests itself in appearances. But again, we do not mean "appearance" as in the shallow surfaces of superfluous embellishment or beautification, or inauthentic decorative kitsch.

These are among the appearances of manufactured beauty, which is indeed occupied with the mere surface.

Aphrodite or Venus, the archetypal goddess of love and beauty, points to the inner and meaningful connection of appearance and beauty. Hesiod's version of the Aphrodite myth calls her the "foam-born" goddess—the one born at the ocean's surface from the bubbling foam, a medium of indefiniteness and mystery. In Botticelli's *The Birth of Venus* (1486), which allegorizes the theme of beauty and art, the goddess is riding on the outer surface of a giant scallop shell, lifted up from the ocean's depths. Here we discern the meaning that beauty born from the depths appears at the surface and reveals itself to be the inner essence of an outer surface appearance. And insofar as Botticelli alludes to the foam motif, he underscores the connection of appearance and the epiphany of meaningful beauty. It is worth noting as well Botticelli's incorporation of the goddess Hora, who is about to wrap Venus/Aphrodite in a marvelous red cloak. In this garment we have a sumptuous surface that resonates with the presence of meaning-making Eros.[90] Such "Aphrodite" qualities shimmer through in the details of Dürer's shirt—in its intricate surface folds and seeming inner radiance—which together convey the presence of numinous beauty.

Bearing in mind the idea of appearance and meaningful surface, what meanings might we discover in the asymmetrical lighting of Dürer's shirt? Taken together, the radiant right side and the shadowed left side might bespeak Dürer's awareness that the realm of beauty self-evidently and always incorporates uncanny darkness and decay. The German poet Rainer Maria Rilke (1875-1926) captures this reality in the previously cited stanza from *The Duino Elegies*: "For beauty is nothing but / the beginning of terror, / that we are still able to bear, / and we revere it so, because it calmly disdains / to destroy us."[91] Rilke's meaning is, of course, much more fully mirrored in Dürer's *The Desperate Man* (Fig. 11). Nevertheless, if we accept Dürer's shirt as a symbolic picture of this dual reality, then we might say in general that the creative force manifests itself especially in the medium of appearance—through imagining, envisioning, through playing with images and possibilities, through striving for beauty in language, knowledge and visual expression. Creativity can only begin to unfold in the medium of appearance. There it finds the colors and sounds, music and images to discover and express its truth.

We can now compare the depiction of Dürer's bared breast and his otherwise clothed torso. Here we see a conjunction of opposites that suggests how the creative impulse is set in motion and nurtured. First, there is the "naked" fact of nature, or the concrete bodily reality, which enables and compels self-transcendence through creative expression. Second, there is the "beautiful appearance" of imagination, which nourishes creativity with its subtle suggestions. Each of the two—true nature and beautiful appearance, body and imagination—comprise a fundamental condition for the experience of the creative force.

Now, there is a paradoxical mediation between body and imagination that characterizes the creative force fundamentally, in its primal being. In Dürer's self-portrait this arrangement is symbolized in the golden ribbon, which, adorning the shirt neckline, joins a pair of opposites and thus appears as an image of the alchemical *complexio oppositorum*. On one hand this ribbon shares the shirt's sensuous quality and suggestive appearance, doing so with the enhancement of its sublime golden radiance. At the same time, the ribbon displays a decorative pattern that unfortunately is visible only with a close-up view. Consisting of an embroidered chain of circles or rhomboids, the pattern corresponds with the idea of clearly defined individuality, which is expressed as well in the motif of Dürer's exposed breast. Yet as the pattern links a whole row of geometric forms—symbols of the Self—it concerns not one but many individuals or individualities. We can interpret this to mean that creative activity entails above all a sublime process that configures both individuality and types. Creative interest and ability are indeed characterized by the propensity to explore character, types, archetypes, and other primary forms—or to retrieve from the magma of imaginative possibilities the remaining structures and basic constants.

It is now time to amplify on the motif of Dürer's head. Earlier we assumed that it describes symbolically specific aspects of the creative process. We noted especially its suggestion of a process that takes place in one's head, generating and bringing forth creative ideas. An idea is creative insofar as it is new, unexpected, surprising, enlightening, or reconceives existing ideas according to new and visible evidence.

We have already several times asked about the validity of subjecting an artist's self-portrait to symbolic interpretation. Does the imagery not simply aim to reproduce aspects of the artist's objective reality—and nothing more, such that the portrait leaves no room for symbolic interpretation? The question presses all the more with regard to Dürer's head, a motif which, in its highly accurate portrayal of the man's visage, would appear to be concerned with nothing but realistic representation. We note the particularities of his hair, his beard, and characteristic gaze, and can't help but wonder, might the image intend more than to reflect Dürer's objective appearance at the time?

In answer to the question it can be said that the facial features do indeed realistically mirror Dürer's appearance in 1498. However the composition envisions his head through a special lens that suggests some playful leeway on Dürer's part and thus invites interpretation. This becomes evident especially in a comparison of this self-portrait with the one completed two years later, *Self-Portrait at Twenty-Eight Years Old Wearing a Coat with Fur Collar*. Here Dürer depicts himself in a full-frontal view, with this and other attributes developing his resemblance to the iconic Christ. Despite portraying the same man, the two portraits convey very different impressions. At this juncture we recall not only the Jungian perspective that all pictures contain symbolic dimensions, but also Dürer's known symbolic approach, both of which invite the onlooker to muse about deeper meaning. As Paul Klee put it,

> In the final analysis, a drawing simply is no longer a drawing, no matter how self-sufficient its execution may be. It is a symbol, and the more profoundly the imaginary lines of projection meet higher dimensions, the better.[92]

With this, we can focus on Dürer's visage. The initial impression conveyed that of a quietly absorbed man, one who is listening inwardly, as if wanting to attune to or sound out some unknown force or voice. He appears to be on the verge of receiving rudimentary inspiration or an intuitive idea. A specifically creative way of understanding things can thus be characterized, first, by receptivity to insight and inspiration coming from within.

Dürer's fine nose suggests the function of intuition to lead the way, to sniff out the good thought, the fruitful concept, the interesting idea. Even when the final aim of the exploratory journey is yet unknown, intuition anticipates the possibilities of new insight or design with startling and seemingly groundless certainty. Creative intuition antecedes thinking in the setting of a goal. Or, we can say, the aim may be only dimly perceived, but its pursuit is charged with creative zeal and curiosity.

Another aspect is Dürer's voluminous hair, spilling in long ringlets down to his shoulders. The image as such symbolizes the man with a wealth of imagination, thoughts, and playful impulses. In terms of the creative process, it points to the value of brainstorming, free association, and openness to gradually emerging new ideas. The light reflecting in Dürer's hair on both sides would seem to say that creative impulses may come from the outside and the inside. The creative factor or the third compelling thing that bridges the two sources is the capacity to play, or the ability to associate and assimilate disparate ideas. Jung put it this way:

> The creation of something new is not accomplished by the intellect, but by the play instinct acting from inner necessity. The creative mind plays with the object it loves.[93]

How might Dürer's full lips, framed by his mustache and beard, fit into the symbolic picture? This image could stand for the imminent impulse to articulate tentatively a subjective perception related to the creative process. We can speak of a "propaedeutical phase," a phase of initial articulation that moves a vision from its raw, inner conception to some kind of communicable form, be it in language or image, or in any other medium.

In this picture, Dürer's eyes, gazing on the onlooker and seeming at the same time to look inward, express an especially essential aspect of creative vision. These eyes imply a three-dimensional view that sees the perceived object, but that also holds necessary distance. The object is brought into a focus that is neither too close, nor too far. It is a suspended gaze like that of a cat hovering before a mouse hole—as if all at once alert and nonchalant. It is this gaze alone—the active and the receptive—that is capable of perceiving the radically new dimension of a creative idea. It is a creative gaze that corresponds with bi-focal or stereoscopic vision. The greatest hindrance to creative knowledge is the ego's monoscopic lens. Focusing on pinpointed ideas and goals, the ego obscures the view of unexpected and unknown contents. At the same time, creative consciousness relies on the ego to bring its perceptions into sharp focus. So, we can say that creative insight is brought about by the paradoxical tension in dreamily looking away and paying close attention. In the motif of Dürer's eyes we encounter this hovering look, which is typical for creative perception.

Inspiration, intuition, associative ability, the translation of subjectively perceived contents into perceptible form, and stereoscopic vision have been described as five means that can help to surpass trusted modes of thinking, and to open oneself up to the incarnation of new ideas. These are the two challenges for a creative individual—and Dürer is a good example. First, how is it possible to imagine something that wants to or has yet to be imagined? How does one avoid arbitrary schemes, and follow instead those germinal thoughts, images, and insights that exist in the background and want to be brought into the foreground? And second: How does one get off the track of habitual thought and lift one's self into the realm of creative insight? Dürer's self-portrait alludes to the paradox and countermotion constellated by these two challenges: His whole visage, seeming to emerge into the light from within the dark background chamber, suggests the subject's role of mediating and revealing a hidden content or meaning. At the same, this "bust," replete with its voluminous curls, suggests a pyramidal or upward striving motion that points to the aim of obtaining uplifting sublime insight. The answer to these challenges lies in the above-described bridging means that mediate between the foreground and the background, the known and the unknown, the ordinary and the creative.

Let us now turn to Dürer's fashionable cap. For all the evident elegance, its drooping peak recalls a fool's cap. Now, a head covering functions objectively as protection from the cold and heat, and it can also signify occupational standing and social status. With the given design, Dürer designates himself to be an accomplished painter and a creative individual. What more might this cap tell us about Dürer's self-perception? Which elements symbolize his specific charisma and artistic calling?

With this kind of cap Dürer identifies himself not as a simple painter or craftsman, but as an artist with a special calling, one with a recognized destiny. Signaling a sublime spiritual status, this cap communicates Dürer's perception of his high function or leadership task. Such a cap is analogous to the king's crown, the bishop's miter, and the magician's hat—all of which symbolize the wearer's status as the mediator between the higher spheres and the human realm. Dürer's vision of himself as a priestly mediator of the sacred and profane worlds comes across in his own words,

> It is difficult to achieve the real art of painting. So anyone who does not find himself gifted for it should not attempt it. Because it wants to come from divine inspiration.[94]

Insofar as Dürer's cap projects the fool, it signifies the wearer, the creative individual, to be unlike ordinary people in yet another way. Creative individuals feel themselves to be untethered from collective norms and laws. They seem unable to conform to prevailing rules, which bespeak collective agreement as to what is fitting and important for all. Their fool's status inheres in their feeling of being outsiders, of being somehow at odds with society. The image of the peculiar and comical fool seems to necessarily underlie creative service to a higher purpose and finding one's self in critical or even unwilled distance to the collective. In the same vein, the creative life entails loneliness and the feeling of being without a home. It should come as little surprise, then, that so many artistic works have taken inspiration from the fool, a figure that embodies the existential condition of being Other. In this context I recall the proverbial fool's scene captured in the picture of Albert Einstein sticking his tongue out when a photographer tried to coax a smile out of him for a press portrait. Perhaps the world's best-known snapshot of Einstein (Arthur Sasse, 1951), it documents him as the mad scientist with unfettered disregard of collective convention.

Now, to continue with the cap motif, we can say that it marks the top-most point and "capping off" of Dürer's figure. It thus symbolizes the epitome of Dürer's self-image, or points to the sum of his artistic principles and experiences, the pinnacle of his artistic self-perception. He understands himself accordingly as author, creator, and the co-creator of God's creation.

Three details in Dürer's cap give us an excellent symbolic view of the innermost tripartite dynamic of the creative force: the rolled front brim; the central crown consisting of four stripes alternating in black and white; and the drooping peak with a tassel at its tip.

An essential feature of the rolled front brim is its wave-like contour or motion. This motif suggests the dynamism of the initial impulse, a movement ex nihilo, which here appears as the differentiation of two parts—a dark one, receding into the background, and a bright one welling up in the foreground. The image thus recalls the biblical story in Genesis, where the Creation begins with God's separation of light and darkness, sky and earth, and air and water. We think also of the splitting-up of the original parental couple, a motif that appears in the Mesopotamian creation myth, as in so many others. What such great myths hold in common is their imagining of a primordial act of creation that inheres in the differentiation of a whole into two opposite parts.

This primary creative act of differentiation manifests itself in creative individuals in more or less subtle ways. Basically, it amounts to the igniting of creative energy by a kind of Ur-repudiation of prevailing ideas and images. Such initial acts of differentiation take shape implicitly or explicitly in concrete artworks, in written works, and also in the evolution of life works. An example is found in the Swiss psychiatrist and proponent of *Daseinsanalysis* Medard Boss (1903-1990), who opened each of his lectures and books by drawing firm lines between his predecessors' positions and those of his own. Boss evidently gained from this process the energy to differentiate and develop his own new ideas. Similarly, one of the twentieth century's greatest Roman Catholic theologians, Karl Rahner (1904-1984), opened most of his talks and essays with long discourses on the themes he would *not* cover. His prophylactic "cleansing" certainly clarified his thematic purposes—but it also launched his own creative imagination. In other words, it was not just a logical operation that served to order his thoughts and perspective. It amounted as well to a mental ritual that stimulated his creativity. Thus in Rahner's procedure we discern the faint echo of the mythological creation of the cosmos, set in motion by the separation of the elements and the Ur-parents. An abundance of examples illustrate how this primary act of differentiation ignites also the beginning of lifeworks. The spark can take shape in an initial critique of prevailing ideas, or in the establishment of a counter position.

Friedrich Nietzsche (1844-1900) exemplifies both tendencies. His lifework was set in motion with the publication of *Untimely Meditations* (1874). In one chapter title, "On the Use and Abuse of History for Life," we gain a glimpse of his cultural critique and polemic approach. But already 1872, Nietzsche had published his book, the *Birth of Tragedy from Music*, in which he distinguishes between the Apollonian and Dionysian modes. A further example can be found in Jung's groundbreaking essays published in *Symbols of Transformation*, where he begins with the already often mentioned distinction between "directed thinking" and "non-directed thinking" or fantasy-thinking."[95] Although it is of general interest, the distinction seems oddly out of context in the passage in which it appears, and it does not appear again in later chapters of this volume. An explanation might be found in the title of the volume's original translation, published in 1916, *Psychology of the Unconscious, A Study of the Transformations and Symbolisms of the Libido [...]*. This title suggests that Jung's initial perception of the two kinds of thinking functioned fundamentally to open his creative exploration of the libido and the creativity of the soul, which forms his larger focus both in this volume and subsequent ones.

The Red Book, begun in 1915 and completed around 1930 but withheld from publication until 2009, is seminal to Jung's lifework. As previously noted, this volume begins with Jung's distinction between a "Zeitgeist," or the spirit of the time, and a "spirit of the depths."

Returning now to Dürer's cap, we will focus on the central crown, which consists of four stripes alternating in black and white. Here we have a symbolization of creative energy expanding from the initial impulse, gaining in surface appearance, and unfolding in four stages. It is a rudimentary picture of the creative force concretizing itself and taking on perceptible form within a process. Still part of the innermost creative dynamic, this process no longer concerns that initial impulse that comes from nothing or breaks out of the darkness, but now manifests itself in space and time. The creative force appears in sequential stages of coming-into-being and dissolving-back-into-nothingness (symbolized by the alternating white and black stripes). It thereby enlarges itself, and resolves with one structure or pattern consisting of four distinct shapes. This resolving image points to the gestalt comprised of the four differentiated creative temperaments.

In what ways might the creative force in this second phase manifest itself in the works and self-images of creative individuals? Remaining for now with the example of Dürer, it is discernable in several of his woodcut cycles that, read sequentially, express creative processes—and also in many pictures that represent individuals within typologically differentiated structures. Among his nine cycles amounting to a total of one hundred thirty-six woodcuts, I would here mention, The Apocalypse of St. John (fifteen woodcuts); The Life of the Virgin (nineteen woodcuts); The Large Passion (eleven woodcuts); and The Small Passion (thirty-six woodcuts). Then there are Dürer's single works that manifest the four-fold structures of typological differentiation. They in particular incorporate the motif of the temperaments: *Four Witches* (1497); *The Four Horsemen of the Apocalypse* (1498); *The Desperate Man* (1515), which we have discussed (Fig. 11); and the painting, *The Four Apostles* (1526), which we have also thoroughly explored (Fig. 15). In the "story" series and in the structural patterns, the creative energy manifests itself as form-engendering force. It is as if the creative force would want to display this function especially in such processes and stories, or respectively in such structures and typologies.

The creative force's structuring or shape-giving function abides in Dürer's very understanding of his artistic task, that of translating inwardly perceived gestalts into outer, visible images. In this calling he saw himself as the perpetuator of God's work. As he wrote,

> It is God who brought forth all art. Because a good painter is inwardly full of figures, if he could live forever, then he would always be able to convey something new from the inner ideas of the kind Plato describes.[96]

Dürer's manuscripts on perspective and proportion may also reflect his perception of himself as an artist with the creative calling to contribute to the correct representation of figure and space.

Now to the third part of the cap motif, the drooping peak. Almost comprising the whole cap crown, it tapers off with a tassel consisting of many fringes bundled together. In the image of the cap as whole we can discern symbolically a third stage of the creative process. But let us first review: In the rolled front brim we observed the symbolic appearance of an initial creative impulse, an unmitigated beginning in an act of division. In the striped crown we saw the emergence of perceptible forms, and their coming-to-being alternating with stages of dissolution. As we shall see, the drooping cap peak describes symbolically the principle of unity and differentiation.

As Dürer pictures it, the peak seems to originate at the center of the cap crown, from which it flops arc-wise to one side, and almost covers or seems to make up the entirety of the head covering itself. The floppy peak in its over-arching appearance symbolizes the unifying principle. At the same time, the peak tassel, comprised of so many bundled fringes, stands for a plethora of creative energies that are differentiated and held together as a whole. The cap peak thus characterizes the basic ability to perceive connections between disparate things and to differentiate and to individualize them. It entails, on one hand, the creative ability for associative perception that links together a range of seemingly disparate contents. On the other hand it entails the ability to value each single content, to heed coincidental events, to make sense of seemingly superficial things, and to discover general meaning within particular facts.

This creative ability to unify and differentiate is very present in Dürer's work. It manifests in his wide choice of motifs, in his explorations of them, in the variety of his techniques and compositions. It is evidenced as well in his meticulous devotion to minute, sensuous surface detail, in his painterly mastery of his tools, and in his attention to the portrayed person. The self-portrait at hand exemplifies Dürer's sublime gift, his exquisite capacity to join in one painting so many different ideas and elements. In our efforts to unravel the meanings, it is this gift that causes our difficulty, but also our delight. At the same time Dürer's genius reveals itself in his devotion to observable detail, in his attention to the present moment, in his resplendent rendering of the sensuous qualities of skin, hair, fabric, and other material things, and in his interest in the person's unique expressive features.

The great creative individual is especially marked by this gift of integral vision that discerns the whole in the variety of parts, and by the ability to value the essences of each single part. Alongside the example of Dürer we think of Hegel, who developed a comprehensive philosophical system and who, in his first work, The Phenomenology of Spirit, describes all possible aspects of spirit in its whole scope. At the same time, he uses the lens of a "naïve consciousness" to view phenomenologically the so-called "'figures" of the mind, and to carefully explore and describe the individual components that add up to the mind's full experience of itself. The creative force's characteristic conjoining of subtle detail and grand unifying vision is beautifully present in Hegel's work. The same force evidences itself C.G. Jung, for instance in his discovery of the collective unconscious and in his focus on individuation as the pathway and goal of personal development. For him, these two dimensions are equally important— the universal archetypes that are common to all people and times, and the specific reality of the Self that characterizes a person in his or her unique being. In the individuation process, according to Jung, we each need come to terms with the archetypes that hinder and further our unique development.

In the examples of Dürer, Hegel, and Jung, we discern the shared sense that the whole necessarily goes hand-in-hand with its parts, and that the whole and the parts co-determine each other. We see it in Dürer's grand compositions incorporating his love for detail;

in Hegel's vision of truth as a whole realizing itself in the many perspectives of the experiencing mind; and in Jung's perception of underlying constants that both characterize all of humanity and give rise to individual developmental potentials. Thus all three of these men express the particular creativity that is symbolized in Dürer's drooping cap peak and tassel, that is, the gift of holding differentiated parts within a unifying vision.

At this juncture I wish to summarize the rich symbolism we have observed in the cap motif. Insofar as it appears in analogy to the fool's cap, it expresses the creative individual's otherness and artistic license in relationship to the world determined by behavioral norms and thought conventions. Insofar as it likens a religious head covering, it expresses the particular charisma and calling to mediate high, essential insight. As a top-most head covering, it signifies the highest principle to which the creative individual submits, or the highest reality he or she serves, that is, the creative force in its highest, most unmediated, and transcendent manifestation—the creative force in its core, original, and sheer essence. In the cap's three parts we recognized the symbolization of three archetypal creative movements: first, from out of nothingness, ex nihilo, the spontaneous division of opposites that ignites the coming-to-being of something new; next, the emergence of individual figures and vivid processes; and finally, the creation of general connections and individual differences.

As Dürer's cap symbolizes the creative force in its innermost essence, it comes as no surprise to find the image corresponding with the Christian idea of the triune Creator God, beginning with the cap's three-part composition. It is rather improbable that Dürer consciously intended it, but the symbolism occurs perhaps by virtue of his aim to achieve an authentic and lively self-likeness, and by virtue of his religious experience in general. The cap's rolled front brim, with its wave-like contour and bright and dark tones, evoked our association to the Biblical creation narrative and God's separation of the light from darkness, heaven from earth, air from water. In this respect the cap brim motif parallels the appearance of the creative force as God the *Father*.

In the motif of the central cap crown we recognized the symbolization of the creative force appearing in processes and in four perceptible gestalts, which we noted to represent the four temperamental types. The cap peak in this sense parallels the narrative

of God's incarnation on earth, in space and time, in the human figure
of the Son. God, the primordial force of creation, now manifest in
Jesus's mortal body, appears in the life process of birth, teaching,
and death—and then the miraculous resurrection, as witnessed by
the four Apostles.

In the cap tassel we noted the symbolization of the creative force
effecting the creation of a new whole comprised of many differentiated
and integrated parts. In this respect Dürer's tassel corresponds with
the theological understanding of God the Holy Ghost. For the Holy
Ghost is the unifying spirit in whom and with whom the Father and the
Son abide as one. In further similarity, the Holy Ghost is said to work
in the earthly here-and-now, bestowing from above "seven spiritual
gifts" that renew, strengthen, and inspire human endeavors. An image
of the creative inspiration par excellence, it is this epiphany to which
Dürer refers when he writes about the outpouring Holy Ghost.

When we consider Dürer's intention to explore in his self-
portrait the essential mystery of creativity itself, then we should not
be surprised by the allusions to the Triune Creator to whom Dürer
is overtly and deeply indebted. In Dürer's view creative energy was
creative spirit, and indeed, divine creative spirit. The devout Dürer
was not alone in feeling a divine calling and closeness to the divine
source of creation. Paul Klee's reflections allow us to submit that such
a "credo" is common to other creative individuals, across space and
time. Klee, however, refers not to one "Creator" behind all creation,
but to the essence of creation within the creation itself:

> The chosen artists are those who dig down close to the
> secret source where the primal law feeds the forces of
> development. What artist would not like to live where
> the central organ of all space-time motion, call it brain or
> heart of creation as you will, activates all functions? In the
> womb of nature, in the primal ground of creation, where
> the secret keys to all things lies hidden? But it is not the
> place for all men. Let each man go where his heartbeat
> leads him.[97]

As an aside, I wish to emphasize several points. To begin, we can
interpret Dürer's cap to symbolize the basic substance or three-fold
essence of the creative force, and say that this force is alive today,
even if we witness it above all in the "great individual." This is the
perspective we have applied. But a different perspective, a theological
view, might see in the cap motif a surprising symbolic expression of

the Trinity, the essential nature of which was debated for centuries by Church Councils. They argued, for instance, about the three persons united in one and about the utter distinctness of each person; about the Holy Ghost connecting Father and Son and remaining at the same time distinguished in itself; and about the revelation of God incarnating in the Son, in the time and course of the Son's earthly life, as described in the four apostolic writings. In this sense, both Dürer's cap and the Christian Trinity are symbols that—like other symbols—inspire our meditations and lead us to discover surprising inner connections.

On much closer inspection of Dürer's cap we discover a fourth part, a design flourish that appears as a complement to the Trinitarian reality or the three-fold creative force. It takes shape in a detail of the rolled cap brim, namely in the minute ribbing that decorates the upper border of the wave-like shape. Visually, this ribbed border connects with the other three cap parts and yet it stands as a separate and different motif. Apparently originating at the wave's "crest" and sharing its color, the ribbing connects with the father principle, that is, with the *ex nihilo* movement. At the same time, the ribbing overlaps the cap crown, and takes on its striped patterning, and thus connects with the realm of things coming-into-being, or the sphere of the "Son." Finally, as the ribbing appears to give rise to the cap tail, by extension it connects with the tassel and its symbolization of the unifying and differentiating principle and the presence of outpouring of the Holy Ghost, or the creative force in the here-and-now.

Now, what we might detect in this fourth element, the ribbed border, is a subtle symbolization of the Great Mother, a feminine counterpart to the three-fold masculine image. Christian theology does not conventionally recognize a feminine match to the Triune God. Yet the divine feminine is present in the figure of Mary, Mother of God, who in the narrative appears in analogy to the Son, Jesus in a historical dimension. A feminine counterpart is also recognized in Sophia, the embodiment of divine wisdom, which is said to have existed before the Creation and to have created the world according to God's design. Sophia thus comes closest to being a feminine equivalent of God the Father. Not last, in many mythical narratives the feminine creative force manifests itself as the apocalyptic woman or the eschatological presence that from the end of all time intercedes in the creation of present times. In this aspect the feminine principle aligns with the principle of the spirit, or the Holy Ghost.

Yet in all such manifestations, the feminine remains unattributed as a divinity enfolded as a fourth and equally essential "Person" in the masculine "One and Manifold God." Instead of appearing as a central and sovereign person along with the Father, Son, and Holy Ghost, the feminine tends to take shape as a side companion who mediates, reveals, and conveys godly essences. We have seen examples in the figure of Mary, the Divine Mother and conveyor of the mother principle; in Sophia, the conveyor of divine knowledge and design; and in the apocalyptic woman, the conveyor of divine destinies and ends. But still, such figures are not central to the Christian Triune God. As Dürer's ribbed cap border suggests, in its Christian epiphany the feminine perspective appears to be pushed to the periphery.

However, we might want to consider that this peripheral position need not amount to an undervaluation of the feminine. It could express an inherent quality or an essential aspect of the feminine, which would be to operate from the periphery of the visible world, to operate on its outer shape and appearance. In this light, we should note that Dürer's placement of the ribbed border is such that it crowns his forehead and corresponds with the midline of his visage. This composition implies Dürer's foremost consciousness and central and high estimation of the feminine creative principle.

Again and again, I am amazed by artworks that consciously or unconsciously compensate and correct prevailing views and teachings. Just as Dürer enhanced the Christian Trinity with a fourth dimension, so does Michelangelo's famous painting of the Creation in the Sistine Chapel bring fresh perspective. In Michelangelo's vision, God the Father creates with his right hand while embracing in his left arm the figure of Sophia, who personifies the primal ground of creative imagination from which the creative Father calls into being all life forms. While Michelangelo's painting contradicts the Book of Genesis, it overtly esteems Sophia's divinity and her co-creation of the Creation. In this and many other examples we discover the purpose of art to lie in tapping the wellspring of the collective unconscious to compensate a given epoch's prevailing thought and its forgotten, undervalued aspects. As Jung put it:

> Therein lies the social importance of art! It is constantly
> at work educating the spirit of the age, conjuring up the
> forms in which the age is most lacking. The unsatisfied
> yearning of the artist reaches back to the primordial image

in unconsciousness, which is best fitted to compensate the inadequacy and one-sidedness of the present.[98]

Leaving behind conventional theology, we need ask: in what sense might the creative principle incorporate this postulated fourth element? How might the feminine transcendent reality of creativity be visualized and experienced?

It is found, above all, in the dimension of beauty. Beauty is, to begin with, the mysterious *numinosum* that accompanies artistic endeavors and ushers their products into being. The imminent presence of beauty may seem self-evident, in that art is generally ascribed with the task to create beautiful objects. But it holds true also for the contemporary arts, which might be critically declared as "not art" when the demand for beauty seems to be unmet. We need hold in mind, however, that such works also spring from an urge to make visible some aspect of beauty. Beauty is an important motif and criterion also in other areas. We think of the beauty of language, the beauty of an idea or fantasy, the beauty of an insight or argument, the beauty of a project or good deed. These all represent different ways in which beauty adds qualitative value and thus releases creative energy.

Furthermore, beauty opens up the higher dimensions of the ideal and the sublime that drive the yearning for insight and the recognition of value in perceived things. As if by magic, beauty allows things to appear in the light of what they actually are, namely, hints and symbols of higher significance. Beauty removes from things their mere matter-of-fact aspects, their naked being and blunt reality. It gives them surplus value and appearance that open up the dimensions of sublimity and special validity.

As concerns art specifically beauty is constituted not only by the artist's composition of outer appearances, but also in the work's manifestation of inner essences. The creative person is captured by the appearing beauty of things, and feels driven to express their primal reality. In this sense, beauty emanates in and as the radiantly authentic appearance of a thing-as-such. The artist who declines the role of the seducer or hustler remains with the authentic "thing of beauty" and allows its reality to manifest in the work of art. This is just as true for the artist of abstract works who doesn't attempt to render the beauty of outer objects, but remains true to the beauty of the fantasies and the expressive potentials they evoke.

Beauty plays a significant role in psychotherapy, too, even if not for the sake of producing a beautiful work of art. In his book, *The Soul of Beauty*, the Jungian analyst Ronald Schenk observes it thusly: In the mutuality of the therapeutic relationship, the psychotherapist works like a "craftsman," attending to "the story of the patient," "sinking into" an "aesthetic" or "contemplative" mode and "becoming at one with the material at hand and the process of the work;" in this way he or she "'wait[s] upon' ... the soul announcing itself or appearing" in all of its "manifestations."[99] When beauty absents itself from the consulting room, when it is not visible in a patient's personality or attitude toward himself, toward other people, or toward life itself, then this kind of therapeutic work becomes difficult. The reassuring gleam of analyst's eye seems to fail, and he or she feels at a loss to discern the person's identity, topics, and psychic *Gestalt*. The opposite is true when beauty lays bare a person's essence—and I do not mean the superficial kind of beauty that presents itself in newspaper headlines and fashion magazines. When the appearance of inner beauty is missing, the individual comes across as being pale, uninteresting, without individual character, and difficult to grasp.

Finally, beauty is a fundamental factor that contributes to the creation and sustenance of the world. After all, nature and animals did not evolve for sheer pragmatic purposes. Had that been the case, it would have sufficed for the creation to limit itself to a bland earth surface, one that could allow the survival of several infinitely reproducible life forms with simple movement apparatuses. Happily for us, some force of creation saw it otherwise. This force reveals itself in the evident luxury and beauty of the creation. It seems to have intended that living things should not only get by, but they should also pronounce and represent their existence. And they all seem designed as parts of a whole that are meant to encounter and engage with each other, thanks to the beauty that activates attraction and mutual interest. In this spirit, beauty stimulates the instinct of reproduction and the progression of life. Likewise it enables the evolution of new species, and with this, also the advancement and differentiation of life.[100]

In all such manifestations of beauty it becomes evident that beauty itself is an essential creative factor. Beauty creates added value in that it manifests itself as appearance, which has a stimulating, attractive and animating effect. Its central and high value as a feminine creative force that works equally from the start alongside the father principle is symbolized in the ribbed border flourish on Dürer's cap brim. The subtle appearance of the feminine in this border motif corresponds with its inherent tendency to work at the periphery, to suffuse the world and its objects with new surface qualities and thus, too, new meanings.

7.4.4. Landscape Symbolism

Now we come to focus on the background landscape depicted in Dürer's self-portrait. Meticulously rendered and resonant with meaning, this landscape is the first one of its kind to have been rendered in the history of western art. It resonates something of Dürer's recently completed Swiss alpine journey, when he was underway from Germany to Italy. It evidences among other things Dürer's absorption in nature and all its appearances, an interest that had begun to register in many of his earlier drawings, engravings, and aquarelles. Among the famous examples are *Wing of a European Roller* (1500); *Young Hare* (1502); *Great Piece of Turf* (1503); *The Large Horse* (1505); and *The Small Horse* (1505). As mentioned before, Dürer's attentiveness to nature reflects his pioneering participation in a new turn of consciousness, that toward a horizontal world, which in the unfolding of the Renaissance would seize the whole collective. Thus first and foremost, this landscape reflects Dürer's participation in the epoch's discovery of empirically perceived nature, an Aristotelian view so to speak. Dürer's genius lay in his artistic ability to observe and to represent the objectively perceived world, an approach that would later be recognized as the genre of figurative art.

At the same time, Dürer was self-admittedly "full of inner figures," i.e. full of ideas in Plato's sense. In this way Dürer was far more than a copyist or documentary illustrator of nature. He gave his inner ideas sensuous appearance and the other way around, he perceived in sensuous appearances the presence of ideas.

Not only Dürer, but the creative individual in general holds this faculty of in-depth empirical perception, that is, the ability to apprehend symbolic value in things as they are. Things are allowed to speak and to be understood and interpreted. This way of relating to things is not the same as mere perception and explanation or utilitarian and technological processing. It is rather an aesthetic approach, which serves not to take possession of things by the application theory or practical handling, but far more, it accepts the appearances of things as such and allows them to open their horizons of meaning. This way of handling things shows up the in range of human creative activity and products, be it literature, the visual and performing arts, or philosophical observation.

(Fig. 24b): Close-up of Land-scape in Dürer, *Self-Portrait with Landscape*

Dürer's works very much emanate the aesthetic approach—the creative relationship to the world constituted in artistic observation and symbolic understanding. We see it in his self-portrait, in the view of the landscape suffused with atmospheric light (Fig. 24b). With this, being as such is apprehended as being full of light and full of meaning, as a being of luminous appearance of creative force.

We note as well that this landscape is an entirely natural one, with no trace of human presence and works. Whereas Dürer's sketches of the Swiss alpine regions portray houses, castles, and people, such objects are not to be found here. Rather than a world shaped by human hands, he now portrays pure being. It is this being, this essence, that Dürer observes and recognizes, and awestruck by it, puts it in artistic form. His is the vision of a creative and descriptive eye, rather than a rational explanation of the world.

Dürer's landscape is divided vertically into two parts, where the background mountain range delineates the earth below and the sky above. The broad earth surface consists of many textured layers, stretching from just beneath the windowsill to the far distant snow covered mountain peaks. It represents the horizontal dimension of worldly being moving from the here-and-now toward a far-away goal. There are obstacles and rifts between here-and-there, now-and-later, this-place-and-that-place. We note also that there are no natural pathways in this landscape. In this sense, Dürer's earth symbolizes human being in its existential ground of finiteness. It depicts a situation of contingent *Dasein* with all its restraints and limitations from which the individual strives for essential being and distant and high goals. Their remoteness and apotheosis take shape in the overwhelmingly beautiful upper half of the image, in Dürer's vast sky, the heavenly sphere of enlightenment and transcendence. It is the sphere of the "infinite lightness of being" that so strongly contrasts the finiteness and heaviness of earthly being.

In this light, Dürer's landscape symbolizes the creative individual's dual reality, which lies in the weighty suffering of broken relationships, illnesses, failures, disappointments, compelled exile to foreign realms—and all of this, conjoined with the intense experience of an illuminating spiritual world. To put it slightly differently, while creative individuals are especially vulnerable to the manifold challenges of earthly existence, they are just as much prone to be recipients of divinely inspired imagination and ideas. It is as if the two would belong together as a pair of mutually determining opposites—on one hand, an existence filled with painful loss and bitter disappointment, and on the other hand, an existence enriched by the transcendent gift of far-reaching inspiration and insight. In Albert Einstein we find a good example of this equation of existential pressure and bestowed inspiration. Einstein's incredibly complicated life came to bear among other ways in his multi-national citizenship, which caused intermittent disruptions in his education and many broken relationships. But at the same time his ingenuity fundamentally changed our understanding of the physical world.

In Dürer's landscape, divine imagination pours down from the heavenly sphere as light that irradiates the earth and reflects itself in the round lake. "Imagination is more important than knowledge," says Albert Einstein; "Knowledge is limited. Imagination encircles the world."[101] Einstein recognizes the same infinite force of imagination that expands on Dürer's sky, illuminates the entire creation, and reflects itself in the Self and in individual human imagining. The motif recalls a 1946 dream of Jung's, recorded in his correspondence with Victor White:

> Yesterday I had a marvelous dream: One bluish diamond
> like star high in heaven, reflected in a round, quiet pool—

heaven above, heaven below. The imago Dei in the
darkness of the Earth, this is myself. The dream meant a
great consolation.[102]

Looking again at Dürer's landscape, we notice many motifs that
show surprising correspondence with motifs appearing in the portrayal
of Dürer himself. It is as if the different aspects of the creative force
that express themselves in Dürer's figure would manifest also in
nature as aspects of an objective creative energy. Let us explore this
impression first from a purely visual angle, beginning with the base
line as we did with Dürer's figure.

Just beyond the windowsill, we see a triangular mound of brown
earth. It is nearly contiguous with Dürer's brown cloak and precisely
mirrors its color and outer contour. The earth mound displays a pair of
knobby protrusions, which, seeming to fold into each other, correspond
with Dürer's folded hands. In the near distance, just beyond the earth
mound, spreads a grassland shining in likeness to Dürer's elegant bright
doublet. The grassland borders the lake, its surface rippling with foam-
crested waves that recall the Aphrodisian appearance of beauty, a motif
we recognized in the sensuous folds of Dürer's white shirt. A curving
line of greenery borders the lakeshore, almost seeming to connect
it with the grassland. Here we have the echo of Dürer's green and
white twisted cloak fastener. In the center of the landscape a convexly
rounded hill with its bedrock quality corresponds with Dürer's bare
upper chest. The foot of the hill is bordered by a bright line, correlating
with the golden ribbon that borders Dürer's shirt neckline.

Just beyond this hill, at a slightly higher elevation, there is a
plateau. On close inspection, and as seen from below, this high plain
appears as if imprinted with a face, a nose, and two eyes. The allusion
to Dürer's own visage is vague. Accepting the similarity, though, we
see the likeness of Dürer's beard in a piece of woodlands running
horizontally below the imagined face. At the plateau's left and right
borders, two fancifully rendered rock formations resemble Dürer's
playful ringlets. The peak of the mountain range, formed by a mighty
snow-covered massif, corresponds with the shape of Dürer's cap.
Arising just to the right, a smaller triangular-shaped massif appears as
if it were part of the greater one, or would stand in unity with it. In this
we see the likeness of Dürer's triangular cap tassel.

Now, what are we to make of such correspondences between
the landscape and Dürer's figure? Whether Dürer intended the

similarities, or whether they resulted independently by the force of necessity in the emerging symbol, is immaterial. The salient meaning lies in the existence of analogies between inside and outside, between the creating subject and the world.

7.4.5. The Analogous Creative Force in Nature

The correspondences between inside and outside tell us that Dürer assumes the existence of one objective creative principle that manifests itself analogously in the world outside and in the creative individual's inner experience. This includes the idea that the creative principle expresses itself in the world outside as nature and the designer of things on different levels: on the primary level of the earth in its raw appearance (the mound of brown earth); on the more developed level of fruitful fields (the grasslands); on the level of water and its circulation (the lake); and on other levels such as those of natural boundaries (the bright line at the foot of the hill, the row of bushes, the strip of woodlands); geological and tectonic formations (the bedrock hill, the high plain, the lateral rock formations); and ultimately, the rocky mountains and the great massif, and meteorological phenomena (the clouds). On all these levels the objective creative force manifests its power of formation and transformation. It acts and expresses itself creatively through all the morphological aspects of the world in which it appears and evolves.

Creative individuals are deeply acquainted with the world as the expression and revelation of this great creative Other. Poets, painters, musicians, dancers who represent the world in their works incorporate it not only as an incidental motif, but as a means of visualizing numinous creative energy that reveals itself in nature's processes of design and transformation.

7.4.6. Correspondences Between Self-Knowledge and Knowledge of Nature

In the correspondences of inside and outside we register as well the interplay of the creativity that operates in nature and that is also "at home" in human consciousness. It is the mutuality of the two that establishes an individual's creative interest in and sensibility for nature. The creative mind, finding itself mirrored in nature, grounds itself in nature and in the will to sustain and advance natural creative processes. At the same time, the creative mind applies its own creative principle as a heuristic tool for understanding nature. As the same creative force inhabits the observer and the observed, the inwardly experiencing mind intuitively grasps the inner life of nature. In a nutshell: The correspondence between the creative mind and the creative force of nature makes of personal self-recognition the basis, the condition, and the means of understanding nature.

The creative force of nature, on the other side, is able to educate and inform the creative mind. The original discipline of alchemy rested on this assumption. In this sense, alchemical practice was a spiritual endeavor rooted in nature. It aimed to understand nature's inner creative processes and gain their use for the creative transformation of inner consciousness. The artist also strengthens his understanding of the creative process and his own task as a creator in the approach to nature, in the deepening of his models, and in his sensitivity for the creative materials. Indeed, creative individuals in general experience the necessity of subjecting themselves to concrete visual material in order to gain creative insight from its inherent potential of stimulation.

7.4.7. The Role of Synchronicity

The correspondence between inside and outside also means that creative consciousness is reflected in the world, which is animated by the same creative principle. As a consequence, the creative individual often experiences coincidence, or more specifically, what C.G. Jung calls "synchronicity." With this Jung refers to processes or experiences in which external and internal events occur almost simultaneously, aligned in time by the act of an objective meaning-making factor. In such cases, connections of meaning between external facts and internal perceptions do not result from the rational or logical succession of cause and effect, but from the constellation of simultaneity, which is grounded in the force of meaning *per se*. However, with the category of sense or meaning as a conditional factor, the connection between external and internal fact is explained, but it remains unclear why or toward what end a synchronistic event occurs. What might the meaning of this meaning-making phenomenon be?

The question can be answered if we understand synchronous events as creative mirroring phenomena that are triggered by a great objective force of creative imagination, one that exceeds the merely human. If we accept this force as an agent, we need also assume that synchronicity is about something that is to be creatively expressed, achieved, changed. In other words, synchronicities are not arranged merely for the sake of staging synchronicity per se, quasi as mere interludes that show off a meaning-making factor. Rather, exceeding these purposes, the force of synchronicity pursues a creative finalistic intention; it wants to produce change and open the mind to something new.

Let us consider the following: As the greater, imagining creative force "stages" itself in the guise of synchronicity, it makes of synchronicities themselves amazing and transformative creative events or works of art. The other way around, artworks themselves may be experienced as synchronous events that stunningly reveal the inner essences and intentions of the creative force. Artworks fascinate because their beauty is suffused with immediacy of meaning, in which the presence of the creative spirit itself is at least implicit or intuitively apprehensible. To divine this presence in an artwork is to experience wondrous coincidence or congruence, that is, a synchronous correspondence of fundamentally differing dimensions: surface and interiority, appearance and essence, sensuousness and sense, beauty and truth. Synchronicity thus comes to play in the transcendent experience of being awestruck by an artwork. While it may be felt only as a diffuse sense stirring from mysterious depths, it is nonetheless the sublime apprehension of correspondence between surface beauty and symbolic depth.

Similarly, even as generally experienced, synchronicities fascinate us because they carry the feeling that some mysterious artist is present and working to shape inner ideas, insights and memories in the form of external occurrences. In the same vein, the sudden appearance of meaning in seemingly unconnected events feels stunningly coherent, mysteriously beautiful and apt, as if they were works of art. It is a symbolic and awe-inspiring happening like that encountered in the beholding of art, but the felt numinosity may be even larger because in the "art" of synchronicity, the "artist" is unknown. As the "work" is ascribed to no artist and no source, it is experienced all the more as a mysterious act ex nihilo. However, in contrast to real artworks, the anonymity and suddenness of synchronicities can cause us to dismiss them casually as nothing but curiosities or odd coincidences, with the result that the things that want to be seen are not seen.

For clarity's sake, we need say that while creative individuals are extraordinarily prone to be led by synchronicity, the experience is not habitual or constant. Rather, it seems to crop up mostly at the start of creative endeavors, as if it would want to serve the origin of a work and provide the sense of finality that sustains goal-orientedness. To put it somewhat differently: Creative activity is charged with the energy of a hidden intentionality that wants to achieve the creative goal, and that supports its realization with synchronistic bonuses. Synchronicities materialize like promotional gifts bestowed by the creative force itself.

Now, we have already considered the likeness of Dürer's window column to the *axis mundi*, by which it obtains symbolically the function of mediation. More than this, the wonderfully diaphanous and yet solidly supporting column beautifully symbolizes the experience of synchronicity as a numinous force and support. We have on one hand the foot of the column, which imagizes the "ground zero" of the here-and-now, or a receptive intuitive mind. From the column top, a brown substance flows downward from an unseen higher source. This substance suggests the objective event that, materializing like a gift or sign from above, coincides with and resonates affirmatively in the here-and-now, in the receptive mind. It bespeaks the actual situation in which a tentative thought or idea gains absolute certainty by the coincidental appearance of a qualitatively matching outer event. Attending feelings of enlightenment and transcendence are expressed in the column's almost spiritual quality of translucence. The central, supporting column in this way evidences the bi-directional flow of energy and the supportive effect of synchronicity arranging an interplay in which the creative force advances the aims of the creative mind.

Let us consider as well the symbolic appearance of synchronicity in the window column's base, the deep windowsill. Strikingly, it is the largest "empty" surface in the whole painting. It thus strongly contrasts the other richly nuanced surfaces, and appears like an empty theater stage. It symbolizes the absolutely open realm of imagination, the inner space of the perceiving and imagining eye. As this "stage" is set between the dark parapet and the illuminated background landscape, Dürer suggests the sphere of imagination to be located in between two realms:

On one side, the dark parapet recalls Plato's renowned cave and metaphor for humanity's entrapment in the realm of the senses. Whether Dürer intended the analogy or not, his parapet is prescient with Plato's meaning, the signs of which may include loss of insight, or the sense of being in the dark and running-up-against a wall. More severely, it can entail depression or melancholia and acedia, the torpor and doomsday darkness that bespeak the utter snuffing out of perspective, creative faculty, and meaning. It is a hellish life that amounts to a radical absence of experienced synchronicity that would otherwise support the realization of meaning in the situation.

On the other side, Dürer's background landscape represents an illuminated world "out there." It proposes an entirely other realm where sensuous objects and one's own sensuous being are full of life vitality and radiant with sense and meaning. In our present way of looking, access to this realm is inhibited, lost, or even prohibited by entrapment in the senses. From this perspective, Dürer's landscape becomes a framed image or stage backdrop that, like a looking glass, points to or intuits something better.

Dürer's vision implies imagination to be the in-between realm and the bridge to the world "out there," to that "something better." Represented by the brightly lit windowsill resembling an empty stage, the space of imagination stands as an open invitation to play. A freely playing mind is by nature receptive to synchronicity and the larger creative force, and its healing and creative effects. The stage of imagination offers a place where synchronicity works to support the individual's apprehension of meaning in the sensuous world, and to transform inner perceptions into coherent, unifying narratives and images. Thus in Dürer's imagining, imagination is the celebrated space in which depleted being—an existence in nothing but the senses— uplifts itself to (re-)unite with the vibrant world.

7.4.8. Further Parallels in the Creativity of Nature and Mind

Dürer's inclusion of the landscape in his self-portrait tells us even more about his perception of himself as an artist. To get at the meaning, we need first consider generally that when artists include landscapes in their self-portraits, they mean to convey some essential meaning about themselves. A landscape is a statement to such effects as, "I feel at one with nature;" or, "I value and feel at home in this particular piece of alpine nature;" or, "I assert nature against the city as my place of belonging;" or, "nature reflects my free and independent spirit." How might we understand Dürer's landscape in this sense? Insofar as he portrays an untouched natural landscape, he identifies himself as the creator or as the co-creator of original nature. Here we recall Paul Klee's idea of artistic vision that reproduces worldly essences ab ovo, in likeness to the egg or origin of creation. In this approach there is no hubris. The point is not to create the real world, but to create an original picture of it, in analogy to the world-creator. This applies to everyone involved in creative processes, because each creative work, likening the initial act of creation that created the world, constitutes the existing world in a new view.

In his self-portrait, Dürer sets his own figure in a spatial position that parallels the background landscape. It is as if he would want to reflect the parallel realities of a human being and of nature in its own being. Yet Dürer's great physiological presence far outweighs the background landscape, so much so, that it would be easy to dismiss the landscape as an incidental decorative element. However, there are a number of reasons to consider the intention of the landscape to acknowledge the role of an essential co-actor. To begin with, the details are portrayed with painstaking meticulousness and devotion, to the effect that the landscape itself features as a kind of autonomous self-portrait of nature. Dürer's achievement in this regard is the first of its kind in the history of art, for up until this time, artists had incorporated elements of nature as a mere staffage and accessory. The parallel spatial positioning of the landscape and Dürer's figure imbues nature with the quality of a bodily appearance that is analogous to Dürer's body, with a corresponding structure and corresponding symbolic meaning of the surfaces. The close proximity of the landscape and Dürer's imposing figure attributes the landscape with the large presence of a personal and equal other. Seen beyond the stage-like windowsill and through the illuminated perspectival view, the landscape gains a significance that far exceeds the implications of its relatively small surface, which occupies only one-tenth of the entire pictorial space. Finally, Dürer's placement of the landscape within the larger pictorial space corresponds with the known fact that a picture's upper right corner automatically compels the onlooker's attention. It bespeaks the natural gravitation of the eye, which holds true not only for the viewing of pictures, but also, for instance, for the viewing of newspaper pages. The overall effect of Dürer's composition, then, is to elevate the landscape and to augment its presence and meaning by lifting the onlooker's gaze and leading it outside, where the landscape is encountered as if it were Dürer's equal.

Dürer's portrayal of himself in a double portrait, paralleling his relationship to nature, suggests that artists and creative individuals in general are aware of a larger and natural creative force that registers its invisible presence and involvement in the creative work. Dürer's portrait in this sense captures the common awareness of an unseeable creative Other who co-directs the creative work, enables insight and design, urges the process on, structures it, and steers the timing. It is this objective and autonomous creative force, which, as mirrored in nature, knows better than people do how to create images of beauty, and how to create life as an interplay of inwardness and outwardness, that is, how to create in such a way that a work becomes alive in a consistency of form and content.

7.5. Henri Rousseau: Self-Portrait from L'Île Saint Louis

Approaching a close to this chapter, let us consider Henri Rousseau's self-portrait, completed in 1890, when he was forty-six (Fig. 25). Rousseau (1844-1910) was nicknamed "le douanier," the customs officer, because until he accepted early retirement at the age of forty-nine, he worked as a toll official, painting only in his spare time. He had no education or training in art. He was entirely self-taught. Many of his contemporaries ridiculed his lacking professionalism and naïve manner. However, Picasso, on his first chance encounter of Rousseau's work, instantly recognized its brilliance. In due course, Rousseau would gain the respect of many others in the *avant garde*. Among them were the poet Guillaume Apollinaire, and the painters Léger, Delaunay and later Kandinsky, Beckmann, and Frida Kahlo. Rousseau became acquainted with Marc Chagall through Alfred Jarry, and at Chagall's atelier he met Mallarmé, Strindberg, and Degas. All of them recognized Rousseau's great portents. Today Rousseau is esteemed as the post-impressionist precursor of modern art and as point of departure for naïve art and surrealism.

In his self-portrait Rousseau depicts himself standing in the middle of a road outside of Paris, on the tiny island of *Saint-Louis*, which lies in the midst of the River Seine. In the background a docked boat displays a profusion of gaily-colored flags, and further back, we see an iron bridge. Rousseau's dark silhouette stands out prominently against the bridge and a vast light blue sky full of fanciful clouds. The large palette in his hand boldly proclaims his artistic identity.

7.5.1. The Artist's Figure

With this setting, Rousseau identifies himself not only as a painter but also as an outsider, standing outside of the main city and outside of Parisian culture, manners, norms, and rules. In this accurate portrayal of his situation, Rousseau shares the status that we have discussed and noted as a basic aspect of creative experience. He was indeed an

(Fig. 25): Henri Rousseau, *Self-Portrait from L' Île Saint Louis*

outsider in being a self-taught painter. But behind his accomplishment was a more pervading and fundamental urge that compelled him to travel his own road, remaining all the while as if oblivious to established norms and collective ideas. In such ways, Rousseau very much embodied the naïve fairy tale Dummling. It was this aspect of his personality and artistic approach that "the avant-garde admired—even as they laughed at it."[103] In December 1908 Picasso threw a party, half in jest, to tribute Rousseau—who was now sixty-four, still untrained and clumsy, but gaining international acclaim as painter. At the raucous event Rousseau lifted an earnest toast, revealing the enormity of his artistic calling and his brash confidence in it: "You and I," Rousseau says to Picasso, "are the two most important artists of the age—you in the Egyptian style, and I in the modern one."[104] Rousseau's boast turned out to be the party's biggest joke and cause for uproarious laughter. But, "In the end," it is said,

> what Rousseau showed Picasso was a way of being an artist. Stubborn and ultimately enigmatic—did he care that people laughed at him? Did he know?—The douanier had an unshakable belief in his vocation... . Rousseau taught him [Picasso] to put yourself on the line even when they laugh at you, or call you a naive fellow traveller.[105]

In line with his self-conception, Rousseau sets himself in his self-portrait like a commemorative statue in a suburban landscape. His ceremonious black suit lends the scene a mysterious, surrealistic air. Apart from facial details, most personal features are nearly erased, such that he appears as none other than the emblematic artist, marked by the attributes of his palette, paintbrush, and beret. The one personal touch is his lapel pin, a stylized pinnate leaf that points to Rousseau's high esteem for nature, which he held to be his main teacher. Considering the group of motifs, we have a picture of a Rousseau unconcerned with personal identity, aiming solely to display his artistic calling and task—perhaps even elevating himself to the status of "Official Office of the Artist." His black suit, bereft of personal flare, points symbolically to non-being, or to empty form and pure functionality. Implied on the whole, then, is Rousseau's sense of being taken into the service of a far larger Other, which we have recognized to be characteristic of the creative personality.

The canvas center is formed by Rousseau's heart- or kidney-shaped palette, itself held at the midriff and center of his figure. The composition as such points to a very central place, that is, the psychic place where outer and inner centers converge. Understood symbolically, it tells us that Rousseau brings his images into the world from the center of his bodily being. They are suffused with his way of experiencing the world, which, as his figure shows us, is from his heart and gut. He aims less to represent the objective world, than to express his subjective experience of it. His point of departure lies not in the outer world, but as it mirrors itself in his psyche.

Rousseau's palette bears the names "Clémence" and "Josephine." With Clémence, his first wife, he had nine children, only one of whom survived. He married Josephine after Clémence's pre-mature death. The inclusion of their names is Rousseau's tribute to the two women who were so important to him, both as beloved marriage partners and as inspirations for his artistic work. In this sense, the two women functioned for Rousseau as animating feminine counterparts. On the whole then, Rousseau's figure portrays him, the painter, being at his core a purely receptive vessel, open to imagination mediated by his anima, and bringing images into the world from the center of his being.

7.5.2. The Boat and Setting Sail for New Shores

Behind Rousseau's figure, a sailboat is anchored at the side of a canal. Displaying a profusion of colorful flags, the boat emanates a joyful levity that sharply contrasts Rousseau's severe black suit, but it well matches the image of the Dummling. It conjures up unlimited dreams of journeys and far-away new shores—but it is not that Rousseau himself ever actually travelled. Unlike many artists of his time, he never once left France. So, this boat symbolizes Rousseau's imagination, which transported him regularly to high seas, dense jungles, and wide deserts, where he encountered all manner of surreal flora, fauna, and human beings. Of the many flags on Rousseau's boat, three allude to and signify two real places—England and France. The abundant others signal sheer territories of imagination.

Remarkably, the French national flag flies at the pulpit, while the British flag flies at the masthead. Evidently Rousseau's imagination sails under the dual signs of his familiar France and foreign England. The symbolic meaning is that Rousseau's imagination is led by oppositional energies, particularly those constellated by the known and the unknown, the familiar and the foreign, the normative and the off-beat, the belonging and the not-belonging. Here we recognize again the tension of opposites that sustains imagination: the play between antithetical perspectives and contrary directions, and the play between the now-here-now-there, and the now-and-then. The ability to entertain all of such sides opens imagination and the space for fresh creative vision.

The sheer number and variety of flags on Rousseau's boat point symbolically to the imagination's inherent manifoldness. "If there were only one truth," says a statement attributed to Picasso, "you couldn't paint a hundred canvases on the same theme." Imagination thrives on the multi-angled view that sees and allows the inner vitality and truth of things to appear. In this spirit, Rousseau was led by a playful and child-like naïve quality of imagination, untrapped by "adult" one-sidedness and absolutism.

Here again we find him embodying the fairy tale Dummling— the fanciful child at play, non-judgmental, and full of imagination, curiosity, and wonder. It is by no means easy to enter this territory, for it is no place of childish inexperience and self-centeredness, but a "treasure hard to obtain," as fairy tale wisdom would have it. Picasso puts the challenge this way: "Every child is an artist. The problem is how to remain an artist after he [or she] grows up."[106]

7.5.3. The Bridge

Uncharacteristically for a self-portrait, Rousseau features a background bridge spanning the entire width of his canvas. Looking down onto the island of Saint-Louis from the perspective of Quai Henri IV, the bridge realistically signifies Rousseau's rootedness in Paris. By the same token, the bridge and the Eiffel Tower arising in the distance reflect Rousseau's genuine fascination with engineering and revolutionary technical invention. Notably, the Eiffel Tower was completed in 1889, just one year before Rousseau's completion of his self-portrait. The third sign of Rousseau's passion for technical invention is the hot air balloon floating in the clouds high above the bridge. All three motifs represent gravity-defying inventions that must have captured Rousseau's child-like and magical imagination—and that in other ways may express the nature of his creative mind. We will amplify on this subject as we go along.

Let us now delve into the symbolism in and surrounding Rousseau's bridge. From its outer reaches, it links two different kinds of neighborhoods. The neighborhood on the right is the one located outside of the main city. Setting his figure here, Rousseau marks his outsiderness—and further, he aligns himself intimately with other qualities and meanings of the place. It appears to be a rather quiet area, characterized especially by the gleaming white hut standing beneath the umbrella of a finely branching tree. With particular relevance for a reflection of Rousseau's creative mind, the white hut and sprouting tree together symbolize the private and differentiated individual. The neighborhood on the opposite side of the bridge is more remote, and we surmise, more remote to Rousseau's being. This area is demarcated first by a lush tree alley, beyond which arises the more distant city, itself distinguished by seemingly endless rows of smoke-stacked apartment buildings. The image as such symbolizes forces that are antithetical to privacy and individuality. These would be the unconscious, represented in the wooded area—and the crowd or the collective psyche, imagized by the city and its unseen but countless inhabitants.

Now, in the cluster of symbolic motifs, Rousseau pictures certain psychic realities that are visible to the human eye only when they appear in and as concrete images. With this in mind, Rousseau's bridge becomes a symbolic conduit for comings and goings between the polarized domains of the individual and the collective, consciousness and unconsciousness, and the time frames of the present, the past, and the future. Indeed, in this view, Rousseau's bridge is a remarkable symbol of the bridging imagination. If his boat symbolizes the voyaging imagination per se, his bridge throws light on imagination's capacity to mitigate and link entirely divergent realms of being that in essence have nothing to do with each other. In this rather surreal function, imagination emerges to be all at once a voyager, a bridge, and the veritable autonomous creator conjuring up images of invisible realities. Standing before the bridge and at it's mid-point, Rousseau suggests that he is fundamentally backed by the bridging imagination, and that he is the "contracted" builder of its paradoxical bridging pictures. And in this endeavor, he is akin to every artist, poet, musician, dancer, and creative individuals in general.

7.5.4. The Sky

Rousseau's figure is further set beneath an endless blue sky that spans the heights and touches the earth. Making his own visage the center of this heavenly cosmos, Rousseau points to his conscious participation in the eternal expanse and fullness of the spiritual universe. It realizes itself within him as inspiration arising from the timeless source of archetypal images.

Rousseau's sky displays clouds of two different kinds. On the left we see mainly the cumulus type, colored in an egg-yolk yellow and foregrounded by a red rising sun. On the right, the clouds are more thinly dispersed, appearing in pale-yellow layers. The black hot-air balloon floats amidst these wispier clouds. The rising sun points to a new day and fresh starts, corresponding with the egg-yolk like clouds beyond it. In contrast, the black balloon alludes to potential collapse, to ends and death, directions that are mirrored analogously in the blanch coloring of the surrounding clouds. Taken together, these motifs symbolize the antitheses of beginning and ending, becoming and passing away, generating and dissolving.

Rousseau's imagined world and lifework typically accentuate such origins and ends. They are perhaps most visible in his jungle paintings that feature abundant nature and its predatory animals. In such clustered images we witness the creative imagination that characteristically delights in making things and negating or destroying them. This kind of imagination is well evident in the playing child, who thrills as much in knocking down sand castles as in building them. Our affinity with creative destruction shows up, too, in the power of scandal, criminal violence, and war to spellbind us. Finally, it manifests itself in the socially acceptable mediums of satire, philosophical critique, journalistic and political polemics, criminal novels, gangster films, and all kinds of provocative art, theater, music, and film. The prominence of this darker energy in our lives goes to show how much creativity encompasses and relies on the presence of oppositional forces.

Let us now re-enter Rousseau's sky, which in its sheer vastness and ethereality appears as a high entity looking down on the material world. In this aspect the sky imagizes the gaze *sub specie aeternitatis*, that is, transcendent vision under the aspect of eternity. In this sense the sky represents not a specific point of view or limited perspective, but the pure, simple, open, and unmitigated eye that sees and embraces things just as they are. It is indeed the child's way of seeing, the untarnished gaze that can be awe-struck and discover creative potential in all things, just so. Such absolutely open sight corresponds with the well-known Zen *ensō*, the empty circle. There is further correspondence in the Zen *Ten Ox Herding Pictures*, especially in the eighth image, which consists of an empty circle representing the complete dissolution of distinctions between subject and object. In this all-embracing emptiness everything can be recognized in its essential being. Hegel's "absolute knowledge" also furthers this unconditional and creative way of seeing, which inheres in the apprehension of things in their unadulterated simplicity and truth.

This quality of vision that appears in Rousseau's sensuously rendered sky manifests itself in his works over and over again. It is most apparent in his jungle paintings, where his absorbed and finely attuned attention is reflected in the details of every leaf and each blade of grass. And in this frame of mind, Rousseau remains undistracted by any concern about the effect the details may have on the painting as a whole. Such painterly devotion that captures a thing's "suchness"— the sheer beauty and truth in its elemental form—corresponds with the aim of the Japanese haiku. This well-known genre relies on contemplation that focuses the mind unerringly on a thing, and allows its essential being to emerge in the form of compressed word-pictures. Two examples by the famous sixteenth-century poet Matsuo Basho follow:

> old pond
> a frog jumps into,
> the sound of water[107]

And:

> summer's night
> the tree spirit follows in
> the sound of wooden shoes[108]

A similar quality of vision appears in the American poet Robert Lax (1915-2000), for instance, in the line of his poem that also entitles his volume, *Turning the Jungle into a Garden without Destroying a Single Flower*.[109] This is one of Lax's laconic poems that best express his capacity to convey the immediacy of being. In this particular poem, Lax almost seems to comment on Rousseau's jungle pictures. Were it the case, it would come as little surprise, because both artists found themselves compelled to relate to the living creative force with unabashed openness and transparency. Lax's medium is a haiku-like compressed or minimalistic language that just as aptly articulates the elemental dimensions of things. In other words, his medium vibrantly conveys his transcendent view of things, through which he sees no "nothing-but-being," but only meaningful being. I intend the double sense here: in Lax's poetic vision, seemingly meaningless things are suffused with intrinsic symbolic meaning, and thus are also flush with the meaning of being esteemed.

Similarly, Rousseau's composition of the sky shimmers with the inherent quality and meaning of sublime, celestial being, or the sphere that is humanly conceived to be the heavenly abode of gods, angels, and other higher beings. We associate it as well with a realm of life after death, a paradise, and a place of eternal bliss. Such ideas commonly reflect the human yearning for a reality that is so much better, so far superior and enduring, that it can only be conceived and felt as an otherworld lying immeasurably beyond and above the earthly here-and-now. The enormity of this meaning is expressed in the wide expanse of Rousseau's sky, and in its height and vertical dominance over the horizontal plane of the earth.

The creative mind typically feels at home in this high and boundless heaven, that is, in elevated and ethereal spheres of infinite imagination. Meaning, too, that creative individuals tend to soar above profane facts and factuality. They find contentment neither in the mere existence of things, nor in their ordinary uses for surviving ordinary bodily and practical life. The creative mind suffocates when it is too much, too long, and too exclusively burdened with the mere management of day-to-day realities. It requires the time, space, and quietude to connect creatively with them and to shape them in the light of the creative experience. Whether the process gives rise to new thought or to concrete artistic endeavor, it is only in this way that ordinary things and events can be elevated and distilled to their meaningful essences. The step toward freedom from mere functional being is beautifully illustrated in Rousseau's initial decision to balance his work as a toll official with artistic experimentation. With this, he lifted himself up and toward the heights of creative vision. To follow the gradations of color and texture in Rousseau's sky, his hobby gave him first the needed breath, and then a gradual transition into the upper vaporous spheres of imagination.

The long-standing, indeed archaic idea that makes of the sky the abode of spirits and mighty gods corresponds with the soul reality and experience of inspiration flowing down from sources high above. Again, creative individuals are especially prone to this kind of experience, and feel themselves to be the objects of its autonomous force. Ideas dawn on them. In a flash, insight arises. Discoveries materialize out of nowhere. Or, the sky goes black. Lights are snuffed out. Myth and religion attribute such events to the powers of willful spiritual beings. Poised beneath this meaningful sky, Rousseau assumes the appearance of a visionary prophet attuning inwardly to messages being channeled from above. And with the tools of his trade in hand—palette and brush—he seems on the verge of translating the messages into visible form. Every kind of creative endeavor somehow entails such play between a superordinate creative force and the individual potential of creative expression. It boils down to collaboration between receptiveness and ability, between listening and active doing.

In Rousseau's painting the meaning of the sky as a far-off celestial and unreachable sphere is made palpable in the image's immeasurable expansion and ethereal transparency. All creativity connects with such an otherworldly dimension, not in a metaphysical sense but as a symbolic reality. It fuels the personal striving for the ideal, for that something more, for that "treasure hard to obtain." The creative force, inherently containing the thrust toward the sublime, pushes to realize itself in creations that express the inner essences of things, their vital and enduring truths. Creative individuals hang in the balance, feeling subjugated to this force and its whims. Its otherworldliness manifests in the here-and-now when a creative work achieves the absolute and ideal expression of beauty, and also in the unearthly contentment experienced by the individual creator. The failure to obtain the goal is the cause of utter desperation and the feeling of a terrible void. Goethe's Clara, in his play *Egmont*, expresses this creative dilemma in her verses, "Hoping and fearing / In passionate pain; / Now shouting in triumph, / Now sunk in despair …"[110]

We have already noted the meaning of eternal bliss abiding in the sky. Imagined here is not complacent happiness in fleshly and material being. It is rather a Clara-like feeling of spiritual triumph, or differently, an abiding contentment of soul. Both are sublime and transcendent qualities of being that resonate so splendidly in Rousseau's sky. We take this image again as testimony of the creative individual's central experience of the creative force as such. In its innermost core, creativity inheres in the paradisiacal or awe-striking coherence of discovery and meaning, seeing and seeing-into, and ever renewed efforts to express this experience in a communicable medium.

The real creative hurdle and hard work lies precisely in the matter of concretizing creative vision. Belonging to the labor is the acceptance of limits related to the creative demand and person's means and ability to fulfill it. For instance, Rousseau's palette of eleven colors represents a self-imposed limit and reduction in the painterly medium, but it also foreshadows tough questions of choice and methodological demands to come. Which colors, tones, mixes, and which brush strokes best allow the inner vision to emerge? Which motifs, what size canvas, and where and how should the motifs occupy the limited pictorial space?

It comes down to the question of realizable imagination. This predicament shows up in Rousseau's self-portrait. For, with another look at the outer contours of his body, we see that he had originally envisioned his figure to more largely inhabit his canvas. Traces of the original scale are especially visible in shady areas around his feet and legs. Obviously Rousseau felt compelled to reduce the scale of image within the whole picture, but his visible effort to erase failed to eliminate his original traces. His *malheur* could be dismissed as an incidental lapse, but the need for symbolic understanding urges us to focus on it.

In this spirit, let us recall the boastful remark at Picasso's party, when the naïve Rousseau displayed his large sense of self-importance, revealing a somewhat inflated self-image. With this in mind, we might discern in Rousseau's re-touched self-likeness the expression of an emerging inner change, a dimly dawning recognition of self-limits. But as change in this realm may have started to register, Rousseau reveals himself to have been facing another limit, namely his lack of the painterly skill required to perfectly represent his downsized self-image. Rousseau's meaningful *faux pas* or "slip of the brush" wonderfully illustrates the general creative dilemma in the move from the blissful sphere of the imaginable to the hard reality of the doable. The transition always entails hard the labor of transporting the imagined vision into the concrete world. The perhaps less self-evident dimension, unwittingly made visible in Rousseau's self-portrait, is this: The sacrificial operations of reduction, erasure, elimination, and boundary-setting performed by the creative individual on the outer object mirror the painful spiritual operations performed on the creative individual by the creative force itself.

VIII

CONCLUDING REFLECTIONS
ON THE NATURE OF CREATIVITY

In the foregoing chapters, we studied twenty-five paintings by a variety of artists, using a phenomenological approach to try to understand how the artists themselves experience and express creativity in its multiple dimensions. This final chapter returns to the questions that opened our study, what is the essence of creativity? What makes creativity what it is? Toward this end we will re-examine some of the previously discussed images and concepts, allowing them now to shed some new light on our subject. To follow the discussion, it should be helpful to refer to the overview of illustrations found at the end of this chapter.

8.1. Creativity: Construction and Negation

Creativity is a phenomenon of design, production, and transformation in which not only constructive and synthesizing energies come to play, but also deconstructive or negating ones. The negating aspect engenders the stagnation and paralysis of creative dynamics—and also, it gives rise to distressing psychological states in which the individual becomes determined by anti-creative factors such as somatic illness, emptiness of soul, loss of meaning, and imprisonment in the earthly here-and-now. Such adverse experience is antithetical to the experience of creativity and causes creative people to feel besieged from the outside and deprived of their creative existence. Moreover, it reflects the reality of the autonomous creative force and its power to induce intended experiences of non-creative being.

We encountered creativity of this negating kind in Chagall's *Jew in Green* (Fig. 4) and in his *Jew in Black and White* (Fig. 5). In Dürer's *Adam and Eve* (Fig. 9), too, it is present, here in the figure of the serpent, a symbol of the negating principle that inflicts suffering and pain and thus opposes the principle of divine creation. The dual nature of the creative force is visible also in Julian Wasser's photo, *Duchamp Playing Chess with a Nude (Eve Babitz)* (Fig. 10). Here, the darkly clad Duchamp could personify the negation by which the creative impulse becomes trapped within itself, while his chess opponent Eve Babitz embodies the constructive and nurturing side. Dürer's *The Desperate Man* (Fig. 11) portrays destructive creativity as a central theme, doing so with particular poignancy. In Picasso's *Family of Saltimbanques* (Fig. 12) the angel-like girl with black wings points to the inspiring muse of heavenly origin who can just as well lead to abysmal darkness. In her duality, this muse expresses the fact that creativity can turn around and manifest itself as a realm lacking all creative inspiration, and in an individual's absolute loss of creative capacity. The uncanny destructive dimension is pictured as well in van Gogh's painting, *The Potato Eaters* (Fig. 13) and in Paul Klee's *Carnival in the Mountains* (Fig. 14). In both of these paintings it takes the form of figures symbolizing the archetypal Great Mother, another feminine aspect of the creative force that provides vitalizing images and insights, and at the same time, can blunt the imagination and create conditions of deadly finiteness.

Destructive creative energy manifests itself in the lives of artists like van Gogh (Fig. 17), Poussin (Fig. 18), Gauguin (Fig. 19), and Munch (Fig. 20). As we know, van Gogh suffered madness, and is said to have cut off his own ear and to have taken his own life. Poussin's artistic activity was hindered by his affliction with Parkinson's disease. Gauguin was nearly driven to suicide by a life that was unsettled and fraught with money-worries and problematic relationships. The titles and contents of Munch's paintings often express his consumption by fear, jealousy, melancholy, and other demons. These four artists exemplify the fateful power of an existential destructiveness that often haunts creative people, and they show clearly the creative force itself as the director of such demise. The one and same creative force was at work in both their creative genius and plagued existences. Perhaps one could say that these artists were creative precisely because they were so intimately acquainted with the forces of negation. Or vice versa, they perhaps suffered so much illness and other hardship because they were so creative.

Finally, in Paula Modersohn's *Self-Portrait with Amber Necklace* (Fig. 23) death appears as life's correlative opposite stemming from one and the same primal creative force. The duality takes shape among other ways in the background greenery and blossoms that all at once recall a cemetery and portend new life. We find it as well in the rhizome cupped in the artist's hand, the motif that points to the pomegranate, emblem of the divine Persephone. As Hades's bride and Demeter's daughter, Persephone is associated with the Underworld and death, and also with the earth and spring. As we previously noted, soon after completing this painting Modersohn suffered a tragic death caused by an embolism following the birth of her passionately desired first child. Her biography is thus an especially moving testament to the duality of the creative force and in particular, to the reality of the archetypal Great Mother who both bestows life and ends it.

8.2. Creativity as the Cooperation of Opposites

Constructive creativity amounts to a cooperation of opposites, such as the conscious orientations to the past and the future; "masculine" directed thinking and "feminine" non-directed thinking; the creative individual and the collective unconscious; the ego and life; the here-and-now and the beyond. As emphasized so often throughout our study, fruitful creativity builds fundamentally on processes of transformation by which the sustained tension of opposites yields a transcendent third, a new image that joins and exceeds the dualities. The images may differ in appearance according to the different realms and the kinds of opposites involved in the process. But the aim underlying the unifying thrust always seems to be that of opening the conscious standpoint and transcending it with new and creative powers of perception. Let us re-consider the variety of antagonists:

8.2.1. The Past and the Future in the Realm of Consciousness

First we may appraise the past and the future as they come to play in the realm of consciousness. Two diametrically opposed approaches are implied here: The one oriented by the past receives and internalizes knowledge that is handed down, familiar, and well-known. The other, oriented toward the future, is led by the urge to discover entirely new things, and by curiosity about what is to come, about what could be different and better than things as they are. As we observed in foregoing chapters, creative insight obtains when the two orientations conjoin, to allow both: the reach back to the trusted past, and the view that opens to the future and the unknown.

This particular pair of differing and yet creatively co-operating attitudes is especially evident in the series of Chagall's paintings that we discussed in Chapter III, "Dimensions of Creative Consciousness." In *The Rabbi or the Pinch of Snuff* (Fig. 1), the Rabbi's left hand, resting on the Torah and holding the pinch, symbolizes the reception and honoring of age-old traditional knowledge. His right hand, elevated and poised at his lips, represents the future-oriented modus that senses, establishes, and transmits new findings. Just as Chagall's rabbi personifies in one figure the-receiving-and-the-doing—the-backward-glancing-and-the-forward-looking, so does the Chinese symbol Yin-Yang envision harmonious reciprocity in such antithetical qualities of consciousness. Similarly, in *Jew in Red* (Fig. 2) the old beggar totes on his left arm the bundle symbolizing his *fundus* of inherited and still available ideas and images. His blood-flushed right hand, however, probes the way forward with the help of a walking stick. This gesture represents the other side, the future-oriented ability to probe and set new pathways, as it were. In *Rabbi with Torah* (Fig. 3), it is the tefillin strap wrapped around the Rabbi's left hand and forearm that signifies the individual's binding to history and collective tradition. At the same time, his right arm, covered by his dark jacket sleeve, suggests a future that awaits individual discovery and design. In *Jew in Green* (Fig. 4), the left sleeve of the storyteller's jacket displays many jagged folds and deep crevices that suggest painful and incisive experiences of the past, held by memory in the present. And here again, the right sleeve, darkly shaded and more vaguely defined, suggests future and still hidden developments.

Thus, Chagall's series on the whole supports the idea that creative consciousness and primarily new perceptions arise from the interaction of the two antithetical frames of mind: the one that looks back, honoring and drawing on the past, and the one that looks forward, seeking to discern what future may bring.

8.2.2. *"Masculine," "Feminine," and Symbolic Thinking*

Let us now re-examine a set of opposites that belong to a different realm and that just as much come to play in the appearance of a new creative reality, the transcendent third, symbolic thinking. I have in mind here the interaction of the antagonistic pair, "masculine" and "feminine" thinking. My quotation marks mean to say that "masculine" and "feminine" are not gender-specific. Rather, these terms point at antithetical tendencies that are inherent to men and women alike. "Masculine" thinking is directed thinking, or a rational approach characterized by linear logic, goal-orientedness, methodology, abstraction, and intellectual reflection. "Feminine" thinking is non-directed thinking, or what Jung sometimes calls "fantasy thinking." Referring to our ability to think in images or by inner perception, this approach is non-rational, non-linear, of the moment, spontaneous, unpredictable, and intuitive. In a nutshell, we experience the two, respectively, as a directing consciousness and diffuse imagination. Successfully coupled, the two opposing modes give rise to the transcendent third and creative approach, symbolic thinking. Symbolic thinking is creative in that directing consciousness and diffuse imagination work in unison to discern meanings in images and to convert meanings into images.

Now, in Chapter IV, "Creativity as Interaction between Masculine and Feminine Factors," we dealt with five artworks in which directed thinking and non-directed thinking are indeed *symbolized* in the figures of men and women respectively. Such portrayals beautifully describe the dynamic process that brings the opposing masculine and feminine modes into an encounter and interaction that yields the transcendent third, the symbolic gestalt. In other words, all five paintings show that the creative product results from reciprocal movements between decisive consciousness and the offerings of a vivid, inner imagination. It makes sense that the antagonistic tendencies appear in the figures of men and women, for in the creative process the two modalities often behave as if they were autonomous entities, each with its own viewpoints and opinions, asserting themselves with the vehemence of a real quarreling couple: The masculine side may defend at all costs a fixed idea, an anticipatory assumption, or a claim to the knowledge upon which the successful outcome or the process depends. And in "his" view, the feminine side counters with seemingly absurd imaginings or distracting fantasies, or, like an offended partner, "she" falls silent, or breaks off contact entirely.

The amazing thing is, the quarrel is neither aimless, nor is it merely a battle of self-righteous wills. Rather, the "couple's fight" develops in service of a yet to be realized goal, that is, a symbolic gestalt or symbolic reality. In the course, masculine directed consciousness keeps the goal and logical procedures in sight—and it may thus serve to rein in a sprawling imagination if necessary. Conversely, feminine imagination supplies the wealth of inner images and ideas—and such imagination may infuse and thus correct directed consciousness when it becomes too narrow or rigid. In this way, the two move together toward the production of a symbolic gestalt, guided all along by the autonomous symbol-making factor, that is, the transcendent function.

The images we discussed in Chapter IV can thus be viewed again, now in light of the symbolic gestalt as being the goal of the creative encounter of masculine and feminine perspectives. Exploring the dynamics as they appear symbolically in the figures of men and women, we discover certain motifs—perhaps especially again the hands—that contribute significantly to our understanding of how symbolic gestalts or realities may be produced.

For instance, in Otto Dix's *Self-Portrait with Muse* (Fig. 6) Dix, grasping in one hand his scepter-like staff, represents the masculine thinking that holds the leading idea and directs the creative process with logic and rational method. The other side, feminine imagination, is personified in the muse, whom we take in this case especially to personify Dix's inner imagination. With the motif of the paintbrush guided by Dix's other hand, we have a poignant image of directed consciousness laboring to realize and bring visible contour to this inner reality. Indeed, Dix's cramped fingers imply a rational consciousness struggling to grasp its feminine counterpart. The other way around, the muse's uplifted hand suggests the power of feminine imagination that essentially nourishes and rules over the symbol-making process. In fact, as the muse's hand seems to touch the heavens, her gesture resembles that of a divine creator, and as such, she symbolizes in the truest sense the transcendent function or the creative product of this particular creative process. For the quality of thinking pictured in her figure is one in which the contributions of directed thinking and abundant imagination are not only conjoined, but are surpassed in what we could call sublime creative consciousness.

In contrast to Dix's portrait, René Magritte's *Attempting the Impossible* (Fig. 7) depicts the artist's effortless grasp of his paintbrush. Indeed, Magritte's hand almost seems to float, making a bridge-like connection with the muse's contours. His painterly hand thus here appears to function not only as the instrument of rational consciousness, but just as much as the receptor of contributions from the muse. With this motif, then, Magritte pictures a rather uncomplicated and fluid creative process, vitalized by the relatedness of directed thinking to its counterpart, imagination. It is not by chance that, while the artist and muse appear oppositionally as the contra-sexual man and woman, Magritte portrays them with very similar physiognomies. The harmonious, nearly twin-like couple mirrors the fact that Magritte, with his surrealistic themes, lived very close to the feminine realm of imagination. With this understanding of Magritte's artistic "dwelling place," we surmise that in this painting, the transcendent function is symbolized by artist's floating hand itself. It would represent a magical touch that unifies the opposites and that moreover resonates the air of mystery that is so characteristic of the creativity of the transcendent function.

The painter's hands figure prominently again in Manet's *Luncheon on the Grass* (Fig. 8). Let us note the right hand in particular, which forms the center point of the painting. It imagizes in an extremely condensed way the exchange between the masculine and feminine factors that participate in the creation of the painting itself as a symbolic gestalt: Manet's extended index finger signifies directed thinking with its characteristically active and aimful approach. His three other fingers, folded into his palm, suggest the integration of inspiring ideas received from feminine imagination. The artist's thumb, pointing obliquely toward the background and the bathing woman stands for the realization of the symbol developed jointly in the service of the transcendent function. Indeed, the bathing woman could symbolize the transcendent function itself. Manet would have been unfamiliar with this Jungian concept, but he would have lived the corresponding experience. That is, some mysterious background factor that determines the creative process according to its own intentions, and that mediates between the waters of imagination and the firm ground of consciously perceived objective reality.

We have already observed the wonderfully symbolic interplay between the two main figures in *Adam and Eve* (Fig. 9), a composition that illuminates Dürer's reliance on back-and-forth movements between his directing will and the gifts of his imagination. The gesturing Adam embodies the masculine assertion of an active position. The apple held forth in Eve's hand symbolizes the counter-position, the feminine offering of imagistically revealed knowledge.

In Dürer's picture it is the snake, coiled in the tree and biting Eve's apple, that imagizes the transcendent function, which aptly appears as a central motif and force that materializes in-between the two main protagonists and the respectively associated figures of the deer and the cat. The picture thus offers a highly differentiated representation of the mysterious symbol-making factor that undergirds creative activity. On one hand, the snake symbolizes the dialectic dynamic between the two main protagonists. At the same time it embodies the central force of evil, or the force of negation, or the paradox of "that power which would do evil constantly and constantly does good."[111] In other words, creative experience always involves some degree of grandiosity, exuberant conviction, delusions and mistakes, and correction, hesitation, doubt and self-questioning. Both dynamics are required—self-inflation and self-diminution. For it is the tendency to grandiose exaggeration and even madness that opens consciousness to new perceptions, while hubristic blinding is averted by the opposite tendency to humility, modesty, and self-criticism. Creative endeavors constantly oscillate between such feelings. This is one reason creative people find it so difficult to objectively assess the value of their own work.

As discussed in Chapter IV, the tree itself, representing the Tree of Knowledge, stands for the reality of the eternal becoming and growth of symbolic understanding. Reaching from the earth toward the heavens, this tree resembles the archetypal world axis, which symbolizes the mysterious experience and wisdom of the transcendent function that creates symbolic reality within the midst of an emerging work, within the midst of a life-long process, within the midst of existence, and indeed within the midst of the world. The transcendent function shapes reality into visible and meaningful appearances not only in artistic endeavors, but also in creative processes in general, and in the world itself.

The dynamism between the analogous pairs of opposites is represented on one hand by the deer walking away from Adam toward Eve, and on the other hand by the cat lying at Eve's feet and facing Adam. More specifically, the deer symbolizes collective Logos and spiritual insight, and the cat, the counterparts of sensuous desire and sovereign inner sensory perception. These two basic powers of the soul animate the creative endeavor, blending the antitheses of an animus-instigated search for sense, meaning, understanding, and truth—and an anima-inspired search for sensuousness, coherence, pleasure, and beauty. The two together motivate the curious search and spirit of discovery, and the fulfillment experienced in the emerging product with its successful appearance and form.

As in the self-portraits of Magritte and Manet, Julian Wasser's photograph *Duchamp Playing Chess with a Nude (Eve Babitz)* (Fig. 10) again condenses in the motif of one hand the symbolic dimension arising from the cooperation of directed thinking and diffuse imagination. In this case, Duchamp and Eve Babitz personify the respective opponents. Here the opposites are joined not as painter to muse, but as a pair of game players. Wasser's photograph captures a moment when Duchamp's elevated hand hovers undecidedly over the chess figures and also opens toward his female opponent. It is this gesture that so pointedly imagizes a symbolic third and Duchamp's exemplary creative gift: His approach to the making of art entailed essentially his attention to all kinds of objects in the world, and his fine attunement to meaningful manifestations of the objective imagination abiding in them. Thus with his ready-mades, Duchamp saw himself to be less the artistic designer of symbolic objects than the co-player in a game of chance. In this game, he had to wait for the moments when existing "banal" objects transmitted to him their inherent qualities of imagination and meaning. And then he, with the gained insight, elevated the objects as artworks. The chess timer in Wasser's photograph underscores the element of time that plays in this kind of creative hand. In other words, here, rational consciousness and imagination do not engage like an embattled intimate couple. Rather, they participate like respectful game players who make their moves, each in turn abiding by the time parameters, and availing themselves of opportunities offered by chance or synchronicity.

Where in Wasser's photograph might we discern a symbol of the transcendent function itself? It can be seen in the background display of Duchamp's actual piece, *The Large Glass*, the puzzling picture of what we called a "creativity machine." The transformative dynamism of the transcendent function comes across in this machine's imagined motion: its rotating central rod, and the rising and falling sine curves formed by the movement of the adjoining cone-shaped parts. This image goes to show that creative imagination not only produces new things—it also imbues existing things with new symbolic meanings.

8.2.3. The Creative Personality and the Collective Unconscious

In Chapter V, "The Creative Individual," we explored works that are characterized by their representations of the four-part paradigm of the psychological temperaments. We observed that the four types are always personified with their specific differences—and that each work places the four types opposite a mother figure who is located in or near the lower right-hand corner of the canvas. This place, by the way, is identified in many systems of picture interpretation as the "mother corner." Correspondingly, we noted that, in all of the pictures now under discussion, this corner is occupied by a feminine figure of mythic proportion, a gestalt in which we perceived the personification of the archetypal Great Mother and image of the collective unconscious. This particular gestalt developed our understanding that close proximity to the collective unconscious is among the essential attributes of the great creative personality. It is the influence of the collective unconscious that leads to creative works with epochal significance.

In this sense creativity is a spiritual force that makes use of creative individuals, developing itself through them and making of them vessels of spiritual insight that serves the common good and advances its creative enlargement. Seen in this light, the creative force is a transpersonal reality that benefits the greater community with the help of individuals who are compelled to recognize and fulfill a mission. Such individuals, taken into service by this larger force, avail themselves of particular qualities of charisma. The "demonic" personalities emanate subservience to a daimon that engenders their suffering and subjects them to life-long tasks that are carried out with relentless feelings of necessity. "Muse-inspired" personalities are carried by higher realms of imagination that infuse them with a sense of humanity's needs and what is to come. "Ingenious" personalities benefit from a "genius" that supplies, as if from nowhere, trail-blazing designs and insights. "Alchemical" personalities gain access to inner realms of being, the experience of which changes the perception and understanding of the world. And finally, "missionary" personalities are certain of being called to a task that aims to serve the common good.

From among such befallen individuals, there emerges the expanded individuality of the great creative person. He or she is characterized by the gift of access to *all four* of the temperament-specific modes of experience and expression: the choleric, the sanguine, the phlegmatic, and the melancholic. In the great creative individuals these four different temperaments and ways of being-in-the-world combine to exceed the ordinarily intrinsic one. Remarkably, in the pictures we explored, creative individuality with this kind of augmented vision is portrayed each time in close proximity to the image of the archetypal Great Mother. Let us now review the artistic expressions of her transpersonal nature and reality.

Dürer, in *The Desperate Man* (Fig. 11), describes the transpersonal dimension as a white cloth, one that likens the "cloud fringes" or the "bands of clouds" he used also elsewhere to symbolize transcendent realities. Picasso's *Family of Saltimbanques* (Fig. 12) attributes it with a young woman's heavenly gaze, accented by her crown-like hat and her contrasting rootedness in the earth. Van Gogh's *The Potato Eaters* (Fig. 13) distinguishes the old woman embodying the Great Mother by her large size and thus her elevated meaning among the other figures. Her ambiguous gesture—the one hand giving and the other as if taking—recalls the mother archetype as the source of life and death. Paul Klee captures the Great Mother's elemental great size and earth-boundedness in his *Carnival in the Mountains* (Fig. 14), showing her in her world-constituting and world-imagining aspects. In Dürer's *Madonna and Child with the Pear* (Fig. 16) the archetype appears as the Christian mother of God, her pear symbolizing the archetypal dimension per se. Each of these pictures illuminates the Great Mother as both the creator of the world and the force of imagination abiding within it.

The meaning, in a nutshell, is that for great creative individuals, the close proximity of this feminine Other forms a highly significant counterpart, opening their access to the well of ideas and images stored in the collective unconscious. While drawing from the well, these individuals also add to it with their works essentially new, enduring, and reverberating experiences. They activate the archetypal Great Mother and fill her with new life, even sowing the seeds of new archetypal paths. This interplay illustrates again the contrast between the "masculine mind" and its counterpart the "feminine imagination." It suggests that the deepest foundations of creativity lie in the cooperation of these two poles.

On closer examination, we find that this feminine Other appears not only as the Great Mother and image of the collective unconscious. She is shown more specifically as an archetypal mediator, that is, as one who both nourishes and transforms life, for better or worse. In Dürer's *The Desperate Man* (Fig. 11), the nurturing aspect appears in the mother's breasts. But their depiction as a part of an apparently armored upper body points to the duality of all archetypes. It bears recalling here that the archetypes, and specifically the collective unconscious, represent potentialities that may or may not take shape concretely in an individual's history, or in his or her current or future life. The collective unconscious is particularly active when it is drawn into a creative or spiritual process. Then it gives special emphasis to certain archetypes, exerting an influence that is giving and "to the point," as suggested in the plastically protruding breasts of Dürer's depicted mother. Otherwise, as Dürer's motif suggests, the archetypal Great Mother and image of the collective unconscious remains as if asleep or dead.

In the latter regard we note Dürer's delineation of the mother's dark, concave abdomen that starkly contrasts her illuminated, convex breasts. This aspect of the composition, emphasizing the elemental mother's association with death, points to the potential of the collective unconscious to exert destructive impulses and ideas that can lame or even destroy constructive creativity. Here the Great Mother's anti-creativity comes to the foreground, as we observed in our earlier discussion of this picture. Such an active harbinger of death from the depths of the collective unconscious impacts not only the creative individual, but also the collective at large, which, led under the banner of archetypal ideas, may enter into grandiose spiritual movements or even war.

In Picasso's *Family of Saltimbanques* (Fig. 12) the Great Mother appears more in its transforming aspect as a young woman. It is she who highlights the archetype's potential to imbue the creative individual with special predilections for change and renewal. We see the possibility, for instance, with a symbolic view of her gestures: Her one arm rests upon her lap, as if cradling internalized experience within her own center—while her other arm is upraised and poised against her shoulder, as if about to make something new of the internalized experience. Her conjoined gestures represent the same creative potential that transforms worldly things into symbolic images. It is suggested symbolically in the woman's repose on the bare earth, next to the clay water jug. This motif alludes to a unified being-at-one with the earthly here-and-now, and a being-immersed in the symbolic waters of change. The woman's hat, nearly floating above her head, implies in this unified quality of being the ability to imbue sensuous eidetic things with spiritual meaning. Indeed, Picasso's creative work itself is very much characterized by such transformational dynamics that we have ascribed to the Great Mother. We saw it in many ways, for instance, in his use and reinterpretation of other artists' existing works; in his continuous re-designing of elements within his own evolving works; in his capacity to transform concrete materials into pictures and sculptures; and finally, in his ingenious proclivity for abstraction.

This transformational, often playful, and overall creative quality of the Great Mother or the deep unconscious transmits to creative individuals their abundance of imagination and ideas about change and transmutation. Not only does this aspect of the unconscious provide the great creative individual with inspiration and images—it also realizes its own creative depths within the individual's creative action. It leads, so to speak, to a cumulating quality of fruitful creativity, as can be witnessed in Picasso's vast productiveness. The presence of this unconscious might also explain the otherwise little understood development of Picasso's life work, which evolved not in linear fashion but in jumps and leaps, known as his different periods. These periods represent fundamental changes of direction influenced by the archetypal Great Mother and her creative transformations. To put it slightly differently: Processes of linear consciousness cannot be said to have orchestrated the abrupt and unsystematic replacement of Picasso's visionary horizons and styles—from the concrete to the abstract, from the blue to the red, from the cubistic to the synthetic, from the antique to the non-figurative. Rather, this kind of shifting bespeaks guidance from the depths of the unconscious, itself being a creative and ever-changing force.

Just as we observed in a number of other paintings in this series, so, too, in Picasso's *Saltimbanques* a container symbolizes the creative work arising from the interplay of the creative individual and the realm of the Great Mother. Here it is the flower basket, to which we shall return. In Dürer's engraving, *The Desperate Man* (Fig. 11), it is the pewter tankard, which we understood before to suggest an addictive tendency. A widened interpretation is possible when we consider the tankard occupying a space in-between the phlegmatic man and the mother figure. In this case, the tankard could be seen as an entirely new container resulting from the encounter of the two "actors," the creative individual and the creative depths. It could represent new powers of perception, or a new conception of art, or a radically new technical accomplishment. All such things would correspond with the advent of engraving, the medium that began to allow artists to capture reality with extreme precision and also to reproduce their designs, making them more generally accessible. Thus in the form of the reproducible image, even art itself became a new kind of container. Picasso's flower basket on the other hand, with its many curving lines, appears to stage a different kind of collaboration between the creative individual and the creative unconscious; namely, one characterized by processes of becoming and transmutation in the sense of Goethe's often-cited, "… Formation, Transformation, / Eternal mind's eternal recreation."

8.2.4. Individuation, the Willful Ego, and Oppositional Life

As we have often noted, the autonomous creative force determines the lives of creative individuals and also their emerging lifeworks. Accordingly, over the course of time, an individual's creativity reflects the characteristics of self-realization or an individuation process. The all-encompassing individuation impulse is in the truest sense creative in that it leads creative individuals ever more to re-invent and move beyond themselves—first, to realize themselves as artists per se, and then to continuously pursue new perspectives and artworks that mirror their creative being and the ways it manifests itself in their lives and self-images. Indeed, creative individuation influences lifeworks to the effect that they very much resonate the artists' life experiences and their reflections on life and art itself. We could go so far as to say that a lifework itself amounts to the creative expression of and reflection on a life-long individuation process. Thus it comes as no surprise that lifeworks contain many motifs that refer to personal biographies, individual approaches to art, and previously accomplished artworks.

Holding in mind such influences and purposes of the individuation impulse, let us now add that an individuation process is creative also in that it takes place in-between and transcends opposite poles. The opposition we now highlight is that between the ego and life itself. The ego possesses its own quality of vision, its own ideas about life and work, and its own interests. Life as the opponent counters with its own facts and potentialities, such as inherited factors that determine a person's special gifts, limitations, and extenuating circumstances. Much the same as the coupled antagonists of directed and undirected thinking, "masculine" rationality and "feminine" imagination, and the creative individual and the collective unconscious, so do the willful ego and oppositional life constitute an antithetical pair and creative vessel. Inputs from each of the two contribute to a creative existence, and creative works transcend this opposition.

Works emanating from individuation-based creativity thus often contain the artists' reflections on their lives, their creative processes, and their understandings of art. As self-portraits are deliberate self-expressions, this genre is especially revealing of the artists' lives and individuation processes. With this understanding, let us briefly return to the self-portraits that we explored in Chapter VI, "Creative Existence."

To begin, let us consider van Gogh's *Self-Portrait with Bandaged Ear* (Fig. 17). While the artist's determined gaze conveys the sense of his willful ego, the motif of the bandaged ear alludes to oppositional life or the tragic history that led to van Gogh's alleged self-mutilation and his eventual death. The canvas leaning on the easel in the background underscores the fact that van Gogh made of his individuation process an object of his art, and that in his creative acts of self-reinvention and self-portrayal, he transcended the oppositions of human will and imposed suffering, of ego and disrupting life. Another background motif, the Japanese woodblock, points to the very meaningful biographical event of van Gogh's discovery of Japanese design and technique, which profoundly transformed his worldview and artistic approach. Therefore the woodblock also constitutes van Gogh's reflection on his own previous works and on art in general, and it thus represents a typical element of this type of existential creativity.

In his *Self-Portrait* (Fig. 18) Nicolas Poussin expresses the ego standpoint in his own willful gaze. In the image of the sketchbook supporting his right hand, he signals the painful fact of the Parkinson's disease that was increasingly disrupting his ability to paint. We have already noted the immediate background containing the large, inscribed canvas that points to Poussin's discovery of the capacity to express himself artistically despite the severe conflicts of will versus suffering, of freedom versus constraint. Moreover, we can say that his experience of the creative force led him to transcend his existential dilemma. Another background canvas portrays a woman on the verge of being embraced by some person whom we cannot see but for the outreaching arms. Taking our earlier interpretation a step further, this little portrait might suggest something more than Poussin's loving embrace of his muse; it could stand also as his reflection on his own over-reaching attempt to cling to and possess life itself. This would correspond with Jung's confession of the same dynamic, expressed at the beginning of *The Red Book*. A counter-position and resolution to Poussin's conflict takes shape in-between the portrait of the muse and the artist's own figure. It is, namely, the arabesque-like floral pattern, which bespeaks Poussin's ultimate conviction that as a *peintre philosophe*—a philosophical painter—he was bound to defer to autonomous nature as the real guide for his art and life.

In Gauguin's *Portrait of the Artist with the Yellow Christ* (Fig. 19) the motifs of the artist's far-reaching gaze and Polynesian blue pullover suggest the one existential pole, that of an ego that is open to new experience. The contrasting pole appears as the background Crucifix, symbolizing the artist himself as one who suffers severely limiting life realities. Gauguin thus reflects on a creative existence that entails a clash of human will with excruciating life circumstances. At the same time he foresees and realizes a Christ-like resurrection, that is, the creative potential to transcend the combative forces, to re-discover in himself the existential need for creative expression, and with this, to obtain new life. Like van Gogh's self-portrait, Gauguin's, too, incorporates reflections on the development of his own style. I now have in mind the background motif of the earthenware pot, an object that Gauguin had actually fashioned after a Peruvian pre-Colombian urn. This pot, viewed also in the light of a creative individuation process, refers to the age-old tradition that Gauguin held as an ideal for his own work—and it is equally a proud biographical reference to his Peruvian mother and early childhood in Peru.

Edvard Munch, in his *Self-Portrait: Between the Clock and the Bed* (Fig. 20), projects a confident and deliberating ego, conveyed in his decisive gaze, his friendly facial tones, and in the far background wall rendered in yellow. Hindering life circumstances appear in his figure's drooping shoulders, dangling arms, in the depressing blue tone of his suit, and in the foreground motif of his bed. The latter motif, recalling a hospital bed, alludes to Munch's intimate surroundings and familiarity with illness and death. In Munch's life, the extreme difficulty to reconcile his own will with impinging life circumstances made of creative expression an existential necessity, a real means to survive. It is not by chance that his self-portrait displays an extraordinary number and variety of frames, which include the many picture frames hanging on the yellow wall in the far background; the blue doorframe in the far background; the implicit doorframe in the middle ground; the blue framing of the long case clock; and the framing of the muse behind the open door. Altogether, they illustrate the possibility of creative self-expression in the limited frame of the picture and they suggest Munch's dire need and ability to creatively transform, and surpass his painfully constrained existence.

Munch's reflection on his own work with reference to an existing artwork appears in the motif of the muse at the outer right-hand edge of the canvas. Rendered in blue and with light brushstrokes, this figure is attributed with playfulness, grace, and levity—qualities that starkly contrast Munch's often heavy themes and painting style. Indeed, the blue tones in this little composition stand for a remote and difficult to obtain inner ideal, one that belongs as if to the upper spheres of free being. In the very title, *Self-Portrait: Between the Clock and Bed*, Munch reflects on his life history, thus again representing a typical aspect of the type of painting that emanates from a creative individuation process. Here, he refers to his being as it developed in a tension-filled, in-between realm defined by two poles: that of his creativity, symbolized by the clock—and that of his dire life circumstances, psychological paralysis, and other such conditions, symbolized by the hospital-like bed.

8.2.5. The Individual and Transcendence

As we underscored in Chapter VII, "Creativity and the Experience of Transcendence," creativity inheres in the interplay of an individual's subjective efforts and the objective will of a transpersonal creative force. Creative activity brings about the encounter of the two: the creative intentions and abilities of the individual on one hand— and on the other hand, the creative purposes and potentialities of a more encompassing and autonomous creative force. The two entities co-direct the creative process. The individual supplies personal perspectives, preferences, and designs, drawing on the sources of his or her subjective and limited body, constitution, and biography. At the same time, this specifically defined person confronts the objective creative force and its infinite supply of transpersonal structures and forms. They are gestalts of the kind that are visible in the designs of nature and the entire physical universe. They take shape as well in collective gestalts that characterize the individual's particular era, country, culture, and history. Accordingly, they emerge over time in the form of ideas and images that characterize particular civilizations, philosophies, religions, worldviews, and visionary horizons. As the individual inherits and becomes infused by all such things, he or she participates simultaneously in the designs of the larger creative force and as a member of a collective—and both come to bear in his or her creative processes.

An exchange of a special kind takes place when the two sides work together in harmony—that is, when the creative individual follows his or her personal perspective and the purposes of the greater creative force. In such an encounter the two "directors" unite to combine essentially antithetical influences, for instance, the subjective and the objective; the individual and the collective; the limited and the all-encompassing; and the imminent and the transcendent. With this, the larger creative reality incarnates itself in the individual's creative conditions and emerging works—and the other way around, the individual transcends his or her limited horizons to produce works that are all at once unique, trail-blazing, and imbued with universal meaning.

We observed this kind of dynamic and outcome among other places in Juan Miró's *Self-Portrait* (Fig. 21). This enigmatic work distills the artist's real appearance with his eyeglasses, necktie, and double-vested jacket, accessories that largely emblemize his standing as an average burgher. On the other hand, his figure is portrayed in the large dimensions and uniqueness that characterize a grand creator. Likewise the portrayal of his sensory organs conveys the sense of someone who is in touch with the cosmos and higher understanding. Incarnating itself in Miró's visage with its constellations of stars and other cosmic bodies, the immeasurable universe makes of him a concrete witness to its own existence—and at the same time, Miró the man is transcended to become a creature of cosmic value. The image as such, which could be mistakenly interpreted as an expression of a grandiose inflation, is far more Miró's acknowledgment that his personal creative activity relies on the great creative force that gave rise to and designed the universe. An artist's proximity to this force need not entail his or her identification with it in a clinical sense. Such closeness can just as well explain the portrayal of awe inspired by the great creative force and experienced by analogy in individual creative work.

Chagall's *Self-Portrait with Seven Fingers* (Fig. 22) while abstract, also distills real aspects of the artist's appearance and biography, and schematically points to his calling to fulfill a universal task. Earlier, we observed the motifs here that signify the permeating of Chagall's being with his Russian background and his anchoring in Paris. These cultural determinants, along with his felt artistic calling, transcend the incidental reality of the man Chagall. Nevertheless, they incarnate and realize themselves meaningfully in Chagall's concrete being and activity: The artist's right hand, grasping his palette, signifies a natural and subjective creative impulse. His left hand, mysteriously displaying seven fingers, guides our eye to his work-in-progress, a work that in fact replicates his earlier painting, *To Russia, to the Asses, and to the Others*. It is this aspect of the composition that points to the greater, sublime, and objective creative force. It would be this force that imbued Chagall with enduring impressions of his life in Russia and his immediate experience of Parisian life. In this light, Chagall's self-portrait reveals the two sources of creative inspiration: that of the visceral urge toward subjective expression, and that of a greater calling in service to a collective task.

In Paula Modersohn's *Self-Portrait with Amber Necklace* (Fig. 23) we see again the personal and transpersonal creative forces. There is on one hand the image of the nude, in whose figure Modersohn portrays herself as the imminent creator and author of her work. At the same time, transcendent nature pervades the picture and in the truest sense transcends the individual. In this way, Modersohn's portrait, too, captures the individual with her particular creative capacity involved in an exchange with the autonomous, all-encompassing creative force. Modersohn's hands, too, allude to the presence of the subjective and objective factors: Her left hand, folded in toward her heart and grasping a tuber, corresponds with the individual's elemental need for self-expression from the depths. Her elevated right hand, holding up a blossom that appears to be intended for the crown of flowers in her hair, reflects her connection with the great creative force that brings forth nature itself. The transpersonal meaning in Modersohn's painting and its vivid life and relevance to the here-and-now can be attributed to her integration of both aspects of the creative force—the one abiding in the individual and the other abiding in and as nature.

In Dürer's *Self-Portrait with Landscape* (Fig. 24a), the artist's subjective and grounded view of the life surrounding him is reflected in his clasped hands resting in the foreground upon a horizontal ledge. The other pole takes shape in the fashionable cap that signifies Dürer's artistic standing and also resonates his creative connection with the divine, ever-present, and form-giving God. Thus with the conjoined motifs, Dürer attests symbolically that creativity emerges between the poles of individual technical mastery, and the calling and spiritual sensibility emanating from above. With his portrayal of the background landscape and the analogous elements in his own figure, Dürer sheds light on the parallel realities of inner subjective life and the greater objective world. Here he conveys the personal experience of individual creative power mirroring the objective one that incarnates itself in the outer realities of nature and in the conditions and ideologies of the given era.

Finally, like the other paintings now under discussion, Rousseau's *Self-Portrait from L'Île Saint Louis* (Fig.25) displays the motif of creativity manifesting itself between the horizontal, earthly pole of individual subjectivity and the vertical pole of a transpersonal and transcendent reality. Here, Rousseau poses on a suburban road that extends behind him, first leading toward a near-by flag bedecked boat, then leading underneath a laterally stretching bridge, then beneath the city on the distant hill, and finally into the picture's deepest horizon. With this aspect of the composition Rousseau symbolizes horizontal and finite being with its corresponding mode of creativity, which in reality takes shape in the empirical acts of exploration, discovery, comparison, and insight. Rousseau's vast blue sky supplies the vertical counter-point to such ego-directed activity. As if observing from above, this sky evokes the transcendent source that embodies itself in the individual's spontaneously experienced inspirations, intuitions, revelations, and mystical insights. Rousseau's access to both kinds of creativity is suggested not only by his grounded and yet upright bodily comportment. It shows as well in the paired motifs: the tip of his paintbrush, pointing decidedly earthward and emphasizing the here-and-now, and his gaze into the beyond, toward the heavenly sphere of transcendence. Rousseau's seer-like emanation, corresponding with the ethereal clouds above him, alludes to his prophetic sensibility for things that are nascent or yet to come. His palette, marking the center of the canvas, appears to refer to the sublime creativity that emerges *sui generis* when the two directions of creativity play together, in unison. Insofar as the palette marks also the center of Rousseau's body and the center of his world, we can say that it symbolizes the congruency of the individual and the world. Such congruence implies that the artist's inner creative impulses and presented creative products resonate with his era and the collective's need for particular healing and transformative symbols.

All in all, this is the kind of creativity that is inspired and carried by the interplay of a lofty numinous force and an earthy finite ego, and that imbues the creative individual with a priest-like or mediumistic aura. Embodying this role, artists work within the limits of their earthly abilities, creating rich, universally meaningful images that incorporate qualities of completeness and wholeness received from above. Last but not least: just as Rousseau's pallet is inscribed with the names of his beloved wives, so does sublime creativity incorporate Eros as the central world-creating power that channels both the forces of love and transcendence into human endeavors.

8.3. The Objective Creative Force and the Four Temperaments

In Chapter VI, "Creative Existence," we thoroughly explored the psychological temperaments and their representation of four basically different and archetypal ways of being-in-the-world, each with its own creative propensity: the choleric, the sanguine, the phlegmatic, and the melancholic. As we emphasized, the autonomous symbol-making factor, or the objective creative force, incarnates itself differently in each one, and accordingly it imbues each with its constructive and negating potentials. Individuals experience the effects respectively as an enhancement of their creativity by the spontaneous appearance of symbols and symbolic understanding, or as the impairment or annihilation of their creativity by an equally spontaneous withdrawal of symbols and symbolic understanding. Let us illustrate with a review of Chagall's four paintings, which we have thus far viewed only partially in the light of the four temperaments. How do these pictures portray the temperaments and their specific creative bents? How do they make visible the constructive and destructive inclinations of the creative force?

8.3.1. The Choleric in The Rabbi, or the Pinch of Snuff

In Chagall's *The Rabbi, or the Pinch of Snuff* (Fig.1) we detect the choleric temperament, with the dominant yellow tones corresponding with the conventionally associated bodily fluid and natural element, i.e. yellow bile and fire. Setting aside the questionable science in favor of a symbolic approach, we can infer the following attributes:

In the constructive sense, choleric individuals are characterized by fiery intuition that enables their unmediated perception of new things, or that imbues them with prophetic abilities to discern in their epochs the prevailing trends of good and evil. Representing also light and gold, the yellow tones allude to the choleric's reception of heavenly given values, ideals, and the perfection and enlightenment found in spiritual ideas and principles. The combined gifts of a sharply differentiating mind, sensitive intuition, and original thought processes emanate symbolically in the Rabbi's deep-set eyes, pointed nose, and unruly temple hair. As suggested in the Rabbi's right hand, lifted to his lips, choleric individuals possess also the gift of oratory. This special rhetorical talent and capacity to explore and convey personally experienced ancient wisdom is suggested again in the Rabbi's left hand, resting upon the Talmud. His index finger and thumb, holding "the pinch," as the picture title puts it, convey the choleric's aphoristic talent to bring ideas to the point and make them accessible to general understanding.

When subsumed by the dark or negating side, the choleric's gifts dissolve into extremely narrow subjective conviction, and absolutism staked to one point of view. Such attitudes, suggested symbolically in the Rabbi's stiff and pointed beard, can conflagrate into fanaticism and fundamentalism. These destructive potentialities, arising from the depths of the Self, belong to the choleric's basic tenor and testify to the latent choleric tendency to oppose or lose touch with constructive creativity.

8.3.2. The Sanguine in Jew in Red

Chagall's *Jew in Red* (Fig. 2) represents the sanguine temperament and its correspondence with the color red, which lends the painting its title, dominates the canvas background, and appears also in the old beggar's right hand. Here the color stands symbolically for blood, the determining bodily fluid that endows the sanguine temperament with its characteristic vitality, emotion, and desire. These attributes form the basis of the sanguine bent for discerning meaning in interpersonal relationships, in elemental energies, and in depth origins and effects. The beggar's gaze, all at once inwardly absorbed and alert to the outside, suggests the sanguine propensity to perceive inner essences in outward appearances. His splayed right forefinger and thumb, guiding his walking stick, suggest the subtle sanguine touch for empathic feeling and relationship. At the same time, the motif evokes this temperament's gift of differentiated judgment with the special ability to formulate antitheses, and to ground subjective perceptions in objective reality. The walking stick itself suggests the especially creative potential held in these gifts, namely, the capacity to enlarge on developed ideas by placing them in the context of systematic theory. To put it another way, the walking stick, being the "instrument" that connects hand and foot, symbolizes the sanguine proclivity for bringing hypothesis and fact into relationship with each other.

Now, the beggar's luminous white hand points to a phenomenal sanguine bent for linguistic or visual creativity, as we have seen earlier. Viewed in connection with the beggar's sack, this luminous hand describes the sanguine inclination to dip into the personal unconscious to retrieve memories and bygone experiences, and especially, to articulate the contents creatively and make them a part of consciousness-raising processes.

The element of air appears in the white background wall, upon which the inscribed names of Chagall's esteemed artistic predecessors even seem to float, as if in the air. The motif as such expresses the sanguine appreciation for the gossamer, ethereal realm of the spirit, as it is realized here in Chagall's honoring of his mentors and creative inheritance.

In the lower left-hand corner of the canvas, we see the dark blue house enveloped in the night, a motif that points to the power of negation lurking in sanguine creativity. With its steeply peaked roof, this dark building in one way likens a tomb, while the eerie light emanating from the one window evokes the notion of a cramped, interior prison cell. All in all, it appears as a gloomy place where lively spirituality is reduced and subsumed to a narrow and rigid system; where "blue" intellectual distance reigns over "red" empathy; and where intellect itself serves no purpose but abstraction (see the steep triangular roof). In this view, Chagall's house suggests the potential for the sanguine to enter into a death trap or a prison of spiritual structures that do not illuminate understanding but shroud it in darkness. The creative ability to translate practice into living theory then becomes diametrically opposed by dogma and authoritarianism. The chessboard-like pattern of tiles in front of the house well symbolizes the ground and tight grid of rigid schemata that can lead to spiritual blindness and the drastic narrowing of spiritual horizons.

To sum up thus far: Just as with the choleric and other temperaments, sanguine creativity holds both potentials, the constructing and the negating. The negating and often destructive side manifests itself in the individual's narrowed horizons, over-determination by facticity, and entrapment in the earthly here-and-now. Constructive creativity on the other hand widens one's horizons and opens up and deepens symbolic understanding.

8.3.3. The Phlegmatic in Rabbi with Torah

Chagall's *Rabbi with Torah* (Fig. 3) offers a view of the phlegmatic temperament, traditionally understood to be determined by phlegm or mucus, the bodily fluid, which, in its healthy state, is translucent, pearlescent, or white. It appears here symbolically in the pervasive snowy background, in the rabbi's creamy white prayer shawl, in his moist face, and in his damp beard. Biologically speaking, mucus serves to maintain the moistness and suppleness of the linings of our inner organs, and thus contributes to the body's natural defenses against infection and other irritants. Translated symbolically, these attributes correspond first with the phlegmatic's suppleness in relationships, characteristically expressed in affability and commitment, and in a fundamental openness toward human nature in all of its manifestations. In further similarity, the phlegmatic is prone to psychological self-determination and self-regulation, tendencies, which maintain centeredness in the Self and defend against harmful impingements from the outside. The basic impulses to outer and inner care appear elsewhere in this rabbi, such as in his trusting gaze and embracing arms that convey the impression of sensitivity, authenticity, and acceptance of others. At the same time, his slightly rounded comportment suggests the characteristic inclination to sovereign self-repose.

Constructive phlegmatic creativity inheres especially in the ability to draw from within one's own depths new and generally meaningful insights. As suggested in the rabbi's reverent embrace of the Torah scroll, this proclivity represents a legacy of connection to the fundus of archetypal experience, which becomes visible in the phlegmatic's creation of concrete gestalts or other forms that give outward expression to inner contents. In this sense we are reminded of the Gothic script and other images that Jung so attentively rendered in the Red Book. Jung's example attests that practical or physical creativity essentially involves submission to a higher force that moves the individual far beyond his or her known limits and toward all possible succeeding insights and developments. In this sense, the phlegmatic bent incarnates the aim of the creative force to provide fresh insight from the collective unconscious, working through the individual's hands-on practice and experimentation.

Now, just as the phlegmatic is said to be governed by phlegm, this temperament is also said to be characterized by the element of water. In Chagall's portrait, this moist element appears symbolically along with mucus in and as the snow-bedecked background. Water's symbolic meanings are multifold. Limiting ourselves to the implications for phlegmatic creativity and imagination, we can say that it represents the origin of life and dynamic transformation. Water in this sense symbolizes the phlegmatic concern with the transformation and renewal of consciousness through imagination and symbolic images. However, the element of water in this painting just as much points to the negating potential in the phlegmatic bent. In the form of crystallized and sullied snow, water is a non-flowing and impure fluid that connotes the phlegmatic inclination to succumb to a frozen soul, a stagnating spirit, a blocked body. The condition bespeaks not only a lack of transformational dynamics, but also an overt hindrance of transformation and a state of inertia staged by the creative force itself. Like the sullied snow that pervades the canvas background, it is a cold and inert state of being that can infiltrate the phlegmatic horizon, and it can thus also induce severe depression that deprives the individual of his or her otherwise flexible nature and motivation to develop constructive creative works and insight.

According to the classical concept, negative mood changes are not only inherent in a given temperament and thus determined by the respective imbalance of bodily fluids. In this system negative moods are also attributed to the specific cause of intense creative endeavor. Again setting aside the questionable science, this interesting thought supports our notion that creativity involves both constructive and negating or destructive potentials, each according to one of the four basic temperaments or psychological dispositions. I am ever again astonished by the reality that the one autonomous creative force engenders within us not only constructive energies but also negating ones. We may well experience an inspiring creative spirit—one that vivifies life, aims to open up our symbolic understanding, and supports our bringing forth of new creative gestalts. But we can just as much experience the absence or loss of that spirit and an existence that amounts to little more than lifeless or empty being, or being in sheer materiality, or being in a stagnant and sullied world—all imagized by the darker meanings in Chagall's pervasive snow.

8.3.4. The Melancholic in Jew in Green

In Chagall's *Jew in Green* (Fig.4), the old storyteller, set against a predominantly black background, personifies the melancholic temperament governed by black bile. At this juncture let us note that in all four of Chagall's paintings under discussion here, it is the coloring of the canvas backgrounds that prevailingly represents the temperaments according to their determination by the bodily fluids— yellow bile, blood, phlegm, and now, black bile. These compositions thus illuminate temperament per se as being the emotional background of each of the four approaches to creativity. To put it slightly differently, Chagall's compositions reflect the underlying emotions or moods that determine the four basic ways of being in the world.

Now, as black bile manifests itself in *Jew in Green*, it alludes to the realities of negation, ends, death, and nothingness that belong to the melancholic ground of being. These realities contribute essentially to the melancholic's characteristic pensiveness, inwardness, and his or her metaphysical need to get to the bottom of things, to find a philosophical perspective on life. This mindset contrasts with others that actively engage to change the world. The point of departure for melancholic pensiveness is the experience of objective boundaries and subjective limits. These in turn can motivate the melancholic's creative efforts to overcome, to find solutions, to move beyond personal confines.

The melancholic's particular creative abilities are symbolized in *Jew in Green*, for instance by the storyteller's large green head, which points to a "green" intellect, or one close to nature. As previously discussed, the mode of thinking is not abstract, but phenomenological. It aims to grasp the objective spirit that is manifest in the appearances of things, be they in nature, in art, in religion, or in other cultural phenomena. To borrow from Hegel, the melancholic grasps meaning by achieving sense-certainty. We alluded to this "green" approach when we explored Chagall's composition of the storyteller's hair, which, as it were, frames the five senses by which melancholic individuals gain their orientation to the world. For them, the senses function like antennae that pick up the inner meanings of things.

In this chapter we already observed the storyteller's jacket sleeves, noting the left one with the many sharp folds that suggest a life characterized by just as many ruptures, hard hits, turning points, and periods of disillusionment. These meanings correspond with the melancholic life, and point to the melancholic's ability to experience it as an essential consciousness-transforming process that can open the way to new creative vision. We observed as well the creative potential symbolized by the second sleeve, which we may now take to represent another special melancholic gift—namely, the capacity to create novel things or ideas with nonchalance and spontaneity. The pair of sleeves, then, represent opposing tendencies that come into play with each other to characterize the melancholic's creative dynamics and style: on one hand, the predilection for being both the object and the director of consciousness-making forces—and on the other hand, the penchant for carefree creative work.

Let us consider as well the sheets of religious text upon which the storyteller sits. These allude to the melancholic proclivity to make of age-old spiritual texts and traditions the basis of personal enlightenment, to integrate these sources, and to invest them with new life. In this spirit, the melancholic is prone to draw inspiration and ever new surprising insight from the creative products of antiquity and by-gone centuries, be they in the form of philosophies, artworks, myths, fairytales legends, literary works, or scriptures in the Bible, the Koran, or in the Upanishads.

The storyteller's cap, too, tells us something about the melancholic temperament and its particular creative calling and abilities. It has to do with the topic of creativity as such. In this sense the melancholic feels compelled to witness the objective creative force, to thematize it, and to bring it to mind. Indeed, throughout our study we have tried to see how this greater creative force is manifest and palpable in works of art. Whether it occurs explicitly or implicitly, artworks themselves become intermediaries in that they contain and convey the creative force's vitalizing attributes. Staging in the artwork its own site of appearance and laboratory, the creative force here immediately engenders creative insight, new perceptions of the world, fresh self-awareness, and in particular, awareness of one's own creativity.

Just as the other temperaments are associated with natural elements, the melancholic is associated with earth, which appears symbolically in the angular shapes on the right-hand side of the canvas. This motif suggests the melancholic preference to abide in immediate earthly being, and to relate to the realities of this finite, concrete, outer world. Melancholic individuals thus take their cues for creative work and meaning from the given outer social situation, from the necessities and possibilities of the times, from the concrete conditions of the world, and from unexpected events and coincidences that life itself throws into the mix. Accordingly, these individuals stake special value in their effectiveness in the concrete world and the given time.

Where might the destructive aspect of the melancholic show in *Jew in Green*? The clue lies in the dark silhouette or shadow arising behind the storyteller's figure. Indeed, this shadow almost seems to personify the ever-present potential for the melancholic's creative vision and sense of meaning to succumb to non-meaning. The real malaise, the *furor melancholicus*, takes shape in the overwhelming experience of absolutely annihilating meaninglessness. This is when the melancholic is befallen by a tormenting "nothing-but" world, a world deprived of all creative breadth, depth, height, and constructive inspiration, because symbolic understanding is utterly repressed. The biblical Job similarly falls prey to some diabolical force, which our present understanding allows us to call the autonomous and all-encompassing force of negation.

It is far beyond the lone-struggling ego to avoid or overcome such metaphysical experience. A certain creative attitude is required, one that is coded into *Jew in Green* in the form of the previously noted Kaddish prayer: "He who makes peace in His heights, may He make peace, upon us and upon all Israel." To enter into the meaning of these words is to set aside deliberate ego efforts, and to hand oneself over to the creative force *sui generis*, the sovereign one that works as if in the unreachable heavenly heights to make peace, or that makes possible the transcendence of one-sidedness and polarization.

From this one and only creative force ensues the creative attitude that exceeds ego-induced resolve and from which ensues the following dialectic: a quality of creativity that, freed of one-sided ego desire, appreciates both the differences of opposites and also the effect of transcendent forces that enable the creative reality of peace between them.

Overview of Illustrations

Chapter III: Dimensions of Creative Consciousness

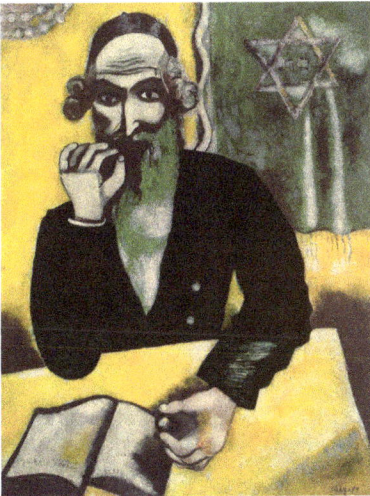

Figure 1

Figure 2

Figure 3

Figure 4

Figure 5

Chapter IV: Creativity as Interaction Between Masculine and Feminine Factors

Figure 6

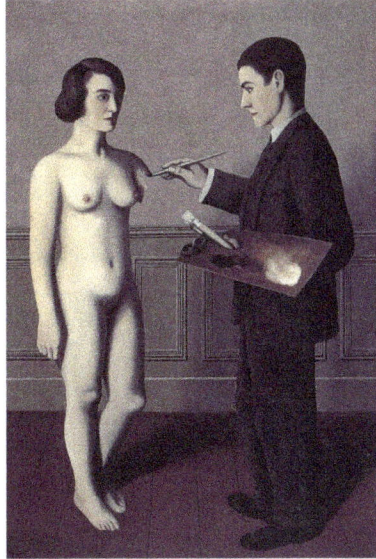

Figure 8

Figure 10

Figure 7

Figure 9

Chapter V: The Creative Individual

Figure 11

Figure 12

Figure 13

Figure 14

Figure 15

Figure 16

Chapter VI: Creative Existence

Figure 17

Figure 18

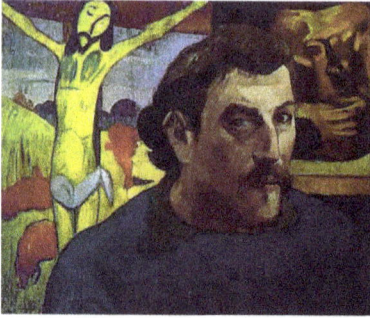

Figure 19

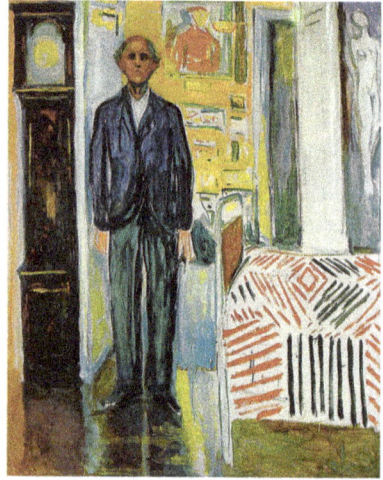

Figure 20

Chapter VII: Creativity and the Experience of Transcendence

Figure 21

Figure 22

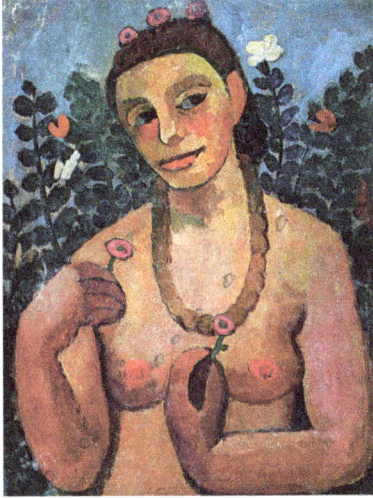

Figure 23

Figure 24

Figure 25

NOTES

CHAPTER I
INTRODUCTION

1. C.G. Jung, "The Problem of Types in the History of Classical and Medieval Thought" (1921/71), in *Psychological Types, The Collected Works of C.G. Jung*, vol. 6, eds. Sir Herbert Read, Michael Fordham, Gerhard Adler, William McGuire, trans. R.F.C. Hull, H.G. Baynes, Ninth printing (Princeton, N.J.: Princeton University Press, 1990), §93.

2. Mihàly Csikszentmihalyi, *Creativity: Flow and the Psychology of Discovery and Invention* (New York: Harper Perennial, 1996).

3. Melvin Rhodes, "An Analysis of Creativity," in *Delta Kappan* 1961, Vol. 42, No. 7, pp. 307–309.

4. Jung, *Memories, Dreams, Reflections* [1963], ed. Aniela Jaffé, trans. Richard and Clara Winston, Rev. Ed. (New York: Vintage Books, 1989), p. 297.

5. Jung, *The Red Book: Liber Novus*, ed. Sonu Shamdasani, trans. Mark Kyburz, John Peck, Sonu Shamdasani, Philemon Series (New York: W.W. Norton & Co., 2009), p. vii.

CHAPTER II
MANIFESTATIONS OF CREATIVITY
A PHENOMENOLOGICAL SKETCH

6. Sigmund Freud, *Gesammelte Werke*, Volume 15, *Neue Folge der Vorlesungen zur Einführung in die Psychoanalyse* (London: Imago Publishing Co., Ltd., 1940), p. 86.

7. Sigmund Freud, cited in Marcus Pound, "Lacan, Metaphysics, and Belief," in *Belief and Metaphysics*, eds. Connor Cunningham, Peter M. Chandler, Jr. (London: SCM Press, 2007), p. 416. Alternative translation: "Where id was, there ego shall be," Freud, *New Introductory Lectures on Psychoanalysis*, trans. James Strachey (New York: W.W. Norton and Co., 1965), p. 100.

8. Jung, *The Red Book*, p. 245.

9. Ibid., p. 253.

10. *The Spiritual Exercises of St. Ignatius of Loyola* [1914], trans., Father Elder Mullan SJ (Amazon, CreateSpace Independent Publishing Platform, 2014).

11. Johann Wolfgang von Goethe, *Faust, Part One*, trans. David Luke (Oxford: Oxford University Press, 2008), lines 682-684.

CHAPTER III
DIMENSIONS OF CREATIVE
CONSCIOUSNESS IN
EXAMPLES OF PAINTING

12. Freud, in Pound, "Lacan, Metaphysics, and Belief," p. 416.

13. Jung, *The Black Books, 1913-1932*, ed. Sonu Samdashani, trans. Martin Liebscher, John Peck, Sonu Samdashani, in collaboration with the Philemon Foundation (NY: W.W. Norton, publication pending).

14. Jung, *Red Book*, p. 229. On the same page Jung contrasts "the superficial spirit of this time" with "the spirit of the depths."

15. Albrecht Dürer, cited in, author unknown, *"Melencolia I: An Indeterminate Object," Seconds Issue 15*, p.1, uploaded by Peter Lewis, at https://www.academia.edu/7481960/Melencolia_1_An_ Indeterminate_Object (accessed January 19, 2016).

16. "Mourners Kaddish," in *Jewish Prayers* (Jewish Virtual Library), at https://www.jewishvirtuallibrary.org/jsource/Judaism/ kaddish.html (accessed January 18, 2016).

17. Annette Weber, "Marc Chagall," in *Die Sammlung Im Obersteg im Knstmuseum Basel* (Basel: Kunstmuseum Basel, Stiftung im Obersteg, 2004), p. 114.

18. Chagall's remark about the war: "I didn't realize that, before a month was up, that bloody comedy would begin, as the result of which the whole world (and Chagall with it) would be transformed into a new stage on which tremendous mass-scale productions would be given." Marc Chagall, *My Life*, trans. Elisabeth Abbott, 2nd printing, Online edition (New York: Orion Press, 1960), p. 117, at *Questia*, a part of Gale, Cengage Learning, www.questia.com (accessed January 18, 2016).

19. In this sense, says Annette Weber, "[Chagall's portraits of Jews] become symbols of the existence of the Jewish people, who are constantly threatened by persecution and homelessness and nevertheless hold fast to their doctrine." Weber, "Marc Chagall," p. 114, my translation.

20. Jung, *Memories,* p. 297.

21. Johann Wolfgang von Goethe, *The Collected Works, Faust 1 & 2*, trans. Stuart Atkins, 1st Princeton Paperback Printing (New Jersey: Princeton University Press, 1994), lines 6278-6288.

CHAPTER IV

CREATIVITY AS INTERACTION BETWEEN MASCULINE AND FEMININE FACTORS

22. This difference between a single-minded, rational thinking and a dual-minded, creative thinking is not identical with the difference Jung notes between "directed" thinking and "non-directed thinking"

or fantasy-thinking." Jung contrasts directed thinking, which guides the sciences, and effortless fantasizing—while I compare here one-poled thinking with the two-poled thinking that in the sense of Jung's transcendent function elicits a creative third.

23. Jung, "Two Kinds of Thinking" (1911-12/1952/1967), CW 5, §20.

24. In the context of Spanish Flamenco there is the expression, *hay duende*. It designates the sublime moment when a trance seizes and carries the dancer beyond his or her familiar ability—and suddenly the dancer and the audience itself are uplifted by an incomparable, heightened creative energy. In the artist's rendering hand we can discern a similar sense of being led beyond one's own willful efforts.

25. Jung, "Psychological Aspects of the Mother Archetype" (1938/1954), CW 9i, §194.

26. Jung noted both thinking and feeling to be rational functions, in so far as they each operate with judgment. This rational quality is underscored by Manet's emphasis on the two figures' faces and their unequivocal eye contact with the observers of the picture. It becomes especially clear when we compare the other two figures: They stand for the so-called irrational functions of intuition and sensation, which handle or deal with material reality and here lack the conscious eye contact with the observer.

27. The sequence of discovery can differ, though, as can be seen in the example of Marc Chagall's work in 1969 on the stained glass windows for the synagogue at the Hassadah University Clinic in Jerusalem. Each of his wonderfully fashioned twelve windows, symbolizing the tribes of Israel, was carefully developed in four sketches. In the four sketches each single window was worked out according to the special perspectives of the four functions of consciousness. Chagall thereby chose the following sequence: first by thinking (his determination of the motifs); then by sensation (his creation of a black and white, pen and charcoal drawing that conveyed the theme's three dimensional volume); then by feeling (his choice and distribution of the color surfaces); and finally, by intuition (his concrete arrangement of the colors and motifs).

28. See the gesture of the right hand.

29. Henri-Georges Clouzot, *Le Mystère Picasso*, ed. Henri Colpi (1956). Awarded the Cannes Jury prize, the film can be viewed with English subtitles at http://www.openculture.com/2012/04/

ithe_mystery_of_picassoi_landmark_film_of_a_legendary_artist_at_ work_by_henri-georges_clouzot.html (accessed May 20, 2016).

30. In the latter vein the mouse itself is associated with Apollo, the god of Truth and Knowledge. The mouse earns its symbolic proximity to the god because of its instinct to gnaw its way into the light, thus embodying the characteristics of unstinting effort and an appetite for clarity and illumination.

31. Duchamp was in fact an avid chess player, who eventually gave up his art for the game, became a member of the French national team.

32. Duchamp also produced a number of paintings, but for these he never received the acclaim he earned for his ready-mades. That said, *The Large Glass*, his major work, is part sculpture, part painting, and part collage.

33. Goethe, *Faust II*, Act. 1, Scene IV, 6287-88f.

CHAPTER V

THE CREATIVE INDIVIDUAL

34. Friedrich Nietzsche, *Human, All Too Human, Parts One and Two*, trans. Helen Zimmerman, Paul V. Cohn (NY: Dover Publications, 2006), p. 250.

35. Walter L. Strauss, ed., *The Complete Engravings, Etchings, and Drypoints of Albrecht Dürer* (NY: Dover Publications, 1973), p. 170.

36. Erwin Panofsky, *The Life and Art of Albrecht Dürer,* 3rd edition (NJ: Princeton University Press, 1948), p.177.

37. Fritz Riemann, *Grundformen der Angst* (Munich: Ernst-Reinhardt-Verlag, 1990).

38. Plato, "The Apology of Socrates," in *The Apology, Phaedro and Crito*, trans. Benjamin Jowett, ed. Charles W. Eliot, The Harvard Classics, Vol. II, Part 1, §58 (NY: P.F. Collier & Son, 1909-14; Bartleby.Com, 2001), at http://www.bartleby.com/2/1/ (accessed June 16, 2016).

39. Johann Wolfgang von Goethe, Wed., March 2, 1831, *Conversations of Goethe with Johann Eckermann and Soret*, trans. John Oxenford, New Ed. (London: George Bell & Sons, 1875), p. 525.

40. Eckermann, in Ibid., Mon., Feb. 28, 1831, p. 532.

41. Goethe, in Ibid., "Wed., March 30, 1831," p. 406.

42. Mihaly Csikszentmihalyi, Flow: The Classic Work on How People Achieve Happiness (NY: Harper & Row, 1992).

43. David Coppedge, "Cosmic Energy: Creative or Destructive?," in *Acts and Facts*, 2010, 39(5):17, at http://www.icr.org/article/cosmic-energy-creative-or-destructive/ (accessed June 17, 2016).

44. Hermann Hesse, *The Glass Bead Game*, trans. Holt, Rinehart, and Winston (NY: Picador, 1969), p. 371.

45. Albrecht Dürer, Peter Russell, *Delphi Complete Works of Albrecht Dürer*, trans. unknown, Delphi Classics, Book 26, Version I, Master of Art Series, E-Books (Hastings, UK: Delphi Publishing, Ltd., 2016), p. 190.

46. Vincent van Gogh, Letter No. 497, "To Theo van Gogh," Neuenen, Thursday, 30 April 1885, *Vincent van Gogh, The Letters: The van Gogh Letter Project*, trans. Diane Webb, John Rudge, Lynne Richards for the letters in Dutch; Imogen Forster; Sue Dyson for those in French, Web Edition, Amsterdam: Van Gogh Museum, 2007, at http://vangoghletters.org/vg/letters.html (accessed June 28, 2016).

47. Ibid., original italics.

48. Ibid.

49. Ibid.

50. Claude Lévi-Strauss, *The Savage Mind*, trans. unknown, The Nature of Human Society Series, eds. Julian Pitt-Rivers, Ernest Gellner (Chicago: Chicago University Press, 1966), p. 21.

51. van Gogh, *Letters*, No. RM25, Auvers-sur-Oise, Wednesday, July 23 1890; unfinished, unsent letter; earlier version of Letter No. 902.

52. Ibid., No. 226, The Hague, Friday, 12 or Saturday, 13 May 1882.

53. Ibid., No. 371, The Hague, on or about Tuesday, August 7 1883, original italics.

54. Paul Klee, Tombstone inscription, in *The Diaries of Paul Klee, 1898-1918*, ed. Felix Klee, trans. Pierre B. Schneider, R.Y. Zachary, Max Knight (Berkeley: University of California Press, 1968), p. 419.

55. Klee, "The Two Mountains," trans. Stacy Wirth, from "Zwei Berge gibt es" (1903), in Paul Klee, *Gedichte*, ed. Felix Klee (Zürich-Hamburg, Arche Verlag AG, 2005), p. 55. Translation by permission of Arche Verlag for original publication in, Paul Brutsche, "Paul Klee and the Symbol of the Mountain: On the Uncertainties of Human

Existence," in *Intimacy: Venturing the Uncertainties of the Heart, Jungian Odyssey Series Vol. I*, eds. Isabelle Meier, Stacy Wirth, John Hill (New Orleans: Spring Journal Books, 2009), pp. 17-18.

56. Klee, cited in Carola Giedion-Welcker, *Paul Klee*, trans. Alexander Gode (NY: Viking Press, 1952), p. 61.

57. Klee, "Diary IV, March 1916–December 1918," *The Diaries*, §1008, p. 345.

58. Klee, *Paul Klee Notebooks, Vol. I, The Thinking Eye*, trans. Ralph Manheim, ed. Jurg Spiller (London: Lund Humphries, 1973), p. 86.

59. Klee, *Notebooks Vol. I*, pp. 76 and 93.

60. Giedion-Welcker, *Paul Klee*, p. 56.

61. Giedion-Welcker, p. 61.

62. Klee, "Diary III, June 1902 to September 1906," *The Diaries*, §747, p. 194.

63. Ibid., "Diary I, Munich III, 1900–1901," §136, p. 48.

64. Ibid., "Diary IV, March 1916–December 1918," §1008, p. 345.

65. Ibid., "Diary III, Trip to Tunisia [1915]," §952, p. 315.

66. Ibid., *Notebooks Vol. I*, p. 357.

67. Ibid., p. 82.

68. Ibid., "Diary III, June 1902 to September 1906," *The Diaries*, §713/14, p. 190.

69. Albrecht Dürer, "Four Books on Human Proportion 1528," in William Martin Conway, *Literary Remains of Albrecht Dürer*, trans. unknown (Cambridge: The University Press, 1889), p. 247; displayed by the Cambridge University Press Archive, at https://books.google.ch/books?id=Kjs9AAAAIAAJ&dq=Dürer,+four+books+on+human+proportion&source=gbs_navlinks_s (accessed July 9, 2016).

70. Erich Neumann, "Experience of the Unitary Reality" [1952], in *The Place of Creation*, trans. Hildegard Nagel, Eugene Rolfe, Jan van Heurck, Krishna Winston, Bollingen Series LXI-3 (Princeton, NJ: Princeton University Press, 1989).

71. Jung, Erich Neumann, Letter 18J, 22.XII.1935, *Analytical Psychology in Exile: The Correspondence of C.G. Jung and Erich Neumann*, ed. Martin Liebscher, trans. Heather McCartney, Philemon Series (Princeton, NJ: Princeton University Press, 2015), p. 118.

72. We note the band extending from the figure's right hand to the fruit basket. It could emphasize the creative gesture with which this phantasmagoric being conjures fruit and other things into existence.

At the same time it suggests the cooperation that exists between the creative individual and the greater creative reality or symbol-making factor, which enables creative being in the first place.

73. Rainer Maria Rilke, "The First Elegy (1912)," in *The Duino Elegies*, trans. A.S. Kline, at *Poetry in Translation* (© 2004), http://www.poetryintranslation.com/PITBR/German/Rilke.htm#anchor_Toc509812215 (accessed February 15, 2017).

74. Dürer, Letter to the Nuremberg City Council, 1526, English translation cited from Peter Russell, *Delphi Complete Works of Albrecht Dürer*, Masters of Art Series, E-book edition (Domicile unstated: Delphi Classics, 2016), p. 159.

75. Dürer, inscription on *The Four Apostles*, English translation cited from Russell, *Delphi Complete Works*, p. 157.

76. Ernst Kretschmer, *Physique and Character: An Investigation of the Nature of Constitution and of the Theory of Temperament* (1925), International Library of Psychology, 2nd Edition, Digital Printing (Oxon, UK: Routledge, 2009).

77. See Peter Strieder, *Dürer* (Königstein im Taunus: Langewiesche Nachfolger KG, 2012), p. 326.

78. Ibid., p. 322.

79. Erich Neumann, *The Great Mother: An Analysis of the Archetype*, trans. Ralf Mannheim, Bollingen Paperback Edition, 2nd Printing (Princeton, NJ: Princeton University Press, 1955/1974), p. 24.

80. Dürer, "Four Books on Human Proportion," in Conway, p. 179.

81. Jung to Jacobi, 24 September 1948, in Jung and Neumann, *Analytical Psychology in Exile*, p. xli.

CHAPTER VI
CREATIVE EXISTENCE

82. The use of the five senses as a specifically feminine creative device is wonderfully portrayed in *The Lady and the Unicorn*, the famous series of six tapestries created around 1500 and exhibited at the *Musée national du Moyen Age* in Paris.

83. Hans Kaufmann, Rita Wildegans, *Van Goghs Ohr. Paul Gauguin und der Pakt des Schweigens* [Van Gogh's Ear: Paul Gauguin and the Pact of Silence] (Berlin: Osburg, 2008).

84. See the Jungian analyst James Hillman, "On Psychological Creativity," in *Eranos Jahrbuch 1966* (Zürich: Rheinverlag, 1967), p .365 ff.

CHAPTER VII
CREATIVITY AND THE EXPERIENCE OF TRANSCENDENCE

85. The nakedness in this painting gains special meaning with the knowledge that Paula Modersohn-Becker was the first woman in the history of western art to paint a nude self-portrait. See for example John Colapinto, "Paula Modersohn-Becker: Modern Painting's Missing Piece," in *The New Yorker*, October 29, 2013, at http://www. newyorker.com/books/page-turner/paula-modersohn-becker-modern-paintings-missing-piece (accessed January 15, 2017).

86. Susan Bach, Life paints its Own Span: On the Significance of Spontaneous Pictures by Severely Ill Children (Einsiedeln: Daimon, 1991).

87. This phrase is my translation of the German "Hang zum Gesamtkunstwerk," the title of the famous exhibition by the Swiss exhibition designer Harald Szeemann, which debuted in Zürich in 1983 and was later shown in several European museums.

88. Erich Neumann, *Art and the Creative Unconscious* (Princeton, NJ: Princeton University Press, 1959/1974), pp. 86-87.

89. Jung, "Two Kinds of Thinking," CW 5, e.g., §17-18, § 20, §36.

90. For more on the subject of surface, appearance, and beauty see Roland Schenk, *The Soul of Beauty, A Psychological Investigation of Appearance* (Lewisburg, PA: Bucknell University Press, 1992).

91. Rilke, "The First Elegy" (1912), trans. A.S. Kline.

92. Klee, "Diary III, June 1902–September 1906," §660, p. 183.

93. Jung, "II. Schiller's Ideas on the Type Problem" (1921/1971), CW 6, §197.

94. *The Hidden Dürer*, in Strieder, pp. 23–24; my translation of the original Old German: "Zw der kunst recht zw molen ist schwer zu kumen. Dorum wer sich dortzw nit geschickt fint, der vndersteh sich der nicht. Dan es will kumen van den öberen eingissungen."

95. Jung, "Two Kinds of Thinking," CW 5, e.g., §17-18, §20, §36.

96. Dürer, cited in K. Lange and F. Fuhse, *Dürers schriftlicher Nachlass aufgrund der Originalhandschriften und theilweise neu entdeckter alter Abschriften* (Dürer's Written Will Partly on the Basis of Newly Discovered Old Manuscripts) (Walluf Dr. Martin Sändig, 1893/1970), p. 295; my translation of the Old German: "Gott ist es, der alle Kunst beschaffen hat. Dann ein guter Maler ist inwendig voller Figur, und obs müglich wär, daß er ewiglich lebte, so hätt er aus den inneren Ideen, davon Plato schreibt, allweg etwas Neus durch die Werk auszugiessen."

97. Klee, "On Modern Art," Jena Lecture January 26, 1924, trans. Paul Findlay, in *Notebooks Volume I, The Thinking Eye*, trans. Ralph Mannheim (London: Lund Humphries, 1961/1973), p. 93.

98. Jung, "On the Relation of Analytical Psychology to Poetry" (1922), CW 15, §130.

99. Schenk, *The Soul of Beauty*, p. 138.

100. See also Adolf Portmann (1887-1982), *Biologie und Geist* (Biology and Spirit) (Zürich: Rhein-Velag AG, 1956). Portmann was a Swiss biologist, zoologist, anthropologist, philosopher, and a regular lecturer at the Eranos Conferences in Ascona. His researches and publications pointed to animals' outer appearances that could not be explained as survival adaptations, but had to be seen in terms of their "representation mode."

101. Albert Einstein, "What Life Means to Einstein, An Interview with George Sylvester Viereck," October 26, 1929, *The Saturday Evening Post*, p. 117; viewed online, http://www.saturdayeveningpost. com/wp-content/uploads/satevepost/what_life_means_to_einstein. pdf (28 February, 2017).

102. Jung, Victor White, *The Jung White Letters*, ed. Ann Conrad Lammers and Adrian Cunningham, Philemon Series (London: Routledge 2007), p. 60.

103. Jonathan Jones, "When Henri Met Pablo" (29 October, 2005) *The Guardian*, https://www.theguardian.com/artanddesign/2005/oct/29 /art (accessed 14 March, 2016).

104. Henri Rousseau, cited in Jones, "When Henri Met Pablo," https://www.theguardian.com/artanddesign/2005/oct/29/art (accessed 14 March, 2016).

105. Jones, "When Henri Met Pablo," https://www.theguardian.com/artanddesign/2005/oct/29/art heguardian.com/artanddesign/2005/oct/29/art (accessed 14 March, 2016).

106. Picasso, cited October 4, 1976, in "Modern Living: Ozmosis in Central Park," *Time Magazine*, Vol. 108, Number 14. N.b.: "The quotation appears as an epigraph at the beginning of the article, source uncited (Online archive of Time magazine)," source check by Garson O'Toole, Quote Investigator, at, http://quoteinvestigator.com/category/pablo-picasso/ (accessed 14 March, 2017).

107. Matsuo Basho, Nr. 152, *Basho: The Complete Haiku*, trans. Jane Reichtold (Tokyo: Kodansha International, 2013), p. 59.

108. Ibid., Nr. 727, p. 176.

109. Robert Lax, Turning the Jungle into a Garden without Destroying a Single Flower (Louisville, KY: Whitefields Press, 1996).

110. Goethe, *Egmont* (1788), Act III, Scene II, trans. Anna Swanick, The Harvard Classics, 1909–14 (New York: Bartleby.com, Great Books Online, 2001), http://www.bartleby.com/19/3/32.html (accessed 13 March, 2017).

CHAPTER VIII
CONCLUDING REFLECTIONS

111. Goethe, *Faust*, Part One, trans. David Luke (Oxford: Oxford University Press, 1987), verse 1336.

INDEX

www.ingramcontent.com/pod-product-compliance
Lightning Source LLC
Chambersburg PA
CBHW050803270326
41926CB00025B/4522